2000 YEARS AND BEYOND

What, in the inheritance of 2000 years, can carry us forward into the increasingly shared time and space of our fast-globalizing world? How, in the third millennium, should we think of the 'Common Era'?

2000 Years and Beyond brings together some of the most eminent thinkers of our time, specialists in philosophy, theology, social anthropology and culture theory. In a horizon-scanning work, they look backwards and forwards to explore what links us to the matrix of the Judaeo-Christian tradition from which Western cultural identity has evolved.

Their reflections raise searching questions about how we move from past to future – and about who 'we' are. What do the catastrophes of the twentieth century signify for hopes of progress? Can humanism, or its notion of human nature, survive without religious faith? If the 'numinous magic of global enterprise' is our own giant shadow cast abroad, does that shadow offer hope enough of a communal future?

Most crucially: has the modern, secularized West now outgrown its originating faith matrix? Are we truly and finally 'post-Christian' – or just post-millennial and suffering hangover?

Often controversial, sometimes visionary, these new essays ask: how do we tell – and how do we write from now on – the unfolding story of the Common Era?

Paul Gifford is Buchanan Professor of French and Director of the Institute of European Cultural Identity Studies. His books include *Reading Paul Valéry: Universe in Mind* (1999) and *Subject Matters: Subject and Self in French Literature*. **David Archard** is Senior Lecturer in Philosophy and Director of the Centre for Philosophy and Public Affairs; **Trevor Hart** is Professor of Divinity and Principal of St Mary's College and **Nigel Rapport** is Professor of Anthropological Studies. All teach at the University of St Andrews.

2000 YEARS AND BEYOND

Faith, identity and the 'Common Era'

*Edited by Paul Gifford
with David Archard, Trevor A. Hart and
Nigel Rapport*

Routledge
Taylor & Francis Group
New York   London

First published by Lawrence Erlbaum Associates, Inc., Publishers
10 Industrial Avenue
Mahwah, New Jersey 07430

Published 2012
by Routledge
711 Third Avenue, New York, NY 10017
Simultaneously published in the UK
by Routledge
2 Park Square, Milton Park, Abingdon, Oxon OX14 4RN

Routledge is an imprint of the Taylor & Francis Group, an informa business

All rights reserved. No part of this book may be reprinted or reproduced or utilized in any form or by any electronic, mechanical, or other means, now known or hereafter invented, including photocopying and recording, or in any information storage or retrieval system, without permission in writing from the publishers.

British Library Cataloguing in Publication Data
A catalogue record for this book is available from the British Library

Library of Congress Cataloging in Publication Data
2000 years and beyond: faith, identity, and the common era / edited by Paul Gifford [et al.]
p. cm.
Includes bibliographical references and index.
1. Christianity. 2. Religion. 3. Christianity – Forecasting. 4. Humanism. 5. Capitalism – Religious aspects – Christianity. 6. Postmodernism – Religious aspects – Christianity. I. Title: Two thousand years and beyond. II. Gifford, Paul, 1944–

BR53. T86 2002
200′.9′0511 – dc21   2002075160

ISBN 0–415–27807–4 (hbk)
ISBN 0–415–27808–2 (pbk)

To remember is to seek to give a
content to our hope

Paul Ricœur

CONTENTS

	Acknowledgments	ix
1	2000 years: looking backwards and forwards PAUL GIFFORD	1
2	Progress and abyss: remembering the future of the modern world JÜRGEN MOLTMANN	16
3	Enlightenment humanism as a relic of Christian monotheism JOHN GRAY	35
4	Historiography and the representation of the past PAUL RICŒUR	51
5	The future of human nature RICHARD SCHACHT	69
6	The mimetic theory of religion: an outline RENÉ GIRARD	88
7	Second comings: neo-Protestant ethics and millennial capitalism in Africa, and elsewhere JEAN AND JOHN COMAROFF	106
8	Can a premodern bible address a postmodern world? ANTHONY C. THISELTON	127

CONTENTS

9   Conclusion: dialogue on the 'Common Era'   147
    THE EDITORS

Notes   191
Bibliography and further reading   208
Index   220

ACKNOWLEDGMENTS

The editors would wish to express their thanks to the funding authorities who made possible the lectures series '2000 Years' on which the present book is based: the British Academy Visiting Lecturer Fund; the French Institute (Edinburgh); the Goethe Institut (Glasgow); and the University of St Andrews Special Lectures Committee. Thanks are due to translators Robert T. Cornelison and Paul Gifford for their work on Chapters 2 and 4 respectively.

The *Angelus Novus* (1920) by Paul Klee (next page) is used by permission of the Israel Museum, Jerusalem (gift of Fania and Gershom Scholem, John and Paul Herring, Jo Carole and Ronald Lauder).

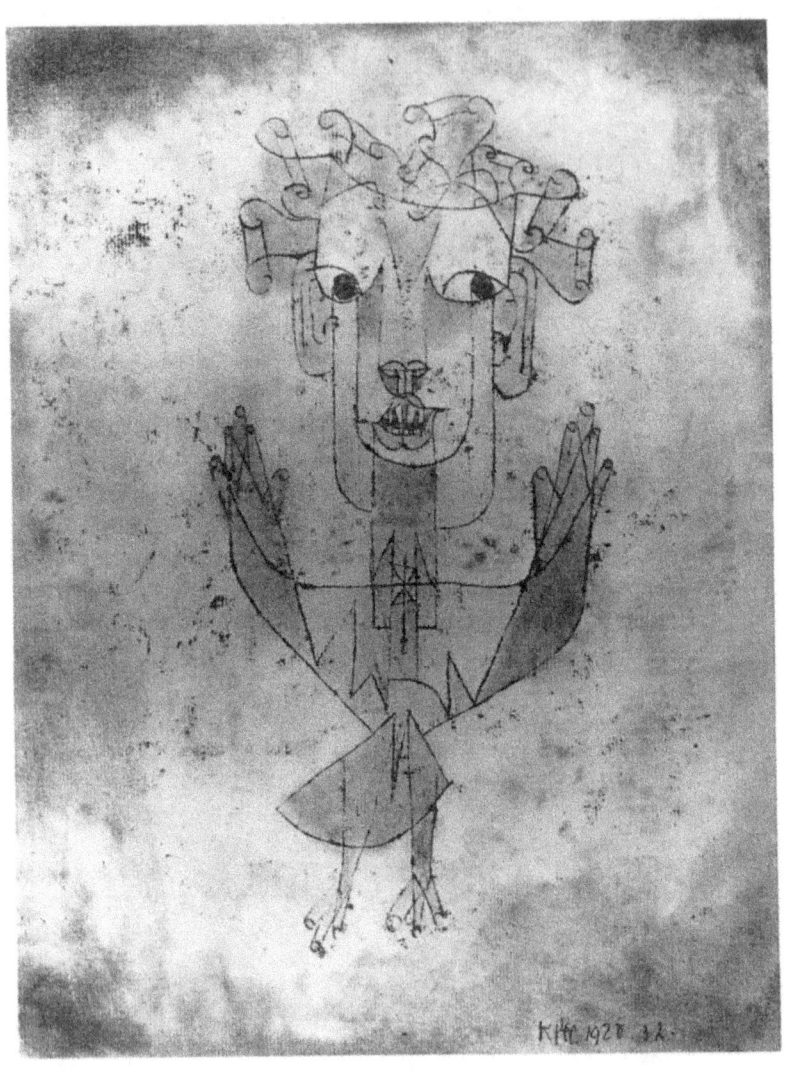

Angelus Novus, 1920, by Paul Klee (Israel Museum)

1

2000 YEARS
Looking backwards and forwards

Paul Gifford

The present volume of essays is an exercise in a neglected art: that of exploring the relationship between evolving secular culture and the matrix of thought, sensibility and social practice derived from the ongoing religious traditions of Judaism and Christianity.

The essays themselves find their origin in a much-followed public lecture series held at the University of St Andrews to mark the bi-millennial year. As the first of our essayists, Jürgen Moltmann, points out, the year 2000 signified very little in its own right, except the poetic stardust of those three noughts. The misadventures of London's Millennium Dome at Greenwich – now fast retreating from memory – no doubt demonstrated the poverty of that slight magic. With the possible exception of its star attraction, the 'Body Zone' (which happened to feature an authentic natural wonder), the Dome failed to address anything vital in collective memory or in spiritual imagination. It offered no point of deeper human self-recognition. It found little to celebrate or commemorate beyond a kaleidoscope of acceptable contemporary images. What it in fact – and briefly – memorialized was the ethos of a passing political moment, and its own monument-making.

Meanwhile, almost unnoticed, the year 2000 offered a landmark of very different interest: a point of overview, properly bi-millennial and pertinently symbolic in character; a point from which to reappraise not the empty arithmetic of one more millennium added to other millennia, but our own collective identity, past, present and future. Symbolically, the year in question invited consideration of this theme with reference to an actual, historically affirmed and dated inheritance of religious belief, value and self-understanding. It was a good time to acknowledge and appraise something much forgotten: the informing presence in our culture of a Judaeo-Christian matrix that has traditionally offered to give human time its horizon of transcultural significance, its deeper intuitions of community and of sense-making.

It is this formative antecedence, together with its programmatic framing or mapping of human time, that is often, albeit imprecisely and ambiguously, evoked by the expression the 'Common Era'. This expression engages, most obviously, a periodization dating the historical era in which we stand from the birth of the – Jewish – founder of the Christian religion. The term is, of course, intensely problematic from many viewpoints, at many levels. Within the Christian faith-tradition itself, the notion is likely to raise ambivalent echoes: of Constantine's state religion, for instance, and of the mediaeval ideal of 'Christendom'. It smacks of a framework of thought encompassing all things temporal within a single spiritual order interpreted and directed by the church. In this sense it is likely to convey, at best, a period-specific account of the relation between culture and faith, time and eternity, the world and God. At worst it might connote the secret confusion between the Kingdom which is 'not of this world' with a socio-cultural dispensation that unquestionably – and often most unchristianly – was. For Jews, of course, the resonance of the 'Common Era' understood in these same terms is largely one of cultural marginalization and exclusion. As one editor of the present volume attests: 'In my Jewish education, we thought of the "common" bit of CE as meaning "vulgar" – the bright and glorious bit was "*BCE*" . . .' Beyond that, Jewish memory may well register a millenarian triumphalism rewriting Jewish messianic expectation; hence, an alienating 'era' of dispossession, insecurity and political scapegoating within an officially Christianized Europe.

As believers or as secularists, our modern ambivalence towards the Common Era is compounded by echoes in collective memory of the countless attempts made to write into the course of human history a secretly millenarian Sense that promised human community and delivered instead some form of political, social or cultural takeover. Not just the attempts pursued by the Holy Roman Empire in the name of Christendom; but also those of the French Revolution, the British Empire, the Positivist Era, the Thousand Year Reich, World Revolution and no doubt even 'the Free World'. We nurture a deep suspicion of any envisaged 'commonality' which, being in and of historical time, is, or looks as if it might be, a sketch for some form of political or cultural hegemony. Only when this potent ghost is exorcized can we recover the deeply desirable principle of 'community' which is also enfolded, hauntingly, within the notion of our 'Common Era'.

The Christian churches have in recent times largely recognized the problem by dropping the public use of the notation AD (*anno Domini*: 'the year of our Lord'). This is a significant adjustment, marking a retreat from the lingering nostalgia for temporal hegemony and cultural privilege; it puts a decent interval of distinction – and of 'Advent'! – between a common era of globalized 'modernity' which is an observable historico-cultural fact and the Kingdom of Heaven. This distinction did not, of course, prevent Christians from marking the bi-millennial year with their own Jubilee celebrations; but it did and does point to the sharp hiatus now existing in the countries of Europe and North America between the (relatively) few who stand in continuity with the matricial faith-tradition (thinking of it as transcultural and inclusive, at least in vocation) and the many who do not (often regarding it as culture-specific, exclusive, even divisive).

Grappling with this hiatus between outlooks, the media (arbiters of the common culture) typically relegated Christian commemoration of the bi-millennium to a 'correct', pluralist marginality. So, for instance, in Britain, Melvyn Bragg's TV series *2000 Years*, which recalled landmarks of Christian history, with following studio discussions, was broadcast mainly in the wee small hours of the morning. In the language of media scheduling, this was a 'minority interest programme'.

What price, then, the question of 'our' own cultural identity – past, present and future? Was it destined to disappear down the gulf between the secular commemoration of one thousand years and the Christian remembrance of two? Could it be addressed at all, in any serious way, in common and in public? Could it, in some form, look backwards to, and forwards from, the shaping antecedence of the faith-matrix that has historically nourished our culture? Or were we – are we – henceforth condemned to unmindfulness of, and disconnection from, our own past?

Uncomfortable reflexive questionings are often the least and the last items of any subject's agenda. Collective cultural subjects (the 'we' envisaged above) are no exception to the rule. Managing a tolerant and tolerable coexistence within our Western multicultural, pluri-faith societies is as much – perhaps more! – than we can cope with; any transcendence of the present seems an unnecessary, and potentially contentious, extra burden. Most characteristically, perhaps, we were and are genuinely at a loss as to how to conceive of a 'Common Era': dubious about how to envisage its commonality, perplexed as to whether its carrying hope of inclusive community may be endorsed or assumed; if so, in *which* terms – and, we feel immediately constrained to add – *whose*?

Is CE just – as Bergson said a century ago of Renan's concept of 'nation' – a convenient notation without definable content? Is it an officialized public memory, merely? an inheritance of great weight, perhaps? even a genuine key to ourselves, but no longer quite receivable as the key to a vocation for the future? Is it something analogous, perhaps, to cultural particularities such as the use of a common language in the 'English-speaking world' or, more broadly, to the shared 'nation-state story' which, from the Renaissance onwards, masqueraded as history and which, within the last 150 years, has served, with sometimes dire consequences, to cement the national identities of the peoples of Europe? What, in that case, of *other* cultures and *their* common eras?

Or are the periodizing and the programme implied in the 'Common Era' something really quite different from the suggestions generated by these hand-me-down analogies: something learned otherwise, known and unknown, narrativized ever anew, ever more deeply and inclusively? Should we, on this alternative hypothesis, think of CE by analogy with changing narratives of the natural world: those given of biological evolution, perhaps; or else akin to the way in which cosmologists are reconceiving the physical universe, which is now recognized indubitably to have, amid the unfathomable complexities of relativity, its own 'common era' . . . ?

Certainly, the notion of *a* 'common era' of Judaeo-Christian antecedence remains entirely intelligible to the cultural historian. It is indeed a fundamental and founding reality of the European and Western past, hence an indispensable dimension of collective self-understanding. The underlying fact remains that the universe of transmitted references, practices and values we call 'culture' has, historically, been massively imprinted with Judaeo-Christian perspectives and values. More invisibly, subtly and tenaciously so, perhaps, than the ready-made analogy with the 'nation-state story' would prepare us to understand; to the point where even our secularizing thought-forms have often represented attempts to reclaim its values, or else to print off, within a 'non-believing' mindspace, secular equivalents for personal or collective use.

Our ethical dilemmas, our difficulties of civilization, have frequently appeared to be symptoms of a loss or lack of the frame of reference furnished to the common culture by this same tradition of religious faith. Our social and political inventions tend to model it allusively, even to reinvent it as an energizing source and resource. The presence of a Judaeo-Christian matrix, arguably, is imprinted in the very logic of secularization itself, so that the simple project of repudiating this matrix seems insufficient quite to efface it. Is it perhaps easier to shift one's rational and discursive ground – as, for instance, the London-based Sunday newspaper the *Observer* has recently begun to do in declaring itself editorially 'post-religious' and 'post-Christian' – than it is to unpick the most intimate constitution and tissue of subject-memory in ourselves?

It seems importantly true, at any rate, that the twentieth century, now closed, brought to most of Western Europe (and, to a lesser extent, North America) the working-out of a deep-seated crisis of cultural identity, radicalizing post-Enlightenment scepticism to the point where it became a normal and norm-setting disaffection for all transmitted and founding programmes of self-understanding. If the problem is posed in sociological terms alone, the possibility clearly exists that the common source and resource constituted by religious faith within our Western culture could be disavowed completely and disappear from view in the next millennium. This prospect is, indeed, embraced by three contributors to the present volume. Nietzsche, one of the undoubted prophets of our 'postmodernity', spoke in very much this sense of the 'death of God', an event in culture which he viewed as the springboard for a heroic adventure of self-invention. 'Post-Christian theologies' have taken up the cry. Jewish and Christian believers will certainly argue that his prophecy constitutes a basic misreading of cultural sources and a misidentification of their own common origins. Yet to them also, Nietzsche is indubitably tonic and pertinent. He addresses the awesome withering *in secularized cultural memory and representation* of the ultimate Referent-Explicator-Respondent of Western inheritance; he focuses dramatically the hypothesis that human identity as such might be entirely established by natural accident and creative human will, within the sole dimension of history.

If anything, however, this comparatively recent development should increase – rather than decrease – the claims to our attention of a *cultural* imprint that survives the modern crisis of identity and of faith. For, as we cross the threshold into the third millennium, the residual presence of this informing cultural matrix is liable to pass purely and simply unrecognized by the majority of those it inhabits. It is open to being misapprehended and misconstrued, by virtue of the very estrangement involved in so significant a dislocation to the continuity of collective memory. It would be instructive – to take a searching and central example (not irrelevant to Nietzsche himself) – to conduct a survey of public opinion enquiring what proportion of our contemporaries consider the 'immortality of the soul' to be a Christian doctrine. The likelihood is of a 90 per cent affirmative response – i.e. of a mistaken and misleading identification. If so, this may imply that enquiring about faith-identities in a postmodern cultural mindspace is likely to involve a crucial element of *quiproquo* and not a little 'blind man's buff'.

The same consideration is relevant, in a more radical sense, if the question asked is no longer that of a residual cultural imprint merely, but now of the distinctiveness of the Judaic and Christian faith-traditions; and, in particular, the question of their ability to address relevantly in the third millennium the common culture which currently stands so estranged from them. By a signal oddity of our times, the same Judaeo-Christian distinctiveness or particularity which is so mistily apprehended by the common contemporary cultural mind, has never been more fully investigated and, perhaps, never more firmly grasped, than by the theologians and the cultural theorists of the age of critical reflexivity. Their task has been to sift out painstakingly (though not without prophecy), within the 'grand narratives' of our Western past – and first of all in the perceptions and practices of former centuries which were culturally and misleadingly labelled 'Christian' – what belongs to the persuasions of the common culture, and what belongs to the transcending continuities of authentic faith. The very foregrounding of the term 'Judaeo-Christian' exemplifies just such a process at work.

Again, the question may be: *what alternative commonality, and from which 'elsewhere'?* Where Nietzsche has passed, many other twentieth-century critiques of the inheritance of the Common Era have also followed. Many 'deconstructions' of Western culture and identity have been practised (Marxist, Freudian, structuralist, Derridian, Lacanian . . .); many forms of fruitful rediscovery explored (feminism, post-colonialism, ecology, alternative spiritualities, to name a significant few); many 'other' faith traditions emanating from other culture zones of our rapidly globalizing time and space have been questioned – so many clues essayed towards a renewal of our 'European' or our 'Western' cultural identity. The future of the 'Common Era' promised by the very globalization of communications, economies and cultural exchanges engages all such viewpoints in a matter of common concern, of common hope.

A pluralism of belief and value may, in the long term, be the best and ineluctable condition of moral growth, enlarged horizons of thought, fruitful Other-recognitions; it may even usher in a common, fully communal – a fully *human* – identity. Yet not, perhaps, without vitalizing reconnection to some human potential that is both before and beyond our merely wishing that it were so. For, of itself, most immediately, our relativistic and pluralist present often appears marked by negativities. It bears, indeed, the symptoms of trauma: amnesia or selective memory in respect of the past, a loss of roots and of the sense of community, an inaptitude for common memory or common hope, an insecure sense of provisionality, together with a widespread confusion about who 'we' are. The common culture right now is a rather Dome-like sort of space...

Given this landscape of dislocation, provisionality and tentative renewal, it has seemed highly pertinent to ask leading academic specialists in philosophy, theology, social anthropology, literature and culture theory to look both backwards and forwards and to give a strategic account of the presence and significance for our times of a Judaeo-Christian inheritance which they may, or may not, see as surviving vitally in the new millennium.

What perspectives of understanding (reflexivity, recognition of cultural diversity, the historicity of knowledge, value pluralism, the advent of feminism, globalization, the imprint of neoliberal capitalism, the vagaries of collective memory itself, etc.) have gone into the making of the modern (and 'postmodern') mind? Can we define its mind-set and temper? Its preferred models of social and personal identity? Most significantly: do these tend to relativize and dissipate 'Judaeo-Christian particularity' or, on the contrary, to disengage, liberate and valorize it?

It is hoped to offer here a representative diversity of views on these questions from many disciplinary perspectives; it being well understood that dialogue on this and all matters of collective subject-identity ('where have we come from, where are we now, where are we headed?') lends itself to an almost infinite variety of viewpoints and voices. There was – and is – no natural limit to potentially valid and interesting contributions on questions of such centrality; and the editors will readily agree with those readers who find themselves regretting the absence here of a direct echo of their own preferred perspective.

The list of actual contributors is, of course, in part contingent. Many eminent names were approached who, though highly sympathetic to the enterprise, were unable in the event to contribute. 'Absent voices' include: Julia Kristeva, Margaret Drabble, Mary Robinson, Martha Nussbaum, George Steiner, Frank Kermode... In other cases, contributors have preferred to keep the reflections they confided to audiences in St Andrews for forthcoming major works of their own: thus Alvin Plantinga on the current relation of religion and science ('Conflict or concord?'), and Zygmunt Bauman on 'Identity and religion in a globalizing world'. The representative credentials of the viewpoints exemplified here cannot, in this sense, claim to be impeccable; and any felt deficiencies are best considered an invitation to further dialogue...

The contributors are, at least, of rare authority in the academic disciplines illustrated.

Jürgen Moltmann is Emeritus Professor of Systematic Christian Theology at the University of Tübingen and one of the foremost names of contemporary Christian theology. His work has had enormous influence in the English-speaking world and the Third World as well as in his native Germany. Moltmann's first major book, *Theology of Hope*, published in 1964, was responsible for restoring to an important place on the theological agenda the Christian hope for the future of the world. He is characteristically insistent upon allowing the treatment of each of his themes to be shaped by the orientation of the gospel (and of Christian faith generally) towards a promised future which is not just of our doing and making, but God's. The theme of hope pervades his writings from first to last: by no means a common feature among the thinkers and writers of the latter end of the twentieth century.

Moltmann argues here that if we are to retrieve something of the hopefulness of the early modern age, it cannot be in disregard of the horrors to which nineteenth-century progress has, in some sense, led in the twentieth century. Hopeful 'bridges' to the future must now 'be built over the abysses of destruction we have experienced in the twentieth century'. The latter is powerfully symbolized for Moltmann by Walter Benjamin's image of the 'angel of history', who is driven into the future by a 'storm from paradise'. With wings outstretched, he faces backward to the past, and sees wreckage piled on wreckage, all the rubble of history mounting up as 'progress' drives history onwards. Driven forward by progress, the angel cannot stop, as he would if he could. He would like to remain in order to lift up the downtrodden, but he is propelled helplessly on. Turning to the transcendent hope of Christian faith, Moltmann sets beside this image from Benjamin a biblical image: the vision of resurrection in Ezekiel's valley of dry bones. The juxtaposition of the two images graphically makes the point that the Christian hope of resurrection offers what the secular hope of the modern age on its own could never provide: hope for the past and for the dead: 'In order to live with this wreckage-laden and victim-laden past without repressing it or repeating it, we need these transcendent hopes of the resurrection of the dead and the healing of the downtrodden... Without hope for the past, there can be no hope for the future.' The transcendent hope of the Christian tradition does not inhibit the smaller hopes of a better future in time; rather it empowers and energizes them.

John Gray is Professor of Modern European Thought at the London School of Economics. He was previously a Fellow at Jesus College, Oxford. He is one of the most distinguished English-speaking political philosophers of his generation, and also an influential political commentator. His early work was markedly libertarian in character and sympathetic to the New Right project of Margaret Thatcher in the United Kingdom and Ronald Reagan in the United States of America. From these early political dispositions he has moved to a nuanced defence of social democratic liberalism and is now a passionate philosophical defender of Tony Blair and New Labour's 'Third Way'. John Gray has offered important book-length critiques of key figures within the libertarian and liberal traditions, namely John Stuart Mill, Friedrich von Hayek and Isaiah Berlin. From the work of the last he has extracted and defended a central claim, namely that liberalism must rest ultimately upon an irreducible pluralism of value. He has also sought to challenge the uniqueness of Western liberal ideals by consideration of Asian societies and their core non-liberal values. At the same time he is sensitive to the impact of globalism and the challenges it presents to justice and the environment. John Gray's many essays – most of which have been collected into widely read books such as *Enlightenment's Wake: Politics and Culture at the Close of the Modern Age* (1995) – provide provocative, scholarly and insightful reflections on our contemporary political condition.

In his new essay for this volume, Gray argues that the core beliefs at the heart of the Enlightenment project are in fact a Christian inheritance – and that they are strictly indefensible in the terms of a genuinely naturalistic world-view. Three such beliefs are examined. The first: the belief in the possibility of progress for the species, not only in scientific knowledge, but also – and more importantly – in ethical and political life. The second is the belief that the growth of human knowledge and emancipation go together, and that knowledge, for individuals and for the species, enhances freedom. The third, presupposed and entailed by the first two, is the belief that, as a result of the growth of knowledge, humankind can attain a rational consensus in the matter of values. The very concepts and categories in which these Enlightenment beliefs are framed were and remain residues of Christian faith; if we now renounce this framework, as the Enlightenment project enjoined, we must also, in any good logic of consistency, renounce these beliefs. Certain conclusions follow. The

Enlightenment itself is to be understood as a phase in the history of one cultural tradition, roughly speaking, that of Western Christendom. It is and always was a strictly local cult, a secular version of Western religion. It also follows that the prospects of Enlightenment humanism, which claimed to be Christianity's successor, are henceforth poor. There is no more reason, in sound naturalism, to expect genuine moral progress from the human species of animal than there is to expect it from whales or tigers. Adopting an authentically naturalistic view means 'giving up the inordinate hopes for it inculcated by Christianity and renewed by the Enlightenment'. Given its antecedence and its dependency, Enlightenment humanism may be expected to sink into insignificance if Christian belief continues to decline. Conversely, only a Christian revival can ensure Enlightenment humanism a future. In his response to the questions posed by the Common Era, Gray himself refers us to a version of liberalism that is, problematically, 'value-pluralist' and, implicitly, 'postmodern'.

Paul Ricœur, who has made peculiarly his own the important modern field of hermeneutic philosophy, is one of the most eminent and versatile French thinkers of the past half-century. His academic appointments have included the Sorbonne, and the Ecole des Hautes Etudes de Sciences Sociales in Paris; and he has taught at half-a-dozen top American universities, including Chicago, of which he is Emeritus Professor. He is the author of ground-breaking works of standard reference in many fields, including *Freud and Philosophy* (1965); *The Conflict of Interpretations* (1969); *The Rule of Metaphor* (1975); *Time and Narrative* (1983); *Oneself as Another* (1990) – the last-mentioned being the fruit of a series of Gifford Lectures given at the University of Edinburgh. He holds the Grand Prix de l'Académie Française for a lifetime's work. His crowning – and possibly last – major book (since he is now nearly 90) appeared in France last year under the title *L'Histoire, la mémoire, l'oubli* to great critical acclaim and lively media interest.

His reflection on the Common Era refers to the hugely important contemporary debate in France about the respective claims of scientific historiography and of the 'lived history' that is collective memory. What can we know of the past? How can we surmount the dissolving effects of postmodern representationalism? Entrapped in historical and moral relativism, how shall we not suffer a loss of the hope of truth? How shall we then counter, for example, negationism about the Holocaust? In a characteristically careful and enlightening evaluation of the respective claims and difficulties of memory and of scientific history, Ricœur defends the thesis that the aim of historical writing – when it deals in its narrative scenarios, which are simultaneously representing and deforming screens – remains to utter the past in an endless approximation which involves an unending labour of rewriting. The case of traumatic events in our national and international past is particularly instructive in this respect: what was once experienced and suffered demands to be uttered. History in the making exerts pressure on the history which is uttered or spoken. Between the faithfulness of memory and the truth of history, there can be no decidable order of preference. The biblical narratives are seen (in his further seminar contribution quoted in the Conclusion to this volume) as expressing these tensions and as offering certain paradigms of response.

Richard Schacht is Professor of Philosophy at the University of Illinois. His main area of scholarly interest is European philosophy of the nineteenth and twentieth centuries. He has published widely on the concept of alienation (from Hegel to Marx and beyond), on twentieth-century phenomenology and existentialism, and on aspects of the philosophy of art, philosophical anthropology and moral philosophy. Anthropological and ethical questions are Schacht's main concern; and Friedrich Nietzsche's challenges to Western philosophical assumptions in these areas have been the catalyst for much of his work, which includes *Nietzsche* (1983), *Nietzsche, Genealogy, Morality* (1994), *The Future of Alienation* (1994) and *Making Sense of Nietzsche* (1995). Richard Schacht is executive director of the North American Nietzsche Society and editor of *International Nietzsche Studies*.

In his spirited and witty chapter, Schacht points out that 'human nature' has had a terrible press over the past century from thinkers and schools who could agree on little else. The 'ban on man' has been endorsed by phenomenologists, existentialists, Marxists, feminists and Foucauld. Not to mention, in the classic account, Nietzsche, who is credited with telling us that 'God is dead' and opening the corollary that the same is true of 'man'. Schacht argues, on the contrary, that Nietzsche not only opens the time of a much-needed 'revaluation of values', but also the project of a naturalistic epistemology and a trail-blazing philosophical anthropology. On this account, the future of human nature is very much the future of 'Hume-and-Nietzsche'. The latter takes us out of the God-shadows and exemplifies a shift towards philosophical anthropology, continuous with the shift from metaphysics to epistemology heralded by Hume. He points to a revolution in evolution, highlighting a 'no-longer-merely-animal animal' and an emergent 'nature' that is plastic and transformational. In an original development looking towards the twenty-first century and beyond,

Schacht himself finally offers a neo-Nietzschean reflection relating to the socio-culturality of biological nature. Defining the key notions which form the agenda of a modern enquiry into human nature – psychosomaticity, objectification, intersubjectivity, embodiment, mentality – he identifies what 'human nature' after Nietzsche, evolutionary yet also developmental, might look like.

René Girard is Emeritus Professor of French and Comparative Literature at the University of Stanford, California; he has also taught at Duke, Johns Hopkins and Buffalo, New York. His early works of literary criticism include books on Proust and Dostoyevsky; but his international reputation was made in the field of cultural anthropology, with the ground-breaking *Violence and the Sacred* (1972), which obtained the Prix de l'Académie Française. His theses on mimetic desire and its relation to violence and to culture have been developed in a series of brilliant and provocative works, including *Essays on Literature, Mimesis and Anthropology* (1978), *The Scapegoat* (1982), *Things Hidden from the Foundation of the World* (1987), *Shakespeare: A Theater of Envy* (1990). He is now an internationally circulating lecturer who holds honorary doctorates from half-a-dozen European universities. The French Academy's Grand Prix de Philosophie has recognized him as one of the outstanding philosophical anthropologists of his generation.

Girard offers us here a recapitulative outline of his thinking to date. He argues that the more fully we grasp the deep structural analogies uniting the various transcriptions of social violence, its crisis and resolution, the more we perceive that we are dealing with the single religious phenomenon of the archaic sacred; and the more we learn to decipher the radical singularity that sets apart the Judaeo-Christian presentation of this same theme. Archaic mythology, as it evolves towards 'civilization', tends to disguise its own allusion to violence. However, since the aesthetic surgery practised remains visible, so does the subtext of violence. What this reveals, according to Girard, is the mechanism of mimetic desire, which induces a contagion of rivalry and tends towards a socially perilous paroxysm, which then discharges itself against a single common object of enmity, the scapegoat. Such patterns can be read in the Old Testament and, in recapitulative principle, in the gospels. The difference is that the Judaeo-Christian presentations of emissary victimization here designate and disarm the disguised transaction involved; the meaning of 'sacrifice' – and the basis of 'religion' – are thereby transformed radically.

John and Jean Comaroff, both Professors of Anthropology at the

University of Chicago, are among the most respected names in contemporary anthropology, renowned for the ethnographic work they have carried out, individually and jointly, among the peoples of southern Africa; also for their theorizing about the place and role of power in the social process, and, specifically, on the relation between religion and politics. They received their PhDs from the London School of Economics and have since then taught largely in the US. Among their publications (individual and joint) are: *Essays on Marriage in Southern Africa* (1981), *Body of Power, Spirit of Resistance: The Culture and History of a South African People* (1985), *Ethnography and the Historical Imagination* (1992), *Modernity and Its Malcontents: Ritual and Power in Postcolonial Africa* (1993). The Comaroffs' work is concerned with the ways religious ritual and symbolism are mediated by seemingly non-religious concerns such as health and healing, the constructions of historical narrative, and the legitimation and delegitimation of law and authority.

The Comaroffs' response to the questions of religion in the Common Era encompasses a wide landscape: an understanding of economy and society, culture and history, faith and identity at the end of the twentieth century. In Weberian vein, they examine the dialectical relationship between economic and religious expression. We are witness, they suggest, to a new moment in the history of capitalism, this time in neoliberal or hyper-rational guise, and on an even more global scale. They describe it as capitalism's 'Second Coming'. Accompanying the new economic moment is a new religious spirit: a spirit rampant in Africa, from where their ethnographic examples are largely drawn. Capitalism itself is taken as a gospel of salvation: millennial, messianic, even magical in potency. As a moral and cultural economy, it is seen to have the capacity to enrich the poor, solve social problems, heal the sick, elicit divine favour and add material value to the commonweal. Why has capitalism taken on these features and how has it reconfigured the wider religious scene in its wake? Why has there been a conjunction of economic hyper-rationalization, on the one hand, and an exuberant spread of innovative cult practices and money magic, pyramid schemes and prosperity gospels, on the other? An answer is to be found, they suggest, in Marxian terms, in the new articulation of production to consumption.

Anthony Thiselton is Canon Theologian of Leicester Cathedral and of Southwell Minster. He is one of the most distinguished theologians in the UK and a scholar of international standing. He has taught in the universities of Sheffield, Durham and Nottingham, and was until recently Professor of Christian Theology and Head of

Department in the University of Nottingham. He has also been visiting Professor in several North American institutions. From 1998 to 2000 he was President of the Society for the Study of Theology. His publications cover an impressive range of subjects. His most substantial contributions have been in the fields of hermeneutics (e.g. *The Two Horizons*, 1980, *New Horizons in Hermeneutics*, 1992, *The Promise of Hermeneutics* [with R. Lundin and C. Walhout], 2000). His *'Scottish Journal of Theology* Lectures' were published in 1995 as *Interpreting God and the Postmodern Self: On Meaning, Manipulation, and Promise*. His most recent, and perhaps most significant work, is a monumental 1,500 page *The First Epistle to the Corinthians: A Commentary on the Greek Text* (2000).

In his chapter 'Can a premodern bible address a postmodern world?' Thiselton tackles his theme through a penetrating inquiry into those characteristic features generally supposed to separate the *pre*- from the *post*modern, and argues that in fact (in the case of the bible at least) the separation is often more apparent than actual. He discusses in this perspective the devaluing and setting aside of universals and of truth-claims based on coherence and rationality as against assumptions that 'truth' is constructed socially; and he offers a critique of 'sequential' accounts of the premodern, the modern, and the postmodern eras. Postmodernity is 'a mood not a period' (Docherty). Similarly, he shows that individualism, progressivism and autonomy are not limited to, or even first discovered by, the secular Enlightenment of the seventeenth and eighteenth centuries: Paul the Apostle encountered such attitudes and placed them under the critique of the Cross. More explicitly, the 'postmodern' elevation of discontinuity, disruption and the denial of stable continuity lay behind early traditions of Greek philosophy. Hence the bible is not in any obvious sense 'premodern' with respect to such things, but already faces and addresses them.

The work of Bultmann on demythologizing and of Barthes, Foucault and Derrida on 'demystification', Thiselton argues, depend in large measure on the (challengeable) assumption that myth and image in premodern religion had insufficient critical awareness to distinguish between, on the one hand, objectified or projected images promoted to sustain primitive assumptions in power-interests and, on the other, the truth-claims of religion or of divine revelation. Further, a semantic and hermeneutical critical awareness is clearly seen in the use of highly sophisticated rhetorical arguments and devices which are demonstrated within the Pauline epistles by modern research (e.g. A. Eriksson). On the sensitive critical issue of boundaries and marginality, Thiselton argues that Jesus of Nazareth shared the postmodern suspicion that 'norms' are too often constructed by a socio-religious or socio-political Establishment to enhance their own elitist power and to marginalize an abandoned or despised group. Nevertheless, the New Testament writers do not merely deconstruct all boundaries as contrived social constructs; they look beyond deconstruction, rather than accepting its spell as the last word on human life and thought.

The postmodern assumption that we have to choose between a comprehensive theory of reference and representation on one side, and radical plurality and indeterminacy on the other, is seen as false. Biblical texts operate with various functions and levels of language, from the most stable to the most suggestive. Fundamentally, grace is 'given', not constructed. It offers a universally relevant foundation, not an ethnocentric 'local' construction, for transformative truth grounded – not merely in what is 'recognized' – but in ontology and eschatology.

In the nature of the case, these diverse and plural reflections which pick their own pathway through the questions of religious faith in its relation to the Common Era do not lend themselves to a tidy conclusion. Nevertheless, a common space of concern is explored, with recognizable patterns of response. The editors, mapping this ground, have therefore undertaken to highlight in a dialogic Conclusion to the volume some of the issues arising from the series as a whole and to mediate some responses of the essayists to the – often challenging – 'live' questions of their academic and general audiences.

At the very least, such reflections must help account for the cultural identity we now have and to say how this is likely to develop beyond the year 2000. At best, it is hoped that they will contribute significantly to a deeper understanding of what links us, with and without faith, to the matrix of the Common Era.

2

PROGRESS AND ABYSS

Remembering the future of the modern world

Jürgen Moltmann

What, then, actually happened on 1 January 2000? Was it 'the turn of an age', with all the weighty solemnity of destiny this implies? Or was it a new millennium in the felicitous progress of the modern world? Was it the beginning of the world's end? Or was it merely a tremendous postmodern New Year's party in Berlin, London, Paris and New York?

Common sense tells us that it was just a night like all the nights before it and after it, without any special significance at all. And yet the year 2000, with its three zeros, does have something magical about it. So what sort of magic? It has to do with the decimal system we have measured time with ever since the beginning of the modern world. From the beginning of modern times, linear chronology has asserted itself, a way of calculating time that takes no account of what happens in it, but simply moves on and on, from one year to the next. It fits our idea of inexorable human 'progress' from the past into a better and better future. That is why at turning points in time, like 1 January 2000, we like to draw up a balance sheet, totting up the profits and the losses of the progress we have made. But about the progress itself there is no question, for it hastens on year upon year, with our calendar, into an endless future. Or so we think.

But why the year 2000 in particular? According to the decimal system, there is evidently something marvellous about everything that ends with zeros, because we think that zero is 'a round number', although in fact it is not a number at all. Every ten years a jubilee, every hundred years a centenary, and so on, whether there is anything to celebrate or not. Why is the zero more attractive than the seven or the twelve? Like the symbol for infinity, the zero only entered our numerical system quite late on, coming to us from India by way of Arabia.[1] The suspended breath or the mystic moment that belongs to what we call zero hour is apparently a difficult and mysterious affair. Can we begin again from the beginning, from zero, so to speak, without a past, and free of memories? With the three zeros of the year 2000 a new year begins, and a new decade, and a new century – perhaps even a whole new thousand years. Fascinating – four new beginnings! We get the impression that the immediate future and the wider future further ahead are both open. What a delightful illusion!

Things look very different if we take our bearings from what happens in time, for real events do not usually take any account of our timescale. What is our situation today, now that the twentieth century is at an end, and the nineteenth before it? The future in the twenty-first century will be determined by these two eras, for they are by no means past and gone, and they confront us with tremendous contradictions. On the one hand we have the nineteenth century (with its twentieth-century extensions), an age of fantastic progress in all life's different sectors: from the steam engine to the aeroplane, from the telephone to the internet, from classical physics to the theory of relativity. It was an age of discoveries and conquests. And on the other hand we have the twentieth century (as distinct from the nineteenth): an age of incomparable catastrophes: Verdun and Stalingrad, Auschwitz and the Gulag Archipelago, Hiroshima and Chernobyl. These names stand for the unimaginable crimes against humanity committed by the progressive Western and modern world. Both these eras are still present today; their progress and their abysses. What once became possible will never again disappear from reality, but will always remain part of it. Today we are globalizing the nineteenth century's world of progress, and at the same time all the weapons of mass destuction developed and employed in the twentieth century are still kept in readiness for mass extermination, which would provide the 'final solution' of the question about the human race.[2]

In the first part of this chapter I shall talk about the birth of modernity out of the spirit of messianic hope, so that we can understand the age of beginnings without end. In the second part I shall describe the age of the end without beginnings which began with the seminal European catastrophe of the First World War. In the third part, I shall ask about the future of Christian hope and hopes for humanity.

JÜRGEN MOLTMANN

I The birth of modernity out of the spirit of messianic hope

The modern world had at least two significant starting points before the advent of the age of Enlightenment. The first was the *conquista*, the discovery and conquest of America from 1492 onwards. The second was the scientific and technological seizure of power over nature by human beings.

(i) The year 1492 saw the beginning of the European domination over continents and peoples. According to Hegel, this was the hour when the modern world was born.[3] Before that the European powers were unimportant, globally speaking, compared with the Ottoman empire, the Indian empire of the Moguls, and the Chinese empire. The Spanish and the Portuguese, then the English, the Dutch and the French 'discovered' America, each for themselves. But what does 'discovered' mean here? America was neither discovered nor perceived as such. It was appropriated and moulded according to the will of its conquerors.[4] 'America', says the Mexican historian Edmundo O'Gorman, 'is an invention of European thinking.' The individual life and individual cultures of the Aztecs, Mayas and Incas have never been perceived for what they were, right down to the present day. They were repressed as something alien, and sacrificed to the conquerors' own notions and purposes.[5] Islands, mountain and rivers were given Spanish names, generally Christian ones. The languages of the indigenous peoples were forbidden. The legal fiction of 'unclaimed property', 'no-man's land', and 'the wilderness' legalized the pillaging and the colonization. With the conquest of America, Christianity came forward as a European religion to rule the world.

(ii) The scientific and technological seizure of power over nature is the other foundation stone of the new world order. In the century between Copernicus and Isaac Newton, the new empirical sciences stripped nature of her magic, as Max Weber put it, and took from her the divine mystery which up to then had been reverenced as *anima mundi*, the soul of the world.[6] This also ended the taboos evoked by reverence for 'Mother Earth' and for the greatness of life.[7] The sciences bring 'Mother Nature and her daughters' to the human being (who is of course a man) in order to make him 'the master and possessor of nature', as Francis Bacon and René Descartes interpreted this process at the time. Science and technology now restored the human being's status as image of God, which had been lost in superstition and idolatry, and in so doing they established human lordship over the earth (*dominium terrae*) which corresponds to the lordship of God over heaven and earth. Here too new discoveries were made (and are being made still) which are adorned, down to the present day, with the name of the discoverer. Recently they have even been patented for the purposes of economic exploitation: the genome researcher Craig Venter wants to acquire the human genome for himself by way of thousands of patents, although he never 'invented' it. For scientific discovery does not merely do away with our ignorance; it also makes us the determining subjects of what we have 'discovered'. Since the beginning of modern times, scientific reason has become what Max Horkheimer calls 'instrumental reason'; that is, reason whose knowledge-determining interest is power and utility. Antiquity's idea of reason as *phronesis* links science with wisdom; but this idea was brushed aside. According to Kant's rationalization of scientific reason, reason 'sees' only 'that which it brings forth according to its own design' by 'compelling nature to respond to its questions' (Foreword to the *Critique of Pure Reason*, 2nd edn). 'Knowledge is power', and scientific knowledge is power first over nature, then over life; today over the future. Through science and technology Europe acquired the instrumentalizing knowledge that enabled it to build up its world-spanning civilization out of the resources of the worlds it had colonized. With increasing globalization, the Christian world became the Western world, and the Western world the modern world, whose historical origins are no longer evident because they look just the same in Tokyo, Singapore, Chicago, London, and now Frankfurt and Berlin too.

What *hope* motivated the European discovery of the world?

It was the vision of 'the new world order'. Columbus was apparently looking both for God's Garden of Eden and for Eldorado, the city of gold.[8] God and gold also provided the most powerful driving force behind the *conquista*.[9] The gold was intended not just for personal enrichment but also (as we know from Columbus's journal) for the reconquest of Jerusalem. For according to Joachim of Fiore's prophecy, 'From Spain will come the one who will bring back the Ark to Zion.' Why Jerusalem especially? Because the Holy City was to be the capital of Christ's Thousand Years' Empire, which will be the consummation of world history.

And why the Spanish? According to the political theology of the so-called Quintomonarchists, the Spanish state theologians, the worldwide Christian monarchy is nothing less than the 'Fifth Monarchy', which Daniel 7 prophesies will replace the four bestial world empires, Rome last of all. This is the kingdom of the Son of Man, in which the saints of the Most High will rule the world and judge the nations. With the stone of Daniel (Daniel 2) or with 'fire from above' (Daniel 7) all the other empires will be destroyed, until at long last humanity is 'one flock under one shepherd'. According to the messianism in Iberian culture, this Christian universal monarchy will last until the end of history. It is 'the new world order', as the Spanish said, long before the United States came into being. This is the 'New World' in the messianic sense. *Novus ordo saeculorum* is impressed on the seal of the United States and printed on every one-dollar note. This is 'the messianic faith of our fathers', this is the 'new world order' which every United States president invokes in his inaugural address.[10] The United States decided the outcome of the two world wars, and after the collapse of the Soviet Union is actually the only Great Power still remaining. It was therefore not without some justification that Henry Luce called the twentieth century 'the American century'. And at the moment the twenty-first century looks no different.

What *hope* motivated modern civilization in the 'Old World'?

It was, and still is, the vision of the 'new time' of modernity. The interpretative framework for Europe's rise to worldwide power, its mobilizing and orientating impulse, can be perceived in two symbols of hope for the future: first, the expectation that history will find its consummation in the 'Thousand Years' Empire', in which Christ will reign together with those who are his, and will judge the nations; secondly, the expectation that history will find its consummation in the 'Third Empire' of the Spirit, which according to Joachim of Fiore's prophecy will replace the empire of the Father and the empire of the Son, and will complete them. We call both these historical expectations chiliastic or millenarian, and their motivation of the present 'messianic'.[11] What they have in common is that wherever their influence is paramount, the past no longer dominates the present, as it does in traditional societies; now the future takes precedence in the experience of time. And thus 'modern society' is born. What is also common to the two expectations is that they see the consummation of history in a historical future, not in a catastrophe outside of or apart from history. And then the past really does become 'the prologue to the future', and successive ages can be divided into stages or steps forward in the direction of time's completion. Like a compass which gives us bearings in space and enables us to master it, 'the eschatological compass gives us orientation in time, by pointing to the Kingdom of God as the ultimate end and purpose'.[12]

From the seventeenth century onwards, waves of chiliastic, messianic and apocalyptic hopes swept through Europe.[13] We come across them in the Jewish messianism of Sabbatai Zwi, in Puritan apocalypticism at the time of Oliver Cromwell, in Dutch 'prophetic theology', and in the expectations of 'better times in the future' which appear at the beginning of German pietism, with Amos Comenius, Philip Jakob Spener and the Württemberg theologians Johann Albrecht Bengel and Friedrich Ötinger. They all fused the hope for the millennium of Christ soon to dawn with the ancient world's expectation of the Golden Age, which they had learnt from Virgil would replace the Age of Iron. There had always been similar expectations about the end in Christianity. But in the seventeenth century, with the beginning of modernity, a new time was proclaimed. Now the time of fulfilment has arrived, it was said, this hope can be realized in the present. Antiquity and the middle ages are past; the 'new time' is beginning, and that is the time of consummation. Now world history will be completed. Now humanity will be perfected. Now unhindered progress in all spheres of life is beginning. There will be no more qualitative changes.

Lessing's famous essay 'On the Education of the Human Race' (1777) became the founding document of the German Enlightenment. Lessing felt that he was the prophet of 'the third age of the Spirit' announced by Joachim of Fiore. The time is coming, Lessing wrote, when everyone will know the truth for himself without the mediation of the church, and will recognize and do the good *because* it is good, not out of fear of punishment. This new time is beginning now, with the transition of men and women from historical faith in the church to general belief in reason. God's revelation in history will become the promise of that which human beings can now perceive for themselves. God's hidden providence will become the manifest pedagogical plan of education for rising and forward-striving humanity.[14]

In Kant too we find the same chiliastic solemnity that heralds the transition of humanity into the new era of pure faith in reason.[15] For devout Christians, the French Revolution was a sign of the apocalypse of the Antichrist. For Kant it was a historical sign that the human race was developing for the better. What had formerly been called the kingdom of God became for Kant the symbol of the ethical goal humanity had endlessly to approach. Part of this chiliasm was also his vision of the perfect civil union of the human race in a league of nations which will guarantee eternal peace; for peace is the promise of what were at that time called 'the rights of man' – human rights.

In view of this messianism of the 'new time' in Europe, it is not surprising that for Kant the religious question was not: 'What links us with our origins in the past?' or: 'What gives us support in eternity?' The real religious question was: 'What can I hope for?' Only a future for which we can hope can give meaning to life in historical time, to historical acts, and to suffering in history. 'All's well that ends well.' In this solemn, religiously charged sense, 'future' became for the modern world the new paradigm of transcendence.

The nineteenth century, which began, as it were, in 1789, after the marked caesura in Europe, and ended in 1914, was indeed an age of beginnings, utopias and revolutions. What earlier had been no more than something to be hoped for was now to be realized. For the first time people saw the alternatives to the faulty condition of the world as it exists, not in the world to come but in the future of this world now, not in an intangible other world but in real alterations to this one.

The French Revolution was the matrix of the democratic vision of popular sovereignty on the basis of human and civil rights, and was the source of the great promise: liberty, equality, fraternity (sisterhood had to be added later). From England came the industrial revolution, sister of the democratic revolution, with its promise of general prosperity and the greatest happiness of the greatest number.[16] The socialist revolution was intended to complete the democratic revolution by producing the classless society in 'the realm of freedom' built up on the industrial 'realm of necessity'.

The sense of progress, fired by ceaselessly new scientific discoveries and technological inventions, trusted in a beginning without an end. Great philosophies of history, like those of Auguste Comte, Hegel and Marx, set historical progress in the context of the perfecting of the world. At the same time the great European Powers divided up the globe into their colonial empires, undoubtedly with the pernicious intention of ruling the world, but also with the benevolent aim of contributing to the education and development of backward, underdeveloped humanity.

Throughout the nineteenth century, the educated classes in Europe cherished the dream of the moral betterment of humanity. This moral optimism too had an ancient apocalyptic premise. According to Revelation 20: 2–4, in Christ's Thousand Years' Empire 'Satan will be bound for a thousand years', so that the good can spread unhindered. Round about 1900, the fulfilment of this dream seemed to be within the grasp of the European Great Powers. After the Boxer rising, they set about dividing up the last still independent country, China. All the Christian missions fell upon the allegedly backward Chinese with the End-time hope which John Mott formulated as: 'The evangelization of the world in this generation'.

The hallmarks of the era were progress and evolution, growth and expansion, utopias and the revolutions of hope.

II The age of catastrophes

Walter Benjamin gave us one of the most moving symbols of the swing from hopeful progress to the appalling catastrophes of the modern world in his image of the angel of history:

> A Klee painting named *Angelus Novus* [*facing page 1*] shows an angel which looks as if he is about to move away from something at which he is staring. He is wide-eyed, his mouth is open, and his wings are spread. This is what the angel looks like. His face is turned to the past. Where we see a chain of events, he sees a single catastrophe which unceasingly heaps up ruins upon ruins, and throws them down at his feet. The angel would perhaps like to tarry, to awaken the dead, and to piece together what has been broken. But a tempest is blowing from Paradise, it is caught up in his wings, and is so strong that the angel can no longer fold them. This tempest is sweeping him inexorably into the future to which he has turned his back, while the heap of rubble in front of him rises up to heaven. What we call progress is this tempest.[17]

Where do we find these 'ruins upon ruins' which our progress has left behind in history? Let us try to find the sources of tormenting memories so that by becoming aware of them we can seek to heal them.

(i) The glossy messianic surface of European history has its ugly apocalyptic downside: the victorious progress of the European peoples in the nineteenth century led to the regress of many peoples, with heavy losses. Only a third of the modern world is the modern First Word; two-thirds of it are the modern Third World. The 'new time' has produced them both, both modernity and submodernity, as I should like to call them. For the oppressed, long-enslaved and always exploited peoples of the Third World, the messianism of modern European times has never been anything but the apocalypse of their destruction. Only the mass enslavement of the Africans from 1496 to 1888 made the colonial latifundia economy in America possible. Sugar, cotton, coffee and tobacco counted as 'slave crops'. It was gold and silver from Latin America that first created the capital used to build up European industrial society.[18] The wealth of the European countries grew out of the triangular transatlantic trade – slaves from Africa to America, raw materials and precious metals from America to Europe, merchandise and weapons from Europe to Africa. But through the slave trade this wealth destroyed Africa's kingdoms and cultures, and through export economy America's subsistence economy; and the peoples there were offered up on the altar of European development.

(ii) Nature did not fare much better. The beginning of modern industrial society was also the beginning of 'the end of nature'.[19] The spread of scientific and technological civilization as we have known it up to now has led to the extermination of more and more plant and animal species. Industrial emissions are producing the greenhouse effect, which is going to change the earth's climate radically in the coming years, with severe consequences. Rain forests are being felled, pastureland overgrazed, deserts are growing. In the last sixty years – my own lifetime – the world's population has quadrupled, and will go on increasing. Foodstuff requirements will grow proportionately, and so will the amount of refuse produced. The ecosystem of our planet is losing its equilibrium. This is not just a crisis of the natural environment. It is also a crisis of the industrial world itself. The destruction of nature which we can see every day with our own eyes is based on the disturbed relationship of modern men and women to nature. It is impossible to make oneself 'the master and possessor of nature' if one is still part of nature, and dependent on it. The modern culture of mastery has produced its own downside, which reveals its catastrophic effects in the disappearance of natural living spaces. Here Benjamin's 'ruins upon ruins' are very evident. If we look at the development of the newest industrial products on show at the EXPO 2000 we get a sense of progress. If we see the growing refuse dumps on earth, in the sea and in space, fears of catastrophe creep in on us. Does our progress really justify these consequences?

(iii) In the First World War of 1914–18, the great Christian powers in Europe destroyed each other. It was a war of extermination without any detectable war aims on either side. Its symbol was the Battle of Verdun in 1916.[20] According to the German idea, this was to be 'a battle of attrition'. It was the idea of annihilation that dominated military thinking, not the hope of victory. The first six months of the war brought over 600,000 dead and almost no territorial gains or losses. Then Germany began the gas war, and gained nothing. The enthusiasm for war in 1914 turned into the naked bestiality of pure nihilism. 'The lamps are going out all over Europe', said Edward Grey, the British Foreign Secretary, 'and we shall not see them lit again in our lifetime.' And it was not just the lamps in Europe that went out; the lights of the Enlightenment and of resplendent progress towards a better world went out too. It was as if progress had turned on itself and had devoured its own children. What we have suffered in the twentieth century, and are still suffering, is an apocalypse without hope, extermination without justification, pure pleasure in torture, rape and murder. The 'Decline of the West' (Spengler's title) was fuelled in Europe by the drive for self-destruction. The age that began in 1914 and whose end we do not know – perhaps it ended with the end of the East–West conflict in 1989 – became what W. H. Auden called 'the age of anxiety'.

The Second World War of 1939–45 continued the modern world's nihilistic work of annihilation. Disguised under those misused symbols of hope 'the Third Reich' or 'the Thousand Years' Reich', in Germany 'the final solution of the Jewish question' was pursued at Auschwitz, while the peoples of eastern Europe were exterminated through labour and hunger. In 1945 Germany's self-destruction was met by cynical comments from its Führer. The expulsion of whole populations began, with millions of victims. Japan was punished in August 1945 by two atomic bombs, which killed hundreds of thousands of people on the spot. In the Fascist dictator cult, naked power – power requiring no legitimation – was idolized, and industrial output relentlessly pursued. In the Soviet Union, Stalin exterminated whole classes and populations, first through hunger, then through labour and disease in his Gulag Archipelago. Mao Zedong adopted the same party system and state terrorism imposed from above. Numerous petty tyrants, such as Pol Pot in Cambodia, learned from them how to murder their own people. Ethnic cleansing became the word – or rather the non-word – of this era. The relapse into forms of personal cruelty against the weak – forms that people thought had long been overcome – in the Balkans, in Africa, and now in Germany too, is horrifying. It would be cynical to go on talking today about the moral progress of humanity through civilization. Hitler and Stalin and all their willing henchmen have convinced us that the power of radical evil is unbroken. That is why end-of-the-world scenarios, catastrophe fantasies and *Apocalypse Now* films seem to us more realistic than the fine, hopeful images of the nineteenth century about the golden age and eternal peace.

The twentieth century brought no new ideas, visions or utopias into the world which could lend history a meaning. We have seen the killing fields of history forbid every attempt to find a meaning for them, and every theodicy, every ideology of progress and every satisfaction in globalization. In this century progress has left in its wake ruins and victims, and no historical future can make this suffering good. No better future can assure us that their suffering was not for nothing. In the twentieth century, a total inability to find meaning in the face of history as it has hitherto been, has replaced the nineteenth century's credulous faith in the future. If the achievements of science and technology can be employed for the annihilation of humanity – and if they can, they will be, some day or other – it becomes difficult to enthuse over the internet or genetic engineering. Every accumulation of power also accumulates the danger of its misuse. But one thing at least the twentieth century should have taught us, as we look back at the nineteenth: it is impossible for history to be consummated in history. No historical future can do that. And it is impossible to complete history if we ourselves are merely historical beings.

III Bridges to the future

I am calling the hopes pointing towards the next thousand years 'bridges to the future' because they have to be built over the abysses of annihilation we have experienced in the twentieth century. They are practically the same hopes that brought the modern world to life in the nineteenth century – in the democratic and the industrial revolutions – but today they are hopes that have become wise through bitter experience. We will no longer be so credulously confident about progress as we once were, when these hopes first saw the light of day, or so blind to the risks. Today our hopes will have to be cautious hopes, and hopes that count the costs. We have to hope and work for the future without arrogance and without despair. The nineteenth century's hopes for humanity have left us living on the mass graves of the twentieth. Whether we look upon the new millennium in exuberant hope or with scepticism, we need to be reconciled with the past of the twentieth century, so that for us that century can become the past, and its catastrophes do not close in on us again.

The future of Christian hope

The raising of the dead: hope for those who have gone

Before I go into the links with the secular hopes for the nineteenth century in the light of the twentieth, I should like to come back again to Walter Benjamin's 'angel of history'. Wide-eyed, the angel sees before him in the past 'ruins upon ruins'; the wreckage of history rises up to heaven before him. He is petrified, 'for the tempest blowing from Paradise' is caught up in his wings, so that he cannot fold them again. But what did this angel really want to do? For what purpose was he sent? 'He would like to tarry, to awaken the dead and piece together what has been broken.' But he is unable to do so as long as the tempest is caught up in his wings. 'What we call progress is this tempest', says Benjamin. So we might conclude, conversely, that if we could interrupt this tempest, and could get away from the wind of progress, the angel would be able to waken the dead and piece together what is broken, and we could remember them, and our memories would be healed.

We find the biblical image behind this in chapter 37 of the book of Ezekiel, which tells of Israel's resurrection and reunification. In the Spirit of the Lord, the prophet is led out to 'the wide field full of dead bones'. That is a reference back to Israel's history of suffering. And the bones 'were very dry'. Then the prophet hears the voice: 'Behold, I will cause a breath [*ruach*, vital energy] to enter you, and you shall live . . . and you shall say to the breath "Come from the four winds . . . and breathe upon these slain that they may live"' (vv. 5, 9). After he has experienced this vision of the raising of the dead, the prophet goes to his people and proclaims: 'Behold they say: Our bones are dried up, and our hope is lost; we are clean cut off . . . But the Lord God says: I will put my Spirit within you, and you shall live, and I will place you in your own land' (vv. 11, 14).

'Waken the dead and piece together what has been broken.' That is a future hope for the past. There is no historical future in which it could happen. It must be a future for the whole of history; and being so, it must have a transcendent foundation. For mortal beings will not awaken the dead, and those who have done the breaking will not be able to put together what is broken. No human future can make good the crimes of the past. But in order to be able to live with this past, with its ruins and victims, without repressing it and without having to repeat it, we need this transcendent hope for the raising of the dead and the healing of what has been broken. Because of the raising of the broken Christ, the Christian hope for the future is at its heart a hope for resurrection. Without hope for the past there is no hope for the future, for what will be, will pass away; what is born, dies; and what is not yet, will one day be no longer.[21] The resurrection hope is not directed towards a future in history; it points towards the future of history, in which the tragic dimensions of history and nature will be dissolved.

But if the future of history is defined by the raising of the dead, then in that raising we encounter our own past too. Among the dead there come to meet us the fallen, the gassed, the murdered and the 'disappeared'. The dead of Verdun, Auschwitz, Stalingrad and Hiroshima await us.

Only the person who remembers can look this future in the face, the future called 'the raising of the dead'. And only the person who looks into this future is able really to remember those who have gone, and to live in their presence. Today many people are asking for 'a culture of remembrance', but such a culture must be sustained by 'a culture of hope', for without hope for a future of the past and those who are past, remembrance sinks into nostalgia and ultimately into a powerless forgetting; or it clings to the remembered so closely that it can no longer free itself, because it cannot let go what it remembers. 'Remembrance hastens the redemption' is written over Yad Vashem in Jerusalem. 'The dead are dead, but we awaken them', said the historian Leopold von Ranke. 'We walk with them and look them in the eye. They demand the truth from us.'[22]

If we compare Benjamin with Ezekiel, we see that the tempest we call progress blows in the opposite direction. It blows 'from Paradise', says Benjamin. That is to say, it drives people further and further from their original home. The tempest of the resurrection does not blow from the past into the future; it blows from the future into the past, and brings back what cannot be brought back – the dead – and heals what is unhealably broken – the ruins. We already feel it in the Pentecostal Spirit that makes us live 'through the power of the age to come' (Hebrews 6: 5).

How are these two tempests, 'progress' and 'resurrection', related to each other? How can the transcendent hope for God be joined with the immanent hopes of men and women? I believe in their opposition.[23] Because (and in so far as) the resurrection hope sees a future for those who are gone, those who are living in the present gain courage for the future. Because of a great hope for the overcoming of death and transience, our little hopes for future better times gain strength, and do not fall victim to resignation and cynicism. In the midst of the age of anxiety we hope 'against hope'; and still do not give ourselves up to despair. We gain the courage to be, in spite of non-being, as Paul Tillich aptly put it.[24] Our limited human hopes for those to come then become a reaction to the divine future for those who have gone.

The future of the democratic revolution

We owe the democratization of political life to the American and French revolutions. With them the nineteenth century began. After tremendous struggles and sacrifices, since 1989 liberal democracy has come to prevail in the Western and modern world, in the face of Fascist tyranny and the communist 'dictatorship of the proletariat'.

But today we have democratic politics under different conditions from those of the nineteenth century.

(i) *Absentee democracy*. Modern democracies today are threatened not so much by totalitarian right- or left-wing parties as by the apathy of the people from whom, when all is said and done, according to the Basic Law or constitution of the German Federal Republic (Article 20.2), 'all state power' issues. The diminishing turnout at elections is only a symptom of this apathy. What is the deeper cause? I believe the reason is that we view democracy as a condition we possess, not as a process we are involved in. But democracy is an open, expanding process of democratization which can never be completed in history, and which requires the active participation, participatory interest and personal commitment of the people. If this democratizing process flags, then the political interest of the people flags too. The participatory democracy that is necessary is replaced by a strange absentee democracy. People withdraw into private life or into their business concerns and don't want to be bothered with politics any longer. They lose interest, and no longer take part. A political class then becomes estranged from the people, and the people lose trust in the politicians. The result, as Richard von Weizshäcker complained, is party rule. The parties by no means fulfil their function of helping to form the will of the people, as the Basic Law requires (Article 21.1); instead they impose their own will on the people.

(ii) Democracy as a process open to the future only remains alive as long as it is motivated and mobilized by *hope for the realization of human rights*. The civil rights guaranteed in various constitutions are just, provided they correspond to the Universal Declarations of Human Rights of 1948 and 1966.[25] As we can see from the struggles for the rights of women, children, the disabled, asylum seekers and other underprivileged groups, the democratic implementation of human rights in the civil rights of our political community has by no means been completed. Many free and spontaneous citizen's action groups on local and regional levels have to be mobilized if human rights are to be realized. Participatory democracy is worth it, I believe, for the sake of the implementation of human rights.

Human rights are universally valid; they apply to all human beings. They are indivisible. It follows that every person is not only the member of a people, the citizen of a nation, the adherent of a religious community, and so forth, but also has 'inalienable human rights'. Today human rights are not just a United Nations 'ideal', as the preamble says; they can be claimed through international courts of law, where these exist. What happened in the Balkans was frightful, but the fact that people responsible for crimes against humanity and infringements of human rights are brought before the international court of justice in the Hague and are condemned by it, is a small step forward. Crimes against humanity and one day – as I hope – crimes against the environment too must be punished, so that human rights and the rights of nature may become the fundamental rights of a global human society.

(iii) The *nuclear threat* means that the peaceful regulation of conflicts between countries is a duty. Nuclear armaments and other means of mass extermination are not military weapons; they are political ones.

The avoidance of the nuclear annihilation of the world (which is possible at any time, even if it is not very probable at the moment) means that an age-old apocalyptic task is again being imposed on the modern state and the community of states as a whole. The power that was to hold back the End-time annihilation was called the Kat'echon. This 'power of restraint' derives from the prophecy about the Antichrist in 2 Thessalonians 2: 7ff.: 'The mystery of lawlessness is already at work; only he who now restrains it will do so until he is out of the way.' For Christians in the Roman empire, the one that now 'restrains' it meant the Roman state; for Carl Schmitt it was the anti-revolutionary Holy Alliance in the nineteenth century and, in the twentieth, the 'anti-bolshevist' Hitler dictatorship.[26] We can forget these two ideological anxieties. Today the annihilation of the human race and the inhabitable earth is the real threat. So every country has the urgent task of restraining humanity's nuclear self-annihilation.

'We are living in the "End-time"', said Gunter Anders, and rightly so, for he did not mean any form of apocalyptic prophecy; he meant the time in which the end is possible at any moment.[27] Consequently the state not only has the power of restraining the nuclear catastrophe; it also has the positive task of gaining time, and extending the time-limit.[28] With every year the annihilation can be put off, we gain time for life and for peace. We do not have endless time. That was an illusion of the nineteenth century, with its credulous belief in progress. We exist in limited time, and must gain time. This is a truly global historical task for the modern state in the shadow of nuclear extermination.

Is there a *Christian hope for the political world* which motivates Christians for responsible cooperation and, if circumstances require it, justifies their resolute resistance?

It is the task of the Christian community to remind the civil community unceasingly, through word, act and presence, of the righteousness and justice of God and of his coming kingdom. The church is not like a sect, separate, and there only for itself. It is there for all human beings, and for nature in this earthly creation. The future for which Christians hope is not the consummation of the church in the downfall of this world, nor the salvation of the redeemed at the world's end; it is the kingdom of God, which will redeem everything and put it to rights, the kingdom which will come 'on earth as it is in heaven'. Consequently the church cannot intervene politically simply on behalf of its own interests. It must above all intervene on behalf of the justice which, in the spirit of Jesus, is there for the poor and the powerless first of all. The church has no 'public claim' for itself, but only for the cause of the kingdom of God it propounds. Its task is not to churchify the world but to prepare the way for the coming kingdom. There is no such thing as non-political Christianity. Indeed, the modern axiom that 'religion is a private matter' was a political decision, directed against the old form of state church and political religion (*cuius regio – eius religio*: a person's religion is the religion of his ruler).

In the history of this still unredeemed world, Christians will not aim to bring about the kingdom of God. God will do that himself. But they will press for parables and correspondences to God's righteousness and justice and his kingdom, and insist that circumstances that are in contradiction to them are diminished. Christianity's motivating vision is the descent to earth from heaven of the *polis* Jerusalem (Revelation 21: 2), in whose light the nations are to live in peace (Rev. 21: 24).

Because Christians know that they have the rights of citizenship in the coming kingdom (*politeuma*, Philippians 3: 20), they will do what is best in the kingdom of the world in which they live, and will contribute their ideas about justice and freedom to their political community. Because of their hope, they cannot escape into the absentee democracy, but will be present wherever political ways out of the perils have to be sought for. In these perils of the world they can show where deliverance is to be found.

The future of the industrial revolution

The industrial revolution awakened the mobilizing faith in progress that was the mark of the nineteenth century. Today we no longer have any need to justify such a belief. Nor do we need to criticize it any more, for the competitive principle makes progress compulsive for all production. Indeed, industries and markets are condemned to a continually accelerating progress. Whatever fails to modernize and rationalize has already lost. Progress has got itself into the acceleration trap. 'The person who rides the tiger can never get off again.'[29]

This means that there is not much point in criticizing progress as such. What does have a point is to question its goals, so as to correct its course, if that is desirable. Progress itself is only a means to an end; it does not itself prescribe humane ends. We generally measure progress by the increase of economic, financial, military and cultural power. But power itself is not a humane goal; it is only an accumulation of the means whereby humane goals can be attained. Every year we are better equipped to achieve what we want – but what do we really want?

Most major technological projects were started not because this was the democratically established will of the people, but because the will of the people was bypassed. In Germany there was no democratic decision about the building of nuclear power stations. And there are no democratic discussions today about genetically modified foodstuffs.

Since the end of the East–West conflict, progress has come to be called globalization. This process already got underway in the nineteenth century and at the beginning of the twentieth. Since 1989, the end of the East–West conflict, we have reverted to the views held before 1914. But like progress, globalization, to be precise, is merely a quantifying term: what once applied to particular cases is now deemed universal. What used to be local is now considered global. Like progress, globalization is therefore only the means to an end, not a humane end in itself. As long as it is merely a matter of acquiring power, the process of globalization does not exist, qualitatively speaking. Initially it is manifestly only a matter of dominating, exploiting and marketing nature. Commerce starts to be shared out between fewer and fewer global players, but these players get bigger and bigger. But if short-term profiteering is not to lead in the long term to the bankruptcy of humanity and the collapse of the ecosystem, we must begin a public discussion about humane goals and the purposes of globalization.

In order to avoid the destruction of the earth through ruthless exploitation, it is good to concentrate on the holism of creation, and to protect life through bio-ethical conventions. It is also important to support sustainable development. But this inevitably ends up as an ethos of conservativism, and conservative ethics are always too late. It is better to develop a counter-model to the globalization of power which concentrates on finding humane goals and purposes for it.

We have a model of this kind for defining humane goals for globalized power, and hence for correcting the course of the modern world's development. We can find it in the inconspicuous term 'ecumenism', which has up to now been used only for relations between the churches.[30] In Greek, *oikumene* is a term of quality and means 'the whole, inhabited globe', a meaning that reflects its root in the word *oikos*, house. From a world inhabited by human beings we can derive the goal of a habitable world for a humanity that is at home on this earth. The 'housekeeping' of this earth requires the keeping of a dwelling place fit for human beings; while, for their part, human beings should be prepared to live in the ecosystem, and no longer stand against and apart from nature as hostile aliens.[31]

If the goal of progress and the globalization of human power is to make the earth habitable, not to dominate and possess it, we must leave behind the modern Western world's God-complex of being 'the masters and possessors of nature', which is what Descartes promised in his scientific theory at the beginning of modern times.[32] The earth can live without the human race, and did so for millions of years; but the human race cannot exist without the earth, for it is from the earth that we were taken. So human beings are dependent on the earth, but the earth is not dependent on human beings. It follows from this simple recognition that human civilization must be integrated into the ecosystem and not the converse – that nature has to be subjected to human domination.[33]

Only interlopers exploit nature, cut down the forests, fish the seas empty, and then pass on like nomads. People who live in these places, and want to live there, are concerned to preserve the foundations on which their life depends, and will preserve their natural environment so that it is capable of sustaining life. They will try to compensate for every intervention in nature, and to establish an equilibrium. Today's economic-ecological conflicts are largely conflicts between foreign corporations and the indigenous peoples – that is to say, they are conflicts between interests in exploitation on the one hand, and the habitability of nature on the other.

Having globalized power, we logically need to globalize responsibility. We cannot stand still at a point where the economy is globalized, but politics are still nationally limited. The economy needs its political correlate, and politics need humane goals about which human beings can unite.

Humanity's scientific and technological potential will have to be developed further, but it must not be employed in a destructive struggle for power. It can also be used to make the earth sustainably habitable by human beings. Then earthly creation will not be simply 'preserved' (to use the conservative vocabulary hitherto employed); it will develop further towards its goal. For it is destined to be the shared house of all earthly created beings, and to be the home and dwelling place for the community of all the living. The earth is even to become the dwelling place of God 'on earth as it is in heaven'.

When the Eternal One comes to 'dwell' on the earth, the earth will become God's cosmic 'temple' and the restless God of hope and history will come to his rest. That is the great biblical – Jewish and Christian – vision for this earth. It is the final promise: 'Behold, the dwelling place of God is with human beings. He will dwell with them, and they shall be his people' (Revelation 21: 3, following Ezekiel 37: 27). The ultimate Shekinah, this cosmic incarnation of God, is the divine future of the earth. In this expectation we shall already treat the earth as 'God's temple' here and now, and cherish its creatures as sacred. We men and women are not 'the masters and possessors' of the earth, but perhaps we shall one day become its priests and priestesses, representing God to the earth, and bringing the earth before God, so that we see and taste God in all things, and perceive all things in the radiance of his love. That would be a sacramental view of the world which would be able to take up and absorb into itself the world-view held at present in science and technology.

3

ENLIGHTENMENT HUMANISM AS A RELIC OF CHRISTIAN MONOTHEISM

John Gray

Introductory

It has long been known that the Enlightenment was a very complicated affair. Within that far-flung extended family of thinkers and movements, arising over several centuries in a number of countries, there were Deists and atheists, empiricists and rationalists, nationalists and cosmopolitans, liberals and anti-liberals – representatives, in fact, of opposing views on virtually all the major philosophical and political issues of the time. Whether freedom of the will is a reality, whether commonsense is a good guide in ethics, how much human behaviour depends on environment and how much on heredity, the importance or otherwise of autonomous choice in the good life – nothing is easier than pointing to Enlightenment luminaries who took up different or opposed positions on these and other great issues. In the light of this enormous variety of views, there are many who say that it makes no sense to talk of anything like an 'Enlightenment project'[1] – a shared enterprise common to all Enlightenment figures.

Ironically, and at the same time predictably, those who deny that there was ever anything like an Enlightenment project are commonly amongst its most passionate contemporary defenders, whilst those who reject it insist that it is what made the Enlightenment a recognizable intellectual movement. I find myself in this latter camp, partly because I believe that Enlightenment humanism was very largely a secular version of distinctively Christian hopes and beliefs.

I do not mean to underestimate the diversity of the intellectual and political movements encompassed by the portmanteau term 'Enlightenment'. The Scottish Enlightenment differed importantly from the French Enlightenment, both differed from the Enlightenment in

America, and all three contained movements and thinkers at odds on basic issues. There is reasonable disagreement about when the Enlightenment emerged as a recognizable tendency in European intellectual history, and equally about when – and whether – it ended. Quite clearly, the Enlightenment is not the sort of thing that has an essence – a set of defining properties that it possesses everywhere. Even so, it is a mistake to think that it signifies nothing more than a range of family resemblances amongst intellectual movements having no shared core beliefs. On the contrary, some fundamental beliefs are shared by nearly all Enlightenment thinkers, whatever their other commitments.

I wish to focus on three such beliefs, and to argue that each of them is a Christian inheritance that is indefensible in the terms of a genuinely naturalistic world-view. The first is a belief in the possibility of progress for the species, not only in scientific knowledge but also – and most importantly – in ethical and political life. The second is the belief that the growth of human knowledge and human emancipation go together: for the species, as perhaps for individuals, knowledge enhances freedom. The third, presupposed and entailed by the first two, is the belief that, as a result of the growth of knowledge, humankind can attain a rational consensus on values.

Each of these beliefs I believe to be demonstrably false; but I do not aim to argue that here. More modestly, I wish to suggest that these beliefs are defensible only in the terms of Christian monotheism. The very concepts and categories in which these Enlightenment beliefs are framed are residues of Christian faith, and cannot survive the adoption of a genuinely naturalistic world-view. If this is so, two conclusions follow of some importance for how we think about the Enlightenment.

In the first place, the Enlightenment must be understood as a phase in the history of one cultural tradition – roughly speaking, that of Christendom, more particularly western Christendom. As MacIntyre and others have represented it, the Enlightenment project was formulated in explicitly anti-Christian terms. It was the project of replacing the traditional morality of the past, which was founded on revelation and the authority of the church, with a new morality, grounded in reason. But precisely because it was framed in such terms the Enlightenment project reproduced some distinctively Christian categories and beliefs.

Unlike the polytheistic cults of the ancient world, Christians hold that there is one god whose commands have authority for everyone. In the same way, Enlightenment values are binding on all of humankind. Almost inevitably, thinkers whose cultural background is monotheistic tend to think that the good life is at bottom the same for all humans. When they oppose Christianity, they do so as post-monotheists, who share with their Christian opponents the belief that one way of life is best for everyone. In contrast, though it acknowledges that some values are universal, a genuinely naturalistic ethical outlook will affirm that humans flourish in many forms of life, some of them incompatible.

It is not only in its strongly universalistic ethical outlook that Enlightenment humanism replicates Christian thinking. More, it holds out to mankind a promise of salvation that is a secular version of Christianity's. History might seem a succession of crises and catastrophes, often tragic and more commonly farcical, in which civilized life in all of its many varieties is recurrently derailed by human folly. But for Enlightenment humanists, as for Christians, this sorry tale is actually the working out of a larger design. The end of history will be a universal civilization, from which tyranny, poverty and superstition have been expunged. This fantastical notion could probably only have been taken seriously by thinkers whose view of things had been deformed by Christian eschatology.[2]

The self-image of the Enlightenment is that of a universal movement. In reality it has always been a strictly local cult, a secular version of a Western religion.[3] If so – and this is my second conclusion – the prospects of Enlightenment humanism are poor. It has always claimed to be Christianity's successor, and in the last analysis it is merely that. Enlightenment humanism embodies a conception of humankind as a peculiarly privileged species that derives not from science but from religion – more particularly, from Christianity.

In any truly naturalistic view, humans are a species of animal. There is no more reason to expect progress from them than there is to expect it from whales or tigers. Unlike whales or tigers, humans have developed methods of scientific inquiry through which they have acquired a degree of power over nature; but they have always used that power to achieve whatever goals and needs were uppermost in their lives, however short-sighted or harmful to themselves and others, rather than to advance their freedom, and there is no reason to think they will do otherwise in future. If humans differ from other animals, it is only in the fact that they can thrive in a greater variety of ways; but for that very reason there is no one way of life that is best for all. Adopting this authentically naturalistic view of the human animal means giving up the inordinate hopes for it inculcated by Christianity and renewed by the Enlightenment.

Because it reproduces so many Christian themes it is reasonable to expect Enlightenment humanism to sink into insignificance if Christian belief continues to decline. Insofar as European thought becomes genuinely naturalistic it makes a humanist conception of the human animal unviable. Contrariwise, probably only a Christian revival can ensure Enlightenment humanism a future.

The idea of progress

Many views of progress can be found among Enlightenment thinkers. This is only to be expected, since Enlightenment thinkers have held to a wide variety of conceptions of the human good. Some have understood it as pleasure or desire-satisfaction, others as self-realization or the full development of human powers. Enlightenment thinkers differ greatly as to the ingredients of the good; even when they agree on a list they often disagree as to the relative weight of its components in the best societies and the best individual lives. Equally, Enlightenment thinkers have taken different views of the relations of the right with the good, with Immanuel Kant asserting the priority of the right over the good in ethics and politics and Jeremy Bentham insisting that rights are fictions, artifices constructed to promote the good. These differences translate into differing conceptions of progress; but they are all of them rival interpretations of a single idea, which marks off the Enlightenment as a whole from other intellectual traditions.

Consider some examples. The French positivist Auguste Comte thought that liberal values were suitable only in a specific phase of human development, and looked forward to a hierarchical, technocratic, post-liberal society in which there would be no more liberty in questions of morality than there is in chemistry. John Stuart Mill believed liberal freedoms, once achieved, to be of permanent value, and condemned Comte's system of ideas as a species of 'liberticide'.[4] Karl Marx – one of many critics of liberal individualism to have been deeply influenced by the French positivists – accepted the Comtean view that liberal values were transitional phenomena in human development, using it to envision another post-liberal regime – one that was classless and egalitarian but equally grounded in the progress of science and technology. These three thinkers held quite different views regarding the future of the species. They diverged radically in their beliefs about what is possible for humankind, and little less about what is desirable. Even so, all three held to the core tenet of Enlightenment humanism – the faith that the future of humankind as a whole can be better than anything achieved by anyone in the past.

In holding out such a prospect before mankind, these Enlightenment thinkers were not unusual, but others were less sanguine about the likely course of human development. Voltaire – the paradigm Enlightenment figure[5] – oscillated throughout his life between fervent hope regarding the possibilities of progress and stoical resignation to the likelihood that the future history of the species would be a repetition of the crimes and follies of the past. Similarly, in the twentieth century, Max Weber and Bertrand Russell were hardly unqualified optimists regarding the human prospect. Yet even the most despairing amongst Enlightenment thinkers have always affirmed that progress – the attainment of a universal condition better than any achieved even by a few in the past – is *possible*. Error and accident might derail the steady march to a better world. The species might advance in a succession of zig-zags, with the danger of relapse never entirely disappearing. Quite conceivably, it might slide into permanent barbarism. Humankind might never actually achieve the progress of which it is capable.

The possibilities of progress might never be fully realized; but it is an unshakeable article of faith for every Enlightenment thinker that they are not illusory. There is nothing in the nature of things or in the nature of the species that stands in the way of a future superior to anything achieved in the past. This was the creed of Condorcet and Paine, Marx and Mill, and it remains the faith of Enlightenment thinkers today. Friedrich von Hayek and Jürgen Habermas, Francis Fukuyama and Richard Rorty may be at odds on a number of issues – though I think they will be found to be points of detail. They are at one in subscribing to the faith that the human condition can be indefinitely improved. In this, they are animated by Christian moral hopes, which any genuinely naturalistic philosophy is bound to reject.

In the eighteenth century, Enlightenment thinkers very often saw themselves as returning to pagan values, but in this they were mistaken. No pagan thinker ever believed that the majority of humankind could achieve the good life. Aristotle is explicit in his view that the best life – a life devoted to philosophical inquiry, as he imagined – was attainable only by a few leisured Greek males. Epicurus took for granted that the happiness he held out to his followers – a sodality of ascetic hedonists conversing tranquilly in a garden – could only ever belong to the lucky few. The mystery religions (such as Mithraism) followed the philosophers in withholding salvation from the many; only an elite of initiates could expect liberation from the world. If they entertained the idea of salvation at all, the religions and philosophies of Greek and Roman antiquity took for granted that the mass of mankind could not be saved – and perhaps was not worth saving. As far as European thought is concerned, the idea of *salvation for all* arises only with Christianity.[6]

The Enlightenment idea of progress is a secular avatar of the Christian idea of the equality of souls. For Christians, all humans are born with the hope of salvation (even if, as Calvin and others believed, most will be damned). To be sure, throughout the history of Christianity this egalitarian faith coexisted with enormous social inequalities – including, for many centuries, the institution of slavery. Even so, the idea of progress is a mutation of *Christian* values. It is nowhere to be found in pre-Christian European thinkers. Among pagan thinkers it is taken as given that the human animal does not change its ways. In Christian and post-Christian thought, affirming the constancy of human nature typically goes with the claim that humans thrive best in one and only one way of life. That was what Rousseau believed: that, because human nature is the same everywhere and at all times, so is the best kind of human life. In contrast, among pagans the belief that human nature is invariant went along with the belief that they would always worship different gods and live in different ways. There were better and worse ways for humans to live; but none that was best for all. In this pagan view, the constancy of human nature does not imply uniformity in its best manifestations. At the same time it means that there will always be many ways of living well.

A similar view of things may be found in early modern thinkers who genuinely rejected Christianity, or who never took it seriously. Machiavelli, Hobbes and Spinoza shared the pagan belief that, because human nature is something fixed, there can be no radical improvement in human affairs. Like the pagans, these early moderns believed that humans cannot surpass the best they have attained in the past, nor is it reasonable to expect them ever to be rid of the defects that have always made the best forms of human life short-lived. In the future, as in the past, there will be eras of high civilization, in which peace, good government, the arts and science flourish; but they will be brief, and succeeded by times of war, tyranny and barbarism. For Enlightenment thinkers, this can only be a desperate view of things. For the pagan philosophers of antiquity and these early modern thinkers, or anyone today who thinks like them today, it is common sense.[7]

That human nature was ineradicably flawed was a feature of Christian thinking, notably in traditions influenced by Augustine. It was not this aspect of Christian belief that shaped the Enlightenment, however, but rather its moral egalitarianism and its view of history.

ENLIGHTENMENT HUMANISM

For pagans, history is modelled on natural processes. Growth and decline, death and rebirth – these are the categories pagans apply to history. This cyclical view of human affairs is seen clearly in Aristotle's *Politics*, with its abundance of biological metaphors, and it is beautifully expressed in Homer's well-known lines:

> Very like leaves
> upon this earth are the generations of men
> old leaves, cast upon the ground by wind, young leaves
> the greening forest bears when spring comes in.
>
> So mortals pass; one generation flowers
> Even as another dies away[8]

In this pagan view, the life of each generation may have meaning, but history as a whole has none. It may well be doubted if a pagan could have thought of writing a history of mankind. A history of the Athenians or the Romans, to be sure – but where does any pagan writer attempt a history of the species? In contrast, Christians have always viewed history as moral drama, a single continuous narrative of sin and redemption in which the salvation of humankind is implicated. In any Christian view, it may not be given us to divine the ways of providence; but it cannot be doubted that history unfolds under its guidance.

The same point can be put in another, and more precise way. Unlike the ancient Greeks and Romans, the Indians and the Chinese, the Japanese and practically every other cultural tradition, Christian cultures conceive history in eschatological terms. It has a beginning and an end and – though we may not be privy to it – a definite plot that involves the whole of humanity. Late mediaeval millenarian movements radicalized Christian eschatology and turned it into a revolutionary project.[9] Later, Marx and other radical Enlightenment thinkers did the same. The Christian, salvific understanding of history is renewed in all the political faiths that have sprung up since the Enlightenment, not least liberalism.[10] Not all liberal thinkers are as hubristic as those who lately announced the end of history. Even so, the very idea of a universal history is a Christian inheritance. In which other culture could Francis Fukuyama's pronouncement have been made[11] – or taken seriously?

The Christian inheritance to the Enlightenment was a combination of two elements, neither of which can be found in pre-Christian European thought – the affirmation that the hope of salvation belongs to all humans, and the belief that the salvation of the species is worked out in history. Taken together, these Christian notions produced the idea of progress. The idea that humanity can advance towards a condition better than any that had ever been known is not a secular idea but rather the very opposite. (As we employ it today, secularity is itself a Christian category; but that is another story.) The idea of progress is a Christian affirmation of the equality of souls fused with a Christian understanding of the meaning of history.

The growth of knowledge and universal emancipation

The idea that truth sets us free is not uniquely Christian. In the European tradition, Plato and his followers held to a mystical philosophy in which what we take to be the world is actually an illusion. Like many other mystical traditions, Platonists linked the condition of delusion in which humans ordinarily live with their propensity to act badly. If the vices have a single cause, it is taking for real what is not; we would not envy another's wealth or power, or devote our lives to acquiring it, if we understood that it is illusory. At the same time, truth contains all that is good. For all true goods are compatible with one another and even interpenetrate one another. This is the Platonic faith that all goods come together in perfect harmony in the Form of the Good.

This account of the relation of knowledge with virtue was given a canonical formulation by Socrates, who claimed – in Plato's account of his teaching, at any rate – that knowing the good and acting in accord with the good were one and the same. In affirming an unbreakable link between knowing the truth of things and living the good life Plato followed his great teacher. So did most of the philosophers of European antiquity. It is hard to make sense of the Stoic claim that a slave may be freer than his master if one does not think that knowledge – in the Stoic case, knowledge of the nature of things and one's necessary place in it – sets one free.

The Socratic faith that knowledge and emancipation go together is one of the cornerstones of classical European philosophy. Christians absorbed this Greek faith and gave it a new content. For Christians, the knowledge that sets us free is not knowledge of the nature of things; it is knowledge of God's will and the teachings of Jesus.[12] The world after the Fall of Man is not perfect; but the God that created it is. Like Plato's Form of the Good, the Christian deity contains all that is truly good; to know that deity is to know the good in its perfection.

True, if humans have free will, they may rebel against the truth. Nevertheless, true belief is a condition of being saved. That is the common view of Platonists and of Christians: to know the truth *is* to know the good.[13]

Unlike paganism and Judaism, Christianity has always made a great deal of belief. In the *Iliad* and the Old Testament, religion has nothing to do with belief, except incidentally. It is to do with practice. To follow one's religion is not to accept any particular, perhaps contested, set of beliefs, it is to perform its rites and worship in its temples. To be sure – and here I anticipate an exceedingly obvious objection – following one's religion in this way carries with it some freight of belief. When I worship at the shrine of Apollo, I must have some beliefs about Apollo and his relations with the world and myself. Even so, it is far from being the case that having such beliefs is what makes me a follower of Apollo. They may be quite unimportant when compared with my faithfulness in performing the rituals of the Apollonian cult and observing its precepts in my daily life. In this, ancient Greek religion resembles a number of religions today. Belief is central neither in Judaism nor in Hinduism. Equally, in Japan and China, belonging to one religion does not exclude membership of another. Buddhists may be followers of Shinto, Confucians may be Taoists, in different contexts and at different stages of their lives. If the core of religion were belief, this would entail inconsistency; but if it is practice, there need be no incompatibility.[14]

It was partly because Christianity attached such a peculiar importance to belief that it aroused such hostility in the ancient world. Precisely because it made true belief a condition of salvation, Christianity was bound to threaten civil cults such as those of the Romans. If all are damned who do not know the one true god, there is an obligation on believers to convert the world. From this standpoint, the Stoic emperor Marcus Aurelius's persecution of Christians does not look so unreasonable.

The Christian insistence on true belief as a condition of salvation was one of the intellectual currents that gave birth to the Enlightenment. Of course the conception of knowledge deployed by Enlightenment thinkers was in many ways quite different from that which Christianity took over from classical Greek thought. It was shaped by science more than by philosophy, and – contrary to Platonism – it affirmed that the mutable material world is real. For Plato, the knowledge that sets us free is knowledge of a timeless spiritual reality. For Francis Bacon, one of the Enlightenment's precursors, it was knowledge of the workings of nature that gave humans power over nature, and thereby – or so he thought – freedom. Later, Bentham affirmed the same, adding only that the most useful knowledge had to do with human nature. For John Stuart Mill, it is the growth of knowledge that drives history, which is none other than the progressive emancipation of the species. This conception of progress in history is at the heart of Mill's liberalism. When he writes in *On Liberty* that his argument for individual freedom will be based not on 'abstract right' but on utility, he is insistent that it is 'utility in the largest sense, grounded on the permanent interests of man as a progressive being'.[15]

What is new in these Enlightenment thinkers is the idea that our knowledge of the world *grows*. What is old – very old – is the faith that the truth shall set us free. Yet there is nothing in the fact of the growth of scientific knowledge that supports Enlightenment hopes. Undoubtedly, science enhances human powers; but that means only that it enables humans better to achieve their goals – whatever they are. As I shall argue in the next section of this paper, it has no tendency to produce a convergence on values.

In holding that the spread of science goes with increasing acceptance of Enlightenment values, humanists today – whether they know it or not – echo the beliefs of an all but forgotten early nineteenth-century philosophical cult. One of the central tenets of positivism was the belief that as the practice of science spreads throughout the world, religion will weaken and there will be a convergence on the values of secular humanism. History has never offered the slightest support to this belief. In reality, science and technology have been appropriated to advance the values of religious fundamentalism and ethnic nationalism and racism quite as often as those of secular humanists. The Taliban warrior threatening to use new weapons of mass destruction in a holy war is an object of incredulous horror in liberal cultures; but he is not a historical anomaly. Modern technology has been used to commit crimes against humanity on a scale hitherto impossible. There have been pogroms throughout the history of Christendom. But only a modern state, equipped with modern technology, could have attempted the Final Solution.

The fact is that the absorption of science and technology into a society carries with it no imperative of convergence on any particular values – least of all Enlightenment values. The belief that they do is part of a philosophy of history that history has itself falsified. As Stuart Hampshire has written: 'The Positivists believed that all societies across the globe will gradually discard their traditional attachments . . . because of the need for rational, scientific and experimental modes of thought which a modern industrial economy involves. This is an old faith, widespread in the nineteenth century, that there must be a step-by-step convergence on liberal values, on "our values" . . . We know now that there is no "must" about it, and that all such theories have a predictive value of zero.'[16] In fact the old faith to which Hampshire alludes has been around a good deal longer than positivism. It is the Platonic-Christian faith that to know the truth is to know the good. The Enlightenment idea of universal emancipation is a mystical theodicy, emptied of its transcendental content and turned into a secular soteriology.

Progress in science and technology is a fact, but there is no reason to think the growth of human knowledge will ever be used to bring about universal human emancipation. History shows science and technology being used to advance the goals and values of a wide variety of movements and projects, liberal and reactionary, civilized and barbarous. Why should the future be any different? Human nature is not greatly different today from what it was three thousand years ago – or, for that matter, thirty thousand years ago. So far as we know, humans have the same needs and emotions. They are as prone to irrational beliefs. They are no less liable to engage in war and genocide than they ever were. The truth they have come to know through the growth of scientific knowledge has not set them free. It has merely enabled them to pursue their goals – however conflicting or destructive – more effectively.

If we think of humans as one animal species among others, this will come as no surprise. In such a naturalistic perspective, truth is one thing, the good – however it may be understood – another, and there is nothing to say they go together. As Isaiah Berlin put it, 'Everything is what it is: liberty is liberty, not equality or fairness or justice or culture, or human happiness or a quiet conscience.'[17] The Platonic-Christian equation of the true with the good presupposes a view of the world in which all goods are finally aspects of a single, perfectly harmonious Good. Very obviously, this is a species of monotheism; but it continues to animate Western philosophers, even – or especially – when they think themselves rid of religion.

The idea that all genuine goods dovetail in a perfect harmony is nowhere found in polytheistic cults, such as those of ancient Greece and Rome. It is a peculiarity of monotheistic religions and monistic mystical philosophies. Today it survives as the Enlightenment faith that the growth of knowledge goes with a growing consensus on values.

JOHN GRAY

The growth of knowledge and the convergence of values

Enlightenment thinkers have always differed widely on the nature of the good, but – curiously, one may think – these differences have in no way dimmed their faith in the possibility of a rational consensus on values. In their view, fundamental divergences in moral judgment are results of ignorance, imperfect knowledge or irrationality. To the extent that humankind accepts the results of scientific inquiry, it will come to have the same conception of the good. As knowledge advances, so will agreement in ethics.

It may be objected that few Enlightenment thinkers held this simple-minded faith; but such an objection would be quite mistaken. It is only because he believed that conflicting conceptions of the good will tend to disappear as knowledge advances that Karl Marx – undoubtedly one of the most formidable and influential Enlightenment thinkers – could have imagined that, in the communist society of the future, the government of men would be replaced by the administration of things. In Marx's utopia, once science has been used to overcome scarcity, there will be no conflicts of value – none, at any rate, that cannot be resolved by rational dialogue. As I have already noted, Marx was strongly influenced by the French positivists. This is nowhere more so than in his conviction that scientific progress tends to yield an ethical consensus. The same positivistic faith is evident in John Stuart Mill, who was rightly concerned that it might be at odds with his defence of diversity in styles of living.

It is not only nineteenth-century Enlightenment thinkers heavily influenced by positivism who have believed that the increase of knowledge yields a consensus on values. The same view is found in eighteenth-century Enlightenment thinkers, including the greatest among them. David Hume is justly renowned as a moral sceptic. For Hume, moral judgments are not the conclusions of the human reason but the expressions of our passions. Once we have established conventions, it is true, we can reason about right and wrong; we can engage in rational dispute about the application of the artificial virtues that have to do with justice. But the root of the natural virtues is in the universal human sentiment of sympathy, not in any of our rational faculties. Take way these human sentiments, Hume famously observed, and there is nothing irrational in preferring the destruction of the world to moving one's little finger.[18] Hume believed that ethical judgments do not track any reality that is independent of human beings; they express human sentiments. At the same time, he believed that the ethical judgments of reasonable people were everywhere much the same. He was able to combine these two beliefs without inconsistency because he held a third. He believed that, in all essential respects, human sentiments were the same everywhere. Hume's version of the Enlightenment project consists in combining an assertion of ethical subjectivism with an affirmation of the invariance of human sentiment.[19]

Hume believed that only religious superstition stood in the way of a rational consensus on values. He was able to do so, consistently with his emotivist account of ethical judgment, only because he underestimated the variety of human cultures – and because of the lingering influence on his thinking of Christianity. As Alasdair MacIntyre has written:

> [All contributors to the Enlightenment project] agree to a surprising degree on the content and character of the precepts which constitute genuine morality. Marriage and the family are *au fond* as unquestioned by Diderot's rationalist *philosophe* as they are by Kierkegaard's Judge Wilhelm; promise-keeping and justice are as inviolable for Hume as they are for Kant. Whence did they inherit these shared beliefs? Obviously from their shared Christian past compared with which divergences between Kant's and Kierkegaard's Lutheran, Hume's Presbyterian and Diderot's Jansenist-influenced Catholic background are relatively unimportant.[20]

Today we know much more than Hume did about the diversity of customs and conventions. We know that the institutions of marriage and the family come in a good many varieties, and property no less so. If it would occur to few philosophers today to attempt – as Hume did – to deduce the particular practices of their own societies from the universal properties of human nature, the reason is that they are known to be only a subset of a far wider range of practices found in other societies. Inklings of the wide-ranging cultural variability of centrally important social practices can be found in a number of eighteenth-century Enlightenment thinkers, including Adam Smith;[21] but few, if any, can be discerned in Hume. To admit such variability would have weakened the largely conservative thrust of Hume's social and political philosophy.

It is no accident that, whether conservative in temper (as in Hume), reformist (as in Bentham), or rigorist (as in Kant), these Enlightenment thinkers are uncompromisingly monistic in their ethical outlook. In conformity with the aim of supplanting Christianity as a universal creed, the Enlightenment sought to propound a single way of life as best for humankind. No doubt inklings of relativism can be found in Enlightenment thinkers such as Montesquieu, whose *Persian Letters* aim to show how the most basic institutions vary across cultures. But I can think of no Enlightenment thinker who does not believe that rational people will hold the same values. This is so, even when Enlightenment thinkers subscribe to a sort of political relativism – as did Voltaire, the prototypical Enlightenment *philosophe*. Voltaire never imagined that a single political regime was everywhere best; time, place and circumstance made enlightened despotism right in some historical contexts, republicanism in others; but he insisted that these regimes be judged in terms of universal values.[22] For Voltaire, political institutions were instruments for the promotion of civilization. Different circumstances necessitated different instruments; but the end was one and the same. One way of life was universally best, even though it could not always be achieved.

The problem faced by Voltaire and by all Enlightenment thinkers who follow him in this belief is why the manifest diversity of ways of living should not be accepted as natural for human beings. Take an analogy from linguistics. Humans are not born everywhere speaking a single tongue. That there are many natural languages, not only one, seems to be natural for them. Why should we not accept a similar diversity in values? By posing this question I do not mean to endorse wholesale value-relativism. It is perfectly possible to recognize some values as anthropological universals while affirming that humans can thrive in quite different ways of life. Indeed, we can view the diversity of particular ways of life as arising partly from different settlements of conflicts among values that are universal.

Some evils are obstacles to any kind of good life for humans. As Hobbes knew, being at continuing risk of violent death stands in the way of any sort of commodious living. So – later liberals added – does being chronically subject to arbitrary power. Anarchy and tyranny are political expressions of generically human evils. But different ways of life stave them off, and resolve conflicts between them, in different ways. Among these various settlements, some may be reasonably judged to be better or worse; but there need be none that is best. No settlement among conflicting universal values can be shown to be uniquely rational, or more reasonable than all others. On the contrary, there may be good reasons for incompatible settlements. Recognizing universal values is not the same as accepting a universally authoritative morality; different moralities will settle their conflicts in different ways. Such are the central theses of what I have elsewhere termed value-pluralism, or objective pluralism in ethics.[23]

Value-pluralism is a controversial position in ethical theory, and not one I need to argue for here. My aim is simpler, and more modest. It is to suggest that the Enlightenment project presupposes the monotheistic belief that only one conception of the good can be finally acceptable, and – as a consequence – only one way of life fully worth living. The project of formulating a universal rational morality does not inquire whether this is indeed so. It takes it as given, and then seeks to demonstrate it. But outwith monotheism there is no reason for denying that humans can live well in very different ways.

In a naturalistic view, variety in ways of life is normal for the human animal. So are conflicts of goods. We know that cultures vastly remote from one another in time and space contain very similar ethical conflicts. Duty versus desire, friendship against justice, loyalty to family at odds with loyalty to country – these are universal dilemmas. From Socrates onwards, European moral philosophers have tried to show that such ethical conflicts are unreal, or else that they have a solution that all reasonable people are bound to agree upon. In much the same way, Christians have always believed that, however difficult or even tragic the conflicts of value we face in the world, they are all resolved in heaven. For a consistent naturalist, all such beliefs are irrational. History and common experience attest that the rivalry of goods and diversity of ways of life are natural for humans. Why not accept what we know to be true?

A genuinely naturalistic view of the species is resisted, I believe, because it suggests that many of the hopes of Enlightenment humanism are delusive, if not spurious. In the past, humans have had many languages, faiths and moralities. There have been many aspirants to a universal civilization, but none has lasted for long. If history is our guide, we will expect the same to be true in future. Enlightenment thinkers reject this lesson of history because they cannot bear to give up the vast hopes for the species they have inherited from Christianity.

If, unlike most Enlightenment thinkers, we seek not to supplant Christianity but simply to set it aside, we will have no reason to formulate a universal morality. If we set Christianity aside, we will naturally relinquish some moral beliefs. As an example, we will no longer believe that human life is somehow peculiarly sacred or overridingly valuable. But we will not thereby share a common conception of the good, or seek to persuade others to adopt our own. We will accept humans as they have always been, with all their miscellaneous moralities.

That does not mean we are bound to leave everything just as it is. We may seek to reform the ways of life in which we are ourselves involved, or try to frame terms of coexistence between different ways of life. But we will not seek to bring into being a universal way of life, or propagate any fantasy of universal emancipation. We will cease to think of human history in terms of the salvation of the species. Unlike the thinkers of the Enlightenment, we will have no reason to be missionaries.

Conclusion

I have argued that Enlightenment humanism presupposes a way of thinking about human life that is inherited from Christian monotheism. The distinctive egalitarian values of the Enlightenment are Christian inheritances, not found in the ancient world. The Enlightenment view of history in terms of progress towards universal human emancipation is a mutation of the Christian view of it as a drama in which the salvation of the species is played out. The Enlightenment belief that humans can flourish fully in only one way of life is a prototypically monotheistic view, scarcely intelligible in pagan terms.

I have not claimed that Christian monotheism was the only important influence shaping the Enlightenment project. The Platonic identification of the true and the good was another, and the view that one way of living is best for all humans – even though only a very few of them can live it – is found in a number of classical Greek philosophers, notably Aristotle. Nor do I want to claim that every Enlightenment thinker is equally in debt to Christian belief. In the twentieth century, Sigmund Freud is worth mention as one whose debts to Christianity are slight.

My aim has been to present the apparently paradoxical thesis that an aggressively secular humanist morality of the sort propagated by most Enlightenment thinkers is defensible only in terms borrowed from Christianity. Without the background of thought provided by Christian monotheism, the universal moral ambitions of the Enlightenment could hardly have been conceived. In defending this seemingly counter-intuitive thesis, I have suggested that a genuinely naturalistic view of humankind would tend to support a more pluralistic view of the good. At the same time it would mean relinquishing many of the Enlightenment's most cherished hopes. What hopes such a naturalistic philosophy might permit is a question I shall leave for another occasion.[24]

4

HISTORIOGRAPHY AND THE REPRESENTATION OF THE PAST

Paul Ricœur

When we read a text purporting to tell us about the historical past, our expectation is that the writer is offering us a 'true account' and not a fiction. This raises questions: is the tacit pact between reader and writer being respected in the case of the writing of history? How, and how far, is it being respected? This is my formulation of the problem I would wish to bring to your attention: the problem of representing the past as history.

I want to argue, first, that the problem does not start with history, but with memory, which is bound up with history in a way I shall describe a little later. The reason I wish to urge the logical priority of the question of representation through memory, rather than that of representation within historical science, is not that I happen to be addressing the themes of a series commemorating '2000 years'; nor that I am taking sides with the champions of memory against the champions of history – such a concern would be entirely foreign to me. It is because the problem of representation – which is the cross the historian always carries – is already there, established at the level of memory; and, indeed, because it already receives, at the level of memory, a limited and fragile resolution which cannot, however, be carried over into historical science. History – and I mean here the writing of history – in this sense inherits a problem which occurs, as it were, lower down, at the level of remembering and forgetting; and its own specific difficulties merely add to the difficulties already inherent in remembering.

Saint Augustine was not the first to formulate the tricky problem of representing the past. He is, certainly, in Books 10 and 11 of his *Confessions*, the initiator of centuries of meditation about the link between the past of things remembered, the present of the things we perceive and the future of things hoped for. Yet it is not Augustine, but Plato and Aristotle, who are the first thinkers to be surprised at the paradox concealed within the notion of 'past things' – what philosophers writing in Latin later called the *praeterita*. Within the classical Greek domain, the problem occurs under the name of the *eikōn*; and already, it constitutes an aporia, an embarrassing question.

In fact, the aporia here is twofold. It consists, first, of an image which seems to be both present to the mind and also an image of something else, something absent. But that is still only half of its enigma (the half it shares, one might add, with fantasy). The other half is the temporal marker, the idea of a 'Before' or a 'Previously' which is the principle separating memory, on the one hand, and fantasy, on the other.

We are indebted to Aristotle for examining this distinctive characteristic of memory in the little treatise which has come down to us in its Latin translation *De Memoria et Reminiscencia* (in the *Parva Naturalia*).[1] As this title indicates, Greek has two words for memory: *mnēmē* and *anamnēsis*. You see the verbal and conceptual double-take, distinguishing memory, properly so-called, from remembrance or reminiscence – the distinction, that is, between (on the one hand) the mere presence in mind of something spontaneously re-occurring and (on the other) the more or less laborious, and especially, more or less successful, search for the thing recalled. This distinction gives Aristotle the opportunity to highlight, within the past thing recalled, the marker 'before' or 'previously' – the *proteron*. 'Memory', writes Aristotle, 'is of time' (*tou genomenou*: literally 'some part of that which has befallen/come to be').[2] More forcefully, he says: we remember 'without things', but 'with time'.[3] In the case of memory, then – and here in counter-distinction to fantasy – the hallmark of the 'before' and the 'after' is imprinted on the thing recalled. This is where the second word for memory – *anamnēsis* – comes into play: the memory of the thing recalled is not always, not even frequently, given; it has to be sought after. That quest is *anamnēsis* – recollection, recall. To the initial question: *what* is recalled? is now added the question *how?* – which brings into play a 'search-capability', conceived sometimes in mechanical terms (as for instance, later, in associationism), sometimes as a more reasoned process, evidenced by the range of procedures of remembering which modern thinkers have parcelled out between both association and the voluntary recall highlighted by Bergson.

Now, under these two headings: memory as mental presence, and memory as mental quest, we have set in place the general framework for a phenomenology of memory. And we have already encountered the question of confidence, which may be expressed in these terms: if memory is an image, how can we avoid confusing it with fantasy, fiction or hallucination? It is here that we come across something which stands at the beginnings of the enterprise which leads from memory to history: namely, an act of confidence in an experience which, in this domain, counts as the basic experience, that of recognition. Recognition takes the form of a declarative judgment, such as: 'that's it', 'he's the one', 'she's the person'. 'No, it's not a fantasm, not a fantasy'. What allows us to be sure of this? Nothing at all except the way the *eikōn* actually presents itself, as being the image of the absent thing under the temporal modality of previousness. Are we making a mistake? Are we being deceived? Often, no doubt, we are. And yet – I would wish to emphasize this point particularly – we do not, in the instant of recognition, have anything more or better than the memory-image. But, can we be sure that something really did happen more or less as the remembering mind represents it? There lies the residual difficulty. That is the issue, the stake, the wager, of the *faithfulness of memory*: the faithfulness which, further on in this chapter, I shall consider in connnection with the claim to truth, however relative, in history – there is an unending dialectic between those two things.

Before striking out towards my principal goal, the representation of the past in historical science, I would like to add two further touches to my summary picture of the problematic of memory: both of them are important for the transition from memory to history.

Firstly, there is the question of the subject of memory: *who* is doing the remembering? Who is engaging in an act of memory by representing things past? We are tempted to reply at once: well, *I* am; it's just *me*. But there is a question here which has become pressing since the emergence in sociology of the concept launched by Maurice Halbwachs in his book *Collective Memory*.[4] The argument is, in this author, driven by the suspicion that individual memory is only an offshoot of, or an enclave within, collective memory. And yet the notion of collective memory has never been immune to criticisms of inconsistency at the conceptual level. Moreover, it has been all the more ill-received in that it appeared to lend justification to a claim by sociology to exercise a hegemony over history itself. For my own part, after long uncertainty, I have come to the conviction that memory, defined by the presence in mind of something past and by the search for such a mental presence, can, in principle, be attributed to all grammatical persons: I, he/she, we, they – etc. It was, indeed, as a result of the slow conquest of reflective certainty by what might be called the school of inner attention, that thinkers were able to identify memory with inwardness. Augustine, at this point, returns centre stage, drawing memory back to the central inner focus-point, in the wake of his experience of avowal and confession. John Locke, in turn, gave even greater prominence to this process of subjectivization by making memory the pre-eminent criterion of personal identity: memory thus becomes something properly mine, my own memory. Husserl takes the decisive step by merging memory and inner awareness of time: memory is then, as Locke had anticipated, merely self-reflection spread out in time. Heidegger, at the end of his philosophic journey, is able to swallow up the experience of memory in his vision of temporality, which is itself sucked into the gravity-field of his being-towards-death, an experience stamped with the imprint of what cannot be replaced or communicated. In the end, memory, now assigned exclusively to the agency of the self, appears as the product of a growing subjectivization, which sacrifices the primacy of the question of 'What is remembered?' to the sole question of the 'Who?' of memory.

After carefully weighing the arguments and counter-arguments, I have, as I say, adopted the thesis that memory is to be attributed diversely, to a plurality of grammatical persons. This standpoint is important for the historian, since he is then able to dialogue untroubled with both individual and collective memory, which are usually entangled together, as we see on the occasion of festivals, commemorations and other forms of public celebration. The historian may, moreover, be interested in the details of the theory of attribution, since he too encounters problems in attributing to social agents memories based on indirect and conjectural signs.

I would like to enter a second qualifying remark which is even more significant for the transition from memory to history. Let us go back to the double form of the problem of memory: this involved, as we saw, both a static presence in mind of the image of something absent, something having previously occurred, but also a dynamic of recall. This recall is a complex operation which may, or may not, succeed. Succeeding here means recognizing the thing remembered; Bergson, in *Matter and Memory*, makes this the basic experience. In this masterwork of his, which we have perhaps been over-eager to leave behind, his great meditation on the resurgent vitality of images of the past turns around this organizing pole. Now recognition appears here as a minor miracle, when we compare its happy outcome with the difficulties which litter the path of recall. These difficulties, which belong to a pragmatics of memory, may be considered under three headings: impeded memory, manipulated memory, obliged or constrained memory. Impeded memory: we think of Freud's writings on repression; or perhaps his explorations of the working-out of grief, as well as of memory. Manipulated memory: that would lead us to examine how the problem of memory intersects with that of identity and look at the many ways memory can be falsified through the stories we tell about the past, with their play of major and minor connections, their emphases and their silences. Dutiful or constrained memory; well, here we must pause a little. I would like to say how important it is not to fall into the trap of what in France is often called the duty of remembrance (*le devoir de mémoire*). Why is this? Because the word duty introduces an imperative, a command, where originally there was only an exhortation made in the framework of filial belonging, traversing successive generations: 'Thou shalt tell thy son . . .' (and, these days, no doubt, also thy daughter . . .). Secondly, because you cannot put into the future tense an enterprise of remembering, that is, of looking back, without doing violence to the exercise itself of *anamnēsis* and, if I may venture to say so, a touch of manipulation. Above all, because the duty of remembering is often summoned up with the design of short-circuiting the critical work of the historian, with the risk of enclosing the memory of this or that historical community within its singular misfortune, of fixing it within the mind-set of victimization, of uprooting it, therefore, from the sense of justice and equity. That is why I propose to speak, not of the duty of memory, but of the work of memory.

These difficulties of recall are handed on from a pragmatics of memory to the epistemology of history. Impeded memory, manipulated memory, constrained memory: these are all themes which re-echo in the ear of the historian as alert-warnings. Against these embarrassments introduced by the difficulties of remembering aright, historical science builds its constraints, its defences, from which derive the achievements I shall detail later; around them it centres its problematic of historical representation. But I must, at this point, enter a word of caution: memory has a privilege not shared by history: 'that's it', 'that's him', 'she's the very one'. What a reward, after the misadventures of remembering and all those arduous efforts expended on overcoming them, to have the assurance of immediate recognition! It is because history does not enjoy this small satisfaction that it has a specific problematic of representation; and for the same reason that its complex constructs aim at reconstructing an account of the past capable of passing muster in respect of the truth-pact with the reader. The small success of recognition is the single, fragile earnest we have of the faithfulness of memory. This success is something which touches even history, which is without it; since this very lack drives historical enquiry – as already suggested in Herodotus' title

The Histories. Historical research, standing in for mnemonic recall, takes in the entire set of historiographical operations leading horizontally from the documentary phase right through to the phase of writing. It is at the end of this journey that the question is raised, in its full problematicity, of representation considered as history; and it is to this form of representation that I would, from now on, propose to give the name 'representancy', hoping by this term to stress its character of mobilized incompletion or unfinishedness – the character that stands in, and does duty for, that unobtainable mnemonic recognition.

The difficulties of historical knowledge begin with the break introduced by writing. In this respect, historiography is aptly named: this term does not point solely to the writing-phase as such, nor even to the reflexive or second-order epistemological stance taken up by the historian; it refers to the entirety of what Michel de Certeau has usefully termed the historiographical operation.[5] In this operation I will in turn distinguish: the documentary phase, concerned with archive material; the phase of explanation and understanding, invoking the varied uses of the conjunction 'because . . .'; and the properly literary or writing phase, which most acutely raises the question of adequate representation.

I

The representing of the past is problematic from the outset because the historian, in his writing, stands back from the field of memory, public or private. This standing back comes into play, however, only when the archive is set up. The archive is the end-point of a complex operation, which takes its point of origin in the very first expressions made, in narrative form, by memory in its declarative stage. Somebody remembers something, says so, tells the tale, gives his testimony. The first thing he says is: I was there. The linguist Benveniste assures us that the Latin word *testis* comes from *tertius*: the witness is a third party alongside the protagonists or between the action and the situation the witness says he has been present at, without necessarily having taken part in it. This declaration of his is at once the assertion of a factual reality which is held to be important and a certification of the declaration by its author. The witness appeals to the credence of another before whom he is witnessing and who receives his testimony. 'I was there.' 'Believe me or not', he adds; 'if you don't believe me, you can ask someone else.' This accreditation opens up the alternative of confidence or of doubt. Thus we have the fiduciary structure of witness accounts. The witness, who is ready to reiterate his account, considers it a promise bearing on the past. The account becomes established. The business of confronting testimonies begins, and, beyond this, controversy between historians. Critical attention to testimonies signals not only the role of challenge but also both the hollow spot of dissension and its educative value at the level of public discussion, which is where history finishes its career as alleged meaning. All this on condition that the account has been written down, writing down being equivalent to the act of filing in the archive. The thing written will pursue its career beyond the witnesses themselves and their testimonies. For want of a designated addressee, it will have the status of the 'orphan text' mentioned by Plato in the *Phaedrus*.[6] But whatever the reliability of the account, we have nothing better than this text to tell us that something happened and that someone was there to witness it. But did it happen as recounted? That is the question of confidence, the test of truth, which the search for documentary proof begins to answer.

Documentary: there's the password. We know, following Marc Bloch,[7] that witnesses who do not intend to bear witness are the most important ones. But their testimonies also are written down among the traces which are rightly termed documentary, many of which are in fact these days no longer witness accounts: vestiges, material pointers, or abstract signs such as the curves of price or wage graphs and other reiterable and quantifiable items. We thus get what Carlo Ginzburg calls 'the indiciary paradigm',[8] which is common to all disciplines of indirect or conjectural knowledge, from medicine and psychiatry to the detective novel. Under this aegis, there occurs a subtle dialectic between testimony and document, the document being for this purpose something akin to a monument. The document thus becomes the unit of accountancy of historical knowledge. Marc Bloch, who was the scourge of the school he called 'positivistic' and which might more fairly be termed 'methodic', went so far as to place it under the heading of observation. A document, however, is not something given, but something sought out, constituted, instituted: the term thus signals anything that can be questioned by the historian with a view to finding in it information about the past, in the light of a hypothesis of explanation and understanding. What we call documents are events which, at the limit, have not been anybody's memory, but which can contribute to the construction of a memory which may be termed, with Halbwachs, a historical memory, so as to distinguish it from memory as such, even from collective memory. Make the documents talk, says Marc Bloch, not in order to confound them, but in order to understand them.

this respect, social history is not one sector of history among others; it is the viewpoint from which history chooses its disciplinary camp, among the social sciences. For my part, I have taken considerable interest in the current of thinking which, following Braudel,[9] has stressed the practical modalities of the way the social bond is constituted and on the problems of identity which spring from this. Hence, as we shall see shortly, my featuring of representations among the prime objects of historical investigation, along with social interactions. To tie things down, I would say that it is by stressing change, and also the social differences or divergences affecting change, that history becomes distinctive among the social sciences and, principally, distinct from sociology. Now, change, difference, divergence from established patterns, all have an obvious temporal dimension. The dialectic between structure, the context of events, events themselves, is well known in this respect, as are the hierarchies of duration explored by Braudel and his school. They are, it is true, constructs in relation to lived experience, which does not spontaneously form the notion of multiple time-frequencies, or scales of duration. What, more particularly, constitutes a construct is the correlation between the nature of the change considered – economic, social (in the limiting sense of that term), political, cultural, or any other, the scale on which it is apprehended and the temporal rhythm appropriate to that scale. But these constructs are indeed presumed appropriate to the nature of the phenomenon considered, and are, in this sense, anything but arbitrary, and therefore not at all fictional. It is implicitly admitted that these constructs are constructs about the historical condition of human beings – *there* is the ultimate referent of historical enquiry, in respect of which the interactions likely to create social bonding are proximate referents. It is thus at the first formal level of the selective framing of the objects of reference that the idea of representing the past is tacitly taken up.

But it is also taken up explicitly, and, we might say, materially (or substantially), when the historian takes as one of his favoured objects of enquiry representations themselves and makes these into a privileged referent alongside things economic, social or political. As we know, it is under the label, much used in France, of the 'history of mentalities' that this theme first came up and then made its weight felt, until the day when it was urged against the label that it was woolly, ambiguous and protean and, above all, that it was, at the outset, compromised by being bound up with the concept of 'primitive' mentalities inherited from Lévy-Bruhl.[10] In these conditions, the idea of representation came in as a replacement for the idea of mentality. It is considers it a promise bearing on the past. The account becomes established. The business of confronting testimonies begins, and, beyond this, controversy between historians. Critical attention to testimonies signals not only the role of challenge but also both the hollow spot of dissension and its educative value at the level of public discussion, which is where history finishes its career as alleged meaning. All this on condition that the account has been written down, writing down being equivalent to the act of filing in the archive. The thing written will pursue its career beyond the witnesses themselves and their testimonies. For want of a designated addressee, it will have the status of the 'orphan text' mentioned by Plato in the *Phaedrus*.[6] But whatever the reliability of the account, we have nothing better than this text to tell us that something happened and that someone was there to witness it. But did it happen as recounted? That is the question of confidence, the test of truth, which the search for documentary proof begins to answer.

Documentary: there's the password. We know, following Marc Bloch,[7] that witnesses who do not intend to bear witness are the most important ones. But their testimonies also are written down among the traces which are rightly termed documentary, many of which are in fact these days no longer witness accounts: vestiges, material pointers, or abstract signs such as the curves of price or wage graphs and other reiterable and quantifiable items. We thus get what Carlo Ginzburg calls 'the indiciary paradigm',[8] which is common to all disciplines of indirect or conjectural knowledge, from medicine and psychiatry to the detective novel. Under this aegis, there occurs a subtle dialectic between testimony and document, the document being for this purpose something akin to a monument. The document thus becomes the unit of accountancy of historical knowledge. Marc Bloch, who was the scourge of the school he called 'positivistic' and which might more fairly be termed 'methodic', went so far as to place it under the heading of observation. A document, however, is not something given, but something sought out, constituted, instituted: the term thus signals anything that can be questioned by the historian with a view to finding in it information about the past, in the light of a hypothesis of explanation and understanding. What we call documents are events which, at the limit, have not been anybody's memory, but which can contribute to the construction of a memory which may be termed, with Halbwachs, a historical memory, so as to distinguish it from memory as such, even from collective memory. Make the documents talk, says Marc Bloch, not in order to confound them, but in order to understand them.

We can readily understand that, looking towards the 'hard' sciences, historians have been led to adopt a tone of assurance which, in relation to our problem, implies a 'heavy' form of confidence in history's capacity to enlarge, correct and criticize memory, at the risk of reducing it from the status of matrix of history to the status of object of historical enquiry, as we shall see in a moment.

But before coming to this point, the historiographical operation, arrested by convention at the documentary phase, is confronted by the question of the epistemological status of the proof claimed for propositions of the type: X did Y at time T and place P. Such propositions, artificially isolated, bear on what may be called attested facts, it being understood that the fact is not the event itself but the asserted content of the proposition of the type I am discussing, which has been put together as the result of various tests involving confrontation and challenge. In this respect the spontaneous philosophy of the historian is a sort of critical realism which faces two sorts of challenge. On the one hand, the historian presupposes the factual nature of the event, in the broad sense of something about which somebody has testified, and which is being talked about in the documents. In this first sense, the historian can find little help in the model of Saussurian linguistics, which reduces the sign to the couple signifier/signified, to the exclusion of the referent. He *can* find help in discourse linguistics in the manner of Benveniste, for whom the unit of sense at the level of *parole* ('utterance') is the sentence, where somebody says something to somebody about something according to codified rules of interpretation. Thus the triad is preserved in principle: the triad of signifier, signified, referent – where the term event applied. On the other hand, the historian knows that his proof belongs to a logic of probability rather than of logical necessity, probability relating here less to the chance character of events than to how reliable the testimony is, and, by extension, to the reliability of all the propositions making up the historical discourse. The fact that this or that happened more or less as recounted is more or less probable. This probabilist character of documentary proof, which is the *terminus ad quem* of the process of emplotting the action, proceeds in the last resort from the fiduciary character of the testimony, which is the *terminus a quo* of the entire process. At any event, this argumentative structuring cannot be eliminated. Of course the historian knows that his proof is not the same sort of proof as in the natural sciences; the critique he makes of testimony remains the model for the whole documentary field, to which the indiciary paradigm applies. Indirect, conjectural: so it remains.

II

Leaving the documentary stage of historiography and venturing deeper into the jungle of the operations of explanation and understanding, we seem to be turning our backs on the question of representation. Could we not say that what is at issue in these operations is perhaps the testing out of the different solutions in the form of 'because . . .' which are supplied in answer to the question 'why?'? Is not the entire field taken up with the question of what meanings obtain within the historian's discourse and the question of their internal self-consistency? We might think so at first sight, and that would lead us to concentrate exclusively on the modes of explanation available in historical science. It has been said, in this regard, that history does not have any method of its own. It combines approximately the ways causality is used in the natural sciences, as can be seen, in particular, in economic history, and by the reasons adduced in political, military or diplomatic history, or else in the negotiations between the protagonists of 'micro-history'. In history, there is no irreducible dichotomy, you see, between explanation and understanding.

Despite this huge displacement of interest towards the modes of explanation and understanding, the question of the representation of the past does not disappear from view in the phase of explaining and understanding the past. It returns centre stage, for a first visit, when the historian talks about dividing up his domain, and determining what is to be explained; and it returns for a second time, in a way which looks unexpected at first sight, in the guise of something which constitutes a favourite object of enquiry in the historical field, namely, the mentality or mind-set of a given period. The term 'mentalities' has largely been replaced in France by 'representations'; so that representations are now the object of historical science. These two reappearances of the question of representation are linked, since what is at stake in the first case is how we specify the immediate referent of historical discourse – what that discourse is *about* – and, in the second case, it is the decision about what slice of the past is to be considered, and, moreover, which representations are to be investigated, as well as which economic, social and political determinants of social reality.

Let us pause for a moment over these two mentions of representation in the framework of the epistemology of historical explanation. Firstly, the way we carve out the area of historical facts is assumed to concern the realities history is referring to; thus, all the explanatory models current in the practice of historians have in common the characteristic that they relate to human reality as a social phenomenon. In this respect, social history is not one sector of history among others; it is the viewpoint from which history chooses its disciplinary camp, among the social sciences. For my part, I have taken considerable interest in the current of thinking which, following Braudel,[9] has stressed the practical modalities of the way the social bond is constituted and on the problems of identity which spring from this. Hence, as we shall see shortly, my featuring of representations among the prime objects of historical investigation, along with social interactions. To tie things down, I would say that it is by stressing change, and also the social differences or divergences affecting change, that history becomes distinctive among the social sciences and, principally, distinct from sociology. Now, change, difference, divergence from established patterns, all have an obvious temporal dimension. The dialectic between structure, the context of events, events themselves, is well known in this respect, as are the hierarchies of duration explored by Braudel and his school. They are, it is true, constructs in relation to lived experience, which does not spontaneously form the notion of multiple time-frequencies, or scales of duration. What, more particularly, constitutes a construct is the correlation between the nature of the change considered – economic, social (in the limiting sense of that term), political, cultural, or any other, the scale on which it is apprehended and the temporal rhythm appropriate to that scale. But these constructs are indeed presumed appropriate to the nature of the phenomenon considered, and are, in this sense, anything but arbitrary, and therefore not at all fictional. It is implicitly admitted that these constructs are constructs about the historical condition of human beings – *there* is the ultimate referent of historical enquiry, in respect of which the interactions likely to create social bonding are proximate referents. It is thus at the first formal level of the selective framing of the objects of reference that the idea of representing the past is tacitly taken up.

But it is also taken up explicitly, and, we might say, materially (or substantially), when the historian takes as one of his favoured objects of enquiry representations themselves and makes these into a privileged referent alongside things economic, social or political. As we know, it is under the label, much used in France, of the 'history of mentalities' that this theme first came up and then made its weight felt, until the day when it was urged against the label that it was woolly, ambiguous and protean and, above all, that it was, at the outset, compromised by being bound up with the concept of 'primitive' mentalities inherited from Lévy-Bruhl.[10] In these conditions, the idea of representation came in as a replacement for the idea of mentality. It is the linkage to interactions within the social field which specifies this use of the concept 'representation' to designate the beliefs and the norms which confer its symbolic articulation on the way the social bond comes into being and on the way identities are formed. One can speak in this respect of a practice of representation, which enables us to extend to the symbolic field of action the step forward accomplished with the notion of a play of timescales mentioned earlier. But above all, it becomes possible to make the notion of social representation benefit from the distinctions developed by a general semiotics of representation: so for instance, there is a fruitful link between representing the absent or dead person, and the lively presence of his image in the here-and-now, as is clear from Louis Morin's analyses on the theme of the King's portrait.[11] These exchanges between the semiotics of representation and the actual history of social representations, especially in the sphere of political power, show themselves to be extremely valuable for analysing the abilities and potencies of the image – *Les Pouvoirs de l'image*, to pick up the title of the book by Louis Marin.[12]

III

Skipping over the arid regions of the causal links which give its proper and varied coherence to historical discourse, we enter the zone of the narrative and rhetorical patterns which govern the literary phase of historiography. It is at this level that the toughest difficulties of representing the past are concentrated. Now, this component of writing is not simply an item added to the other operations of historiography: it runs through every one of its stages, to the extent that these stages have in them something of the general category of things 'written down'. What we shall now consider, more specifically, is writing insofar as it gives readability and visible profile to the historical text looking for its reader. The reading-pact I mentioned earlier is here spelt out; and our opening question returns in full force: has the pact been kept? and could it be kept?

The major difficulty comes from the fact that the shaping narrative and rhetorical patterns of the historian are constraints upon reading: they structure the reader, unbeknown to him; they may play a twofold role – as mediations towards historical reality, but also as intervening screens whose opacity undermines the transparency they claim to offer.

In this way, what comes to the fore are the signs of *littérarité* (Roland Barthes's term, you may remember, for the quality and status of 'literariness', i.e. what makes texts 'literary'). Here, first of all, I rediscover the narrative patterns on which I concentrated in *Time and Narrative*.[13] Since that book, the fear of confusing narrative coherence with connectedness of explanation has led me to put off the task of treating the narrative component of history until the signs of 'literariness' could be properly taken into account. This relative de-classification of historical narrative will have its part to play in my reply to attempts that have been made to blur the frontier between the fictional and the historical. True, I continue to think that narrative is not confined to the order of real events, but is co-extensive with all levels of explanation and the entire set of timescales. But here, the narrative codes are not substituted for modes of explanation; they instead add to these explanatory modes the element we mentioned earlier of readability and visible profile. What creates the difficulties we are now about to consider is the fact that when writing-grids are set up, they can become reading-grids which remain unobserved. True, narrative structures do not merely ensure the movement of historical discourse towards its referent, they offer the resistance of their own opaqueness; but it is then the privilege of the semiotician to bring into view the constraints which may have influenced the writer in his presentation of the facts. It is tempting, at this point, to suggest that these same constraints, which the reader takes on board unawares, keep him prisoner within the nets of a strategy of persuasion which the semiotician is alone competent to unmask. We know the themes of 'reality effect' and of 'referential illusion' developed by structuralist semiotics, in which, as we saw, the referent is excluded in principle from the binary structure of meaning, itself reduced to the couple signifier/signified. Such is the suspicion cultivated at the level of narratology by this particular school of semioticians, and the anti-referential argument drawn from it in respect of historiography.

But it is when we come to the rhetorical analysis of historical discourse that the problem of constraints is most acute, and in fact develops into a frontal assault against what I earlier called critical realism; that is, the view assumed, without any real theorization, by most practising historians. The shaping narrative patterns, which are tributary to a typology of story-patterns, are then framed within a complex architecture of codes, alongside tropes and other figures of discourse and thought; taken together, these figures are held to be the innermost structures of an imaginary which covers the entire class of 'verbal fictions'. The subtle work of Hayden White is a model of this tendency.[14] However, its devastating thrust, directed at the persuasive strategies of the historian, could only strike home in conjunction with the much larger movement known as 'postmodernism', in which the historian's rationality is caught up in the storm-winds shaking all convictions inherited from the Enlightenment, itself taken to be the measure of the modern. So that it really is the self-understanding of our whole era which is being played out in the debate about truth in history.

This discussion, which was for a time threatening to get lost in ideological confrontations lacking any recognized criteria – the idea of criteria being itself in question – was brought back within the limits of a conflict of interpretation about historical knowledge. This happened thanks to one, precisely focused, debate. At issue was the reception of works on Hitler's 'final solution', principally the collective volume entitled *Historikerstreit* devoted to the controversy on this theme between German historians. From the unlimited question of the 'postmodern', people's attention was brought back to a fearsome, but limited question: how do we speak of the Holocaust, of the Shoah, this major event of the mid-twentieth century? The question came to us, framed between two sets of researches, from opposite horizons, suddenly brought up against each other: the horizon posited by the masters of suspicion, with their password of 'referential illusion', and the horizon articulated by the negationists, and their password of the 'official lie'.

There is a book which bears witness to this confrontation, by Saul Friedlander, the title of which has great significance for me: *Probing the Limits of Representation*.[15] This is the only work I examine here, by reason of the emblematic status it holds in relation to the whole problematic of this chapter. Friedlander observes: 'The extermination of the European Jews, as an extreme case of mass murder, must challenge the theorists of historical relativism to confront the corollaries of the positions they hold at an abstract level.'[16] Hayden White, called out, faced up bravely to the challenge, by reiterating his argument and confessing that his tropological rhetoric did not provide him with any criterion immanent in discourse for distinguishing reality from fiction. The distinction, he admitted, must proceed 'from another region of our receptive capacity than that which has been educated by our narrative culture'.[17] On that account, he suggests broadening the field of modes of representation beyond the cultural inheritance which totalitarianism had brought to the verge of exhaustion.

However legitimate this concern of Friedlander's, which indeed finds some echo in the attempts at a renewal of certain forms of expression which have emerged from the breakdown of established mediations, it leaves unresolved the fundamental question-mark against the adequacy of aesthetic forms of expression which aim to represent the Shoah. If one says, with George Steiner, that 'the world of Auschwitz lies outside speech, as it lies outside reason',[18] how can the sense itself of the undecidable and the unrepresentable come to articulation? Carlo Ginzburg, in his moving essay, 'Just one witness!'[19] invokes the power of testimony, a power prior even to its written entry into the archive. In turn, testimony refers to the violence of the event itself and its moral dimension, which Friedlander describes – it is an understatement – as 'inadmissible'.[20] But then we have the living experience of woundedness thrust deep into the process of 'history-making', rising like some outer limit imposed upon representation and creating an internal implosion of all modes of representation – narrative, rhetorical, filmic (and others). The event at the limit is a shock which history-in-the-making inflicts on collective and private memory, which, as in the violent *peripeteias* of Greek or Elizabethan tragedy, governs the referent to which the 'saying of history' directs us. Something terrible has happened, which turns the thing of horror into a negative and symmetrical figure of the sublime; it demands to be uttered, so as not to be forgotten. And part of the happening of the event is the position of the protagonists in relation to it: as executioners, as victims, or as bystanders. That makes three sorts of living history; and nobody can add them together and encompass them as a whole.

Still, it would not be right that some new intimidation, deriving from the immensity of the event and its cortege of complaint, should paralyse our thinking about the historiographical operation. It belongs to the judge to condemn and to punish, and to the citizen to militate against forgetting and for the equity of memory. It is the historian's job to understand without either laying blame or discharging from blame.

If this is so, then the extreme case of the limit-event must help us rework the problematic arising from the rhetorical analysis of discourse. The debate can, in my view, be pushed in two directions: forwards from the text, towards reader-reception – and backwards, towards the prior phases of the historiographical process.

On the side of reception, the reader comes to the historical text, equipped not only with the expectation that he will not be 'told a load of fairy stories', but with an experience as protagonist engaged in history-in-the-making. He it is who provides the addressee of a discourse supposedly taking shape at the intersection of present and past. More precisely, it is the citizen within the protagonist of history who requests from the historian a true discourse capable of enlarging, criticizing, even of contradicting, his own memory. While failing as a true discourse, in the sense current in the 'hard' sciences, it is at least a discourse situated in relation to some intention of truthfulness.

To take the measure of this intention of truthfulness, we have to appeal back from the writing-phase of historical knowledge to the previous phases, to the explanatory/comprehending phase and to the documentary phase. This is what is commonly lost sight of in discussions centred on the rhetoric of historical discourse. The mistake here is to expect narrativity and tropology to fill out the gaps in the argument, meeting its concern to account for the varied and manifold causal connections between attested facts. Getting people to believe things is not a topic peculiar to rhetoric alone. It arises wherever convincing and pleasing meet and entwine, those two things which the old controversies between Socrates and the sophists taught us to differentiate. Here the logic of probability, applied to establishing the reliability quotient of the discourses of the human sciences, and drawing on the analyses of the 'school of suspicion', can help; not to blur the frontier between fiction and truth, but to hunt down that truth amid all its ruses, as Plato, in the Socratic dialogues, sets himself to distinguish between medicine and cosmetics. As far as the special epistemology of historiography is concerned, not everything is played out at the documentary level – though I sometimes feel there is a deplorable neglect of this component in quarrels over truth in history – it works also at the level of explaining and understanding. In this regard, I must not fail to include in the epistemological parameters the major phenomenon of rewriting. Verisimilitude – which is another name for probability – is the meaning-effect produced by the series of rewritings generated by the same event, this sameness being part of the point of the discussion. There is a truth which belongs, not to a book, but to the dossier of a controversy. So it is with us in France over the French Revolution and the small library of writings it has called forth.

What remains open is the question of the competing claims of memory and of history in the representation of the past. Memory has the advantage of recognizing the past as something which has been, although it no longer is; history lays claim to the power of enlarging our vision of things in time and space; it can point to the strength of its critique in the order of testimony, of explanation and of understanding; and, pre-eminently, it allows the practice of equity in relation to wounded memories. Really, in the matter of the competing claims of the faithfulness of memory and the truth of history, neither can finally prevail.

IV

My reflection in this chapter has centred on the question of truth in historical knowledge. How does this help us understand 'Judaeo-Christian particularity' and the Common Era? I would defend its pertinence in the following way: one cannot claim to evaluate this centuries-old tradition without attributing a truth-value to propositions bearing on events, causal links and truly significant trends in history As I have tried to say in public debates in France on the 'duty of memory', there is a duty of truthfulness before and beyond what is due to supposedly equitable judgments redressing the balance of history: what truly occurred? what really happened?

Within the strict limits of my epistemological approach, I believe my contribution has been twofold. Firstly, it carries the plea that a history of representations should form part of the studies accounting for our collective life, alongside economic, political and other histories. Judaeo-Christian particularity, as object of study, is part of that special form of history. Secondly, I hope to have made the case that there are *degrees of truth* to be attributed to the propositions of historians, according to whether they remain close to primary sources or whether they go on to more complex constructions relating to the causes and motives of things, or venture into large-scale extrapolations on, say, 'the French Revolution', 'the Cold War' or 'the Final Solution'. Historical truth is not monolithic; it is graduated on a Richter scale of probability (a thesis I share with Marc Bloch, Stanislas Furet, Carlo Ginzburg, Roger Chartier, Michel de Certeau and others). Historical knowledge of Judaeo-Christian culture itself may have different levels of truth.

This being said, my own manner of addressing Judaeo-Christian particularity specifically calls on considerations which are more fully developed in my book *La Mémoire, l'histoire, l'oubli*.[21] Perhaps I might mention some of them.

Firstly, there is the relationship between the history written by the historian and the history men make (in circumstances they have *not* made, one should add, with Marx). These interact in history at the point where the reading of history is articulated to the writing of history. If historiography is fundamentally retrospective, reading it is the active work of the protagonists of history, who come to their reading with expectations of all sorts; looking forward, linked to the action in hand, plays against the backward-looking historical viewpoint. This dialectic of reading and writing, prospect and retrospect, offers scope for 'heavy' re-evaluations to intervene and to take over the 'true account' that the historian's discourse claims to be. Evaluating the Judaeo-Christian heritage does not escape this dialectic.

Secondly, I would like to mention the linkages emphasized in the triadic structure of my book's title: the connection between history and memory, on the one hand; and, on the other, between the science of history and the historical condition common to all human beings. With both these sets of connections, longstanding problems familiar to Plato and Aristotle, as much as to Kant, Hegel, Nietzsche, Bergson and Heidegger, come to the forefront. As I like to say, all books are open before me, without any imposed chronology. At this point, the 'historicism' summoned up by the history of historiographers finds its limits, whether we are speaking of the historicism of Troetschke, or of the more recent brand peculiar to our own 'postmoderns'. The paradox of the situation created by the Holocaust is to oblige the champions of a rhetoricist interpretation of history to answer the suspicion that they are unable to refute negationism, because of their failure to discover any firm line between fiction and reality in respect of the historical past.

In the light of this discussion, a presumption is created *for* or perhaps (in all senses of the word) in *favour* of continuity, rather than for radical dismissals-and-rebeginnings, in the course of history. I 'recognize myself' in the great texts of my culture. I want to make this affirmation of what Simone Weil called 'the Hebrew source' and 'the Greek source', which I would not wish to dissociate from each other in my own cultural memory. These are 'classic texts' in the sense Gadamer gives to this term;[22] a sense he characterizes by the power such texts have to journey beyond their context of origin while acquiring new configurations of meaning. It is the task of interpretation to bring out the kind of historical identity generated by ongoing, cumulative history. Here, once again, we can learn from the parable offered by the dislocation introduced by the totalitarianisms of the mid-twentieth century; this break makes the assertion of a cultural continuity of the West appear as an act of spiritual resistance. In this respect, Hannah Arendt is right to entitle her great book *The Human Condition*.[23] Her plea for continuity is no doubt an answer to the claim of tyrants to manufacture a 'new man' out of nothing.

Behind these correlations, I would suggest, there is a presentment about the very nature of experienced temporality: is not lived, inner time (*la durée*), that which survives and abides, as much as – and more than – that which changes and passes? Abiding is, I guess, this somehow ontological power of experienced subject-time at the root of cultural continuity, at the root of the cumulative character of historical experience. Such is the recurring presentment, more radical in its persuasion than the contrary prejudice we spoke of earlier. *Abiding* – that is, pre-eminently, how I would describe the Judaeo-Christian 'matrix' of our Western culture.

5

THE FUTURE OF HUMAN NATURE

Richard Schacht

My title is 'The future of human nature';[1] but by this I don't mean to be asking whether our species will be around much longer. Rather: is there anything more than merely biological to the idea of 'human nature'? Does it still make good philosophical sense to think so today? If Michel Foucault and his kindred spirits are to be believed, the very idea of 'man' is an idea whose time has come and gone. *We're* still here; but the idea that 'we' have some sort of determinate nature, about which there is anything interesting to be studied and discovered and said, is purported by Foucault to be a nineteenth-century invention that we ought to drop. Nietzsche famously told us that God is dead; and according to Foucault, he ought to have said the same of 'man'. There is nothing *out there* that has a *divine* nature; and there likewise is nothing *around here* that has a *human* one. Or rather: there are human *natures* aplenty on this planet; but all of them are historically contingent affairs – and this supposedly makes nonsense of the idea that there is anything like a blueprint of humanity that we all either do or ought to exemplify.

This way of thinking has become quite popular in recent years. In fact, the idea of human nature has become one of those ideas philosophers seem to love to hate. It makes strange bedfellows of philosophical sects which, in most other respects, are at each other's throats. Rejection of it just might be the closest thing we have had during the past couple of centuries to a common denominator.

Time was when things were different, at least for a while. So, for example, John Locke did not blush to publish his *magnum opus* under the title *Essay Concerning Human Understanding*; and David Hume went so far as to entitle his, *A Treatise of Human Nature*. Enlightenment *philosophes* in France, with Gallic zest, took up the idea that, whatever else we may be, we are first and foremost *human* beings. In German-speaking Europe Ludwig Feuerbach rallied post-Hegelians to the banner of what he called the 'anthropological reduction' of Hegelian speculative-philosophical talk of *Geist* (or 'spirit') into naturalistic-philosophical talk of 'man' or 'humankind'. *Geist* was out; *der Mensch* was in.

Marx, Kierkegaard and Nietzsche, in their own quite different ways, and with plenty of other company, were also very much concerned with the problem of how to conceive of and understand human reality. Yet they also had deep and significant reservations with respect to ways of thinking about ourselves other than their own; and their philosophical fans for the most part have been more interested in their mentors' reservations than in their proffered alternatives. A movement actually calling itself 'philosophical anthropology' did get going in central Europe in the 1920s; but first Heidegger came along, and then Hitler, and then existentialism, and then Marxism, and critical theory, and then post-structuralism, and deconstructionism, and feminism – and somehow, amid all this high-octane competition, 'philosophical anthropology' never really caught on. *Der Mensch* joined *der Geist* in the attic.

For one reason or another (and in more ways than one), the twentieth century has not been a good one for human nature. Positivists, linguistic-analytic philosophers, phenomenologists, existentialists, Marxists and critical theorists, structuralists and post-structuralists, feminist theorists and analytical 'philosophers of mind' might be able to agree on little else; but one thing they have had in common is the conviction that the idea of human nature has no place in philosophical discourse. They suppose either that it is not the sort of thing philosophers have any business talking about, or that *all* talk about it is much ado about nothing.

When I was an undergraduate (at Harvard, in the early 1960s), some of these philosophical fashions had not yet made their appearance on these shores. But as I went shopping around, hoping to find some philosophical neighbourhood in which inquiry into human nature was not taboo, I was dismayed to discover that there simply wasn't one. There once had been a few – but they had been deconstructed. Hume's talk of 'human nature' was discreetly ignored, or glossed in terms of epistemology and philosophical psychology. John Dewey, who had been one of the champions of a kind of philosophical anthropology, had become a philosophical un-person. And those few who did not despise Marx and Nietzsche were quite sure that *they* were leaders of the opposition, campaigning to relegate the notion of human (as well as divine) nature to the intellectual-historical circular file. The same story could be told about the situation in the better philosophy departments throughout the English-speaking world in those years.

What are we to make of this philosophical misanthropic turn? One possible answer is that the idea of the 'human' must indeed be bankrupt if so many differently-minded philosophical clans all came to think so. In my student days I was more inclined to draw the opposite conclusion, and to think that anything on which *they* all agreed *must* be wrong. But even then I knew that the matter could not really be settled that quickly and easily.

Another possible answer is that fads and fashions change, in philosophy as in other walks of intellectual and cultural life (even in the two Cambridges and neighbouring precincts); and that people just got tired of the idea of human nature, and decided to clean house. There probably is something to this analysis. And if so, then by the same token, we may have only to wait a little longer until, like wide ties and short skirts, the idea comes back into vogue. And that may indeed happen. But this cannot be the whole story either.

A further part of the story may well be that many of those who have talked about human nature – and even about a philosophical anthropology – have given these notions a bad name in the philosophical community, either by what was said about them, or by how it was said, or by things with which they happened to be associated. Sociobiologists and others of even more dubious persuasions make much of it; but with such friends, the idea hardly needs enemies. Feuerbach may deserve an 'E for effort' in his attempt to get a naturalistic philosophical anthropology going; but an E is not generally considered to be a very good grade – and even the most generous and sympathetic of graders of his thinking (like myself, for example) would not give him much more than a C.

Kant and Hegel tower over Feuerbach; and both offer versions of what they actually call 'anthropology' – Kant, in his *Anthropology from a Pragmatic Point of View* and Hegel, in the 'Anthropology' section of the third volume of his *Encyclopedia*. But their 'anthropologies' are only *parts* of their accounts of ourselves. And the dimensions of ourselves and our lives with which they deal in their philosophical anthropologies are at the bottom of their totem poles. Moreover, anyone who actually takes a look at the sorts of things these two giants of philosophy have to say in their writings on the matter is unlikely to be impressed. In fact, if you were to read these things, you might well conclude that, if this is the best that philosophy can do with the idea of human nature, then to hell with it. And that may be exactly how the neo-Kantians and neo-Hegelians towards the end of the nineteenth century reacted.

In any event, mainstream Anglo-American philosophers abandoned it, leaving the so-called 'philosophy of man' to Catholic philosophers and neo-Marxist humanists, who did talk about it; but were generally deemed to be either behind the times or beyond the pale. And their embrace did not exactly boost its stock. It was like the case of a fellow named Harry Tiebout, who taught religion and theology courses in my department when I first arrived at Illinois. He introduced himself to me by saying: 'Hi, I'm Harry Tiebout. "*Phlogiston* Tiebout", they call me – throw *my* weight into the scales, and the scales go *up!*'

The influence of Kant and Hegel themselves is at least partly responsible for the disdain for the idea of human nature in the philosophical establishments on both sides of the English Channel in yet another respect. Each in his own way reinforces the longstanding religious and philosophical prejudice that what is 'human' about us is *all-too*-human; and that, while we obviously *have a kind* of human nature related to our animality and corporeality, *that* nature is what we were put in this world to *rise above*. It therefore is something to be made as little of as possible, and left to doctors and novelists.

The influence of Hegel – and also Marx, and subsequent thinkers such as Dilthey, Simmel and Weber – has made itself felt in yet another respect, of which the line taken by Foucault is a direct descendant. For them we have become what we most importantly are not by *nature* but by *nurture* – that is, in the course of history, and in the context of social, cultural, political, economic and other such historically-developing institutional circumstances. Hegel called all of this by the name of *objektive Geist*, 'objective spirit', and for that reason in German the disciplines concerned with them are called the *Geisteswissenschaften*. On our side of the English Channel they are sometimes called 'the *human* sciences'; but to most people they are 'the *social* sciences'. And if the 'human' is resolved completely into the 'social', the result is the dissolution of any more substantive notion of the 'human' than can be extracted from the idea of 'the social', which isn't much. Hence the derision in which the idea of human nature is held by most social scientists; and hence also Foucault.

A century or so ago, when British and American neo-Hegelians were anglicizing Hegel's terminology, the terms 'spirit' and 'spiritual' were deemed as infelicitous as the terms 'man' and 'human', though for opposite reasons. If 'man' seemed too naturalistic, 'spirit' seemed too *super*naturalistic. It therefore was decided to talk in terms of 'mind' and the 'mental' instead, and subsequently of 'agents' and 'action'. And so we wound up with 'the philosophy of mind' and 'the philosophy of action'. It was simply *bad form* to refer to ourselves in terms like 'human'.

That fastidiousness eventually turned into the conviction that there is something hopelessly superficial, naive and just plain *unphilosophical* about all such talk. The human identity of those whose minds and actions were under consideration was one of the 'unmentionables' in the laundry of the profession that was to be kept out of sight. *Who* was performing the actions? Why, 'agents', of course! *Whose* minds? 'Ours', obviously! To say more would be otiose and vulgar. And to ask for more, as I was roughly informed by several of my more bluntly-spoken professors in my college days at Harvard, was sophomoric, and betrayed a lack of sophistication unbefitting a serious student of philosophy.

The ban on 'man' deriving from this sensibility soon received powerful reinforcements from very different quarters. Phenomenologists objected to the naturalism implicated in the whole idea of taking our nature to be a fundamentally 'human' one, to be understood at least in the first instance in terms of the sort of living creature we are. Existentialists seconded the motion, adding that in our case 'existence precedes essence', and ruling out any meaningful conception of human nature beyond the idea of our 'being' being an issue for each of us. In their book any such conception is a fiction by means of which we try to avoid having to face up to our *Angst*-laden freedom and responsibility for ourselves.

Marxists condemned the idea of human nature as a reactionary ideological invention, intended to thwart recognition of both the possibility of and the need for a profound transformation of the status quo. Structuralists followed suit, taking any and all forms of humanity to be functions of contingent arrangements having no significance beyond the specific contexts in which they are realized. Feminists condemned all talk of our kind in terms of 'man' and 'men' as sexist; and they sometimes even went on to discern sexism in the very idea of a human nature that would apply across the board. And then along came Foucault and the other post-structuralists, for whom the very notion of a human nature is nothing more than the conceptual product of certain nineteenth-century disciplines in search of an object.

In the face of so much opposition, one might well conclude that the only future the idea of human nature is likely to have is that of whipping-boy for whatever else might come down the philosophical pike.

If Foucault is to be believed, Nietzsche was one of the leaders of the pack of its detractors. As *I* read Nietzsche, on the other hand, he has precisely the opposite significance, giving *der Mensch* a new lease of life. Nietzsche published *Beyond Good and Evil* as the turn of the previous century approached, and gave it the subtitle: *Prelude to a Philosophy of the Future*. I credit him not only with launching a much-needed 'revaluation of values' and the project of a naturalistic epistemology, but also with blazing a trail for a viable philosophical anthropology, deserving a central place on the agenda of the 'philosophy of the future' as both he and I envision it. It is my hope and expectation that the coming century will see his prelude come true.

In this respect, as in so many others, Nietzsche is truly one of Hume's heirs. Here are a few of the things Hume had to say in the Introduction to his *Treatise of Human Nature*, published in 1739:

> 'Tis evident, that all the sciences have a relation, greater or less, to human nature; and that however wide any of them may seem to run from it, they still return back [to it] by one passage or another ...
> There is no question of importance, whose decision is not compriz'd in the science of man; and there is none, which can be decided with any certainty, before we become acquainted with that science. In [purporting] therefore to explain the principles of human nature, we in effect propose a compleat system of the sciences, built on a foundation almost entirely new, and the only one upon which they can stand with any security.
> And as the science of man is the only solid foundation for the other sciences, so the only solid foundation we can give to this science itself must be laid on experience and observation ... We must therefore glean up our experiments in this science from a cautious observation of human life, and take them as they appear in the common course of the world, by men's behavior in company, in affairs, and in their pleasures. Where experiments of this kind are judiciously collected and compared, we may hope to establish on them a science, which will not be inferior in certainty, and will be much superior in utility to any other of human comprehension.[2]

Nietzsche undertook to practise what Hume here preaches, in his own inquiries into what makes human beings tick, from his relatively early volumes of aphorisms, beginning with *Human, All Too Human*, to *Twilight of the Idols*, written just before his untimely terminal collapse at the age of only 44. The title of one of his middle-period books nicely describes this kind of inquiry: *Die fröhliche Wissenschaft*, 'The Gay Science' – or better, perhaps, 'Joyous Inquiry'. Like Hume's 'science of man', it revolves around Nietzsche's version of psychology, supplemented by a multitude of other disciplinary (and extra-disciplinary) perspectives and modes of analysis and reflection. So, with what surely is a gesture in Hume's direction, Nietzsche concludes the first part of *Beyond Good and Evil* with what he calls the 'demand'

> that psychology shall be recognized again as the queen of the *Wissenschaften*, for whose service and preparation the other *Wissenschaften* exist. For psychology is now again the path to the fundamental problems.[3]

One of these 'fundamental problems' is how to carry out the 'revaluation of values'. And another is signaled when Nietzsche writes, in *On the Genealogy of Morals*: 'To breed an animal *with the right to make promises* – is not this the paradoxical task that nature has set itself in the case of man? Is it not the real problem regarding man?'[4] This is one of the ways in which he pursues the task he had articulated five years earlier, in *The Gay Science*. After announcing that 'God is dead' but observing that the interpretive 'shadows' cast by the God-gambit linger on,[5] he then goes on to ask:

> When will all these shadows of God cease to darken our minds? When will we complete our de-deification of nature? When may we begin to *naturalize* ourselves [literally 'us humans', *uns Menschen*] in terms of a pure, newly discovered, newly redeemed nature?[6]

This sounds very much like someone who thinks that the naturalistic reinterpretation of ourselves as *human* (*menschlich*) ought to be one of the first and foremost items on the agenda of philosophy, as we secularize and advance our understanding of the nature of which we are a part. And in fact Nietzsche explicitly proclaims this to be one of the main tasks of the 'philosophy of the future' heralded and launched in *Beyond Good and Evil* – even if a rather daunting one, owing to the doubts about many of our most cherished ideas about ourselves to which it may give rise. 'To translate man back into nature', he writes, to see to it that man henceforth stands before man as even today, hardened in the discipline of science, he stands before the rest of nature . . ., deaf to the siren songs of old metaphysical bird catchers who have been piping at him all too long, 'You are more, you are higher, you are of a different origin!' – that may be a strange and insane task, but it is a task – who would deny that?[7]

In short: as I read him, Nietzsche advocates and exemplifies what might be called an *anthropological shift* in philosophy. By this I mean a general reorientation of philosophical thinking, involving the attainment of an 'anthropological optic' and sensibility in thinking about ourselves, and also in thinking about most other items on the philosophical agenda. It thus involves the replacement of epistemology – as epistemology once replaced metaphysics – by a kind of philosophical anthropology as the central philosophical project.

Nietzsche is far from taking our humanity to amount to nothing more than a variation on the general theme of animality. The common view of his general conception of our nature imputes to him strongly reductionist and biologistic tendencies. This view, however, greatly distorts his actual approach to it and understanding of it quite seriously. We began as animals, and animals we remain; and, as Nietzsche has Zarathustra say, '"soul" is only a word for something about the body.'[8] But he also considers human life to have been fundamentally, pervasively and fatefully transformed – and to have become *human* life in the first place – with the advent of *society*. So it is that he devotes most of his attention, from *The Birth of Tragedy* onward, to phenomena associated with human social and cultural life.

Thanks to this revolution in our evolution, we are, as Nietzsche puts it, 'the no-longer-merely-animal animal'. He does contend that what he calls 'the entire evolution of the spirit' is ultimately to be referred back to 'the body' and our physiological constitution. However, he places equal emphasis upon the ways human life has come to be reconstituted and shaped in the course of its development. And in this connection he makes much of the social and cultural phenomena associated with its transformation, in which its emergent nature is manifested, and through which the conditions of the possibility of its further enhancement have been established.

The purported key to all of this, and so to our humanization, was what Nietzsche calls the 'fundamental change' that 'occurred when [man] found himself finally enclosed within the walls of society', and that transformed the 'semi-animals' we once were into the human beings we now are. This for Nietzsche was a crucial step, giving rise (as he strikingly puts it) to 'the existence on earth of an animal soul turned against itself', which 'was something so new, profound, unheard of, enigmatic, contradictory, and pregnant with a future that the aspect of the earth was essentially altered'.[9] The earth now featured a novel sort of creature, with a novel sort of nature. We are that creature, and its nature is our human one.

Nietzsche did indeed repudiate the notion of human nature as a kind of 'eternal truth', as early as *Human, All Too Human* (1878), in which he wrote:

> Lack of historical sense is the [hereditary] failing of all philosophers; many, without being aware of it, even take the most recent manifestation of man, such as has arisen under the impress of certain religions, even certain political events, as the fixed form from which one has to start out. They do not want to learn that man has become, that [even] the faculty of cognition has become...
>
> Now, everything *essential* in the development of mankind took place in primeval times, long before the four thousand years we more or less know about; during these years mankind may well not have altered very much. But the philosopher here sees 'instincts' in man as he is now and assumes that these belong to the unalterable facts of mankind...
>
> But everything has become: there are *no eternal facts,* just as there are no eternal truths. Consequently what is needed from now on is *historical philosophizing,* and with it the virtue of modesty.[10]

Nietzsche then went on to recast the notion of the 'human', and to make much use of it thus reconceived. He clearly supposed that it can and should be *rehabilitated,* and made the focus of enlightened philosophical inquiry of the sort he commended to his 'new philosophers' and sought himself to undertake. It is no objection or fatal obstacle to the enterprise of a philosophical anthropology, for Nietzsche, that our humanity has a history and a genealogy, and that it remains capable of further transformation. In both cases, the moral he draws is not that the idea of human nature is ruled out, or that things human are matters with which philosophy is incapable of dealing. Rather, it is that philosophy must and can adapt itself to the character of these objects of inquiry, in aspiration and method, as it proceeds to deal with them.

It is this kind of thinking about our human reality that I believe can and should have a future, philosophically and humanly. Some of what Nietzsche himself had to say about it – for example, some of what he says relating to heredity, gender, and our psychology – may be confused, unwarranted, or flat-out wrong. But that is less important than his insistence that such matters are relevant to our self-interpretation, and his attempts to develop ways and means of pursuing them. And, further, it is less important than his commitment to non-dogmatic, self-critical rigour and honesty in dealing with them. We need not subscribe to his every pronouncement to embrace the spirit of his enterprise, and to join in the practice of the sort of thinking he preaches.

But enough about Nietzsche. It is time for me to put more of my own cards on the table. Human life, to my way of thinking, is undeniably both a biological and a socio-cultural affair. Its socio-cultural dimensions are obviously anchored in certain of its biological underpinnings, and clearly are importantly conditioned by them. But its biology is equally clearly engineered precisely for *plasticity*. The social and cultural diversity of human existence past and present is undeniable, and stands in striking contrast to the relative constancy and uniformity of our biological constitution. Moreover, the open-endedness of human life with respect to the possibility of the emergence of new socio-cultural forms must at least be presumed. These are among my reasons for supposing that at least a good deal of what goes on in human life, at and beyond the level of socio-cultural phenomena, is not explicable in merely biological terms – even though I readily grant that it is an open question in what respects and to what extent this is so, and have no metaphysical investment in the idea of free-floating, free-wheeling 'free wills' frolicking about behind the scenes.

This socio-cultural supervenience is a profoundly important feature of human reality, and might be called our 'true supernaturalism'. The point is not that we started out supernatural, or are so by metaphysical birthright, but rather that we have wound up that way. We are creatures of nature *and then some*, having bootstrapped our way beyond our original merely natural animality. With the transformation of our proto-human nature that both made possible and was required by our socialization and the invention of culture, human life broke the mould in which it had first been cast. A dialectic of nature and nurture has been going on ever since, to the point that the very impossibility of disentangling them is one of the hallmarks of our humanity. Hence also the fundamentally *historical* character of human life, which likewise is no less real than its inescapable animality, and indeed is intimately bound up with its socio-culturality.

Our kind of animality thus is only a part of the story where our human nature is concerned. The nature–nurture dialectic and our historicality are others. Another is what might be called our *psychosomaticity*. There is little if anything that we experience and do as human beings that is not psychosomatic, in the sense of having both psychological and physiological dimensions that are deeply interconnected. Our senses, our emotions, and our sexualities are all cases in point – and so are our arts, sports, uses of language, interpersonal interactions, and even our religions and sciences, insofar as they are ongoing pieces of human life, having to do with forms of human activity and experience. Nor do they take shape and go on in a vacuum: the dynamics of the interrelations between the psychosomatic and the socio-cultural are the heartbeat of the human.

Another cardinal feature of our humanity might be called *objectification*. It has to do with the interplay of experience and its expressions in human life. In this ubiquitous dialectic, subjectivity both finds objective form and undergoes transformation under the impact and through the appropriation of objectivities that have thus been humanly produced. This is how art works. This is how culture more generally works as well. And this is how human life elaborates itself.

No less significant is the phenomenon of human *intersubjectivity*. It pertains to those relations and interactions constituting our interhuman relationships, impersonal as well as personal. Human life is interpersonal to the core. And as such it is *communicative*, on a number of levels and in a variety of ways – all mediated to one degree or another by symbols, conventions and institutions, but not fixed by their forms and structures.

Then there is our *embodiment*. Our relation to our own bodies is a very perplexing and by no means simple one, and is another basic feature of our human existence. A human body is neither simply what a human being *is*, nor simply something one *has*, but rather is both at once inseparably, even if also dynamically – and sometimes awkwardly, and even distressingly. Hence the boundedness of human reality by death, and the cogency (if not the plausibility) of the idea that, for immortality to be humanly meaningful, it would have to involve re-embodiment ('reincarnation') rather than the mere survival of 'the soul'.

One last example of such things: a number of these features of our nature converge upon and frame the problem of human *mentality*. We obviously have brains. But we also obviously have 'brains', in the figurative sense in which it is beyond dispute both that we are talking about something other than sheer quantities of grey matter inside our skulls, and that we are not all comparably endowed. How are we to understand what goes on in our 'brain-processes' in relation to what goes on 'in our minds', even if – and indeed particularly if – we understand both expressions to be more than a bit metaphorical? And how are we to understand both sorts of goings-on in relation to what goes on in our lives? We may not have a monopoly on this sort of thing in the universe; but there can be no doubt that much about the way it all goes in our case is inextricably bound up with the genealogy of our humanity. I shall return in a moment to this issue, in which I have a considerable interest.

This is only a very partial inventory of topics on the agenda of the sort of inquiry into human nature I believe has a future. But it should serve to help indicate what I am talking about, and to suggest why I find it interesting as well as intellectually respectable and important. As I have indicated, I take myself to be making common cause in all of this with Nietzsche, and to be very much in the spirit of Hume as well. But I believe that Nietzsche and I have gone beyond Hume in certain important respects; for human beings as Nietzsche and I understand them are more complicated than what I might call 'Humean beings'. Outgrowing Nietzsche himself may be the *next* order of business; but, to my way of thinking, that is going to take some doing, since few among us have even caught up to him yet.

How does a Nietzschean version of a human being differ from others in the philosophical-historical inventory? Let me refresh your memory. A Platonic being might be thought of as a soul in a body. An Aristotelian one is a potentially rational animal that fares best in something like a Greek polis. The Christian version is either an embodied soul or an ensouled body, depending on whether it favours the Platonic or the Aristotelian side of the family. A Cartesian being is a mind hooked up to a body. The Hobbesian model is a body with a brain. Its Humean cousin is a physiology with a psychology and a social life. Their Kantian rival is that *plus* a self capable of rationality, autonomy, duty, and immortality.

A Hegelian being is a bit player in the self-transformation of reality from the natural into the spiritual by way of the socio-cultural. How about a Heideggerian being? Well, you'd better not try this one at home, but a Heideggerian being has the character of (and I more or less quote the master) 'being-in-the-world-ahead-of-itself-with-thrown-facticity-alongside-entities-among-others-towards-death'. (It is no better in German!) A Sartrean being, on the other hand, is just a

THE FUTURE OF HUMAN NATURE

recycled Cartesian duality, redescribed as a 'being' and a 'nothingness' – or, as Sartre playfully puts it, it 'is what it is not and is not what it is'. (In contrast to the Heideggerian formulation, I can explain *this* in a single lecture – but not on this occasion.)

And a Nietzschean being? A Nietzschean being might be characterized as a Humean being with its psychology scrambled by socialization, and with a penchant for sublimation resulting from a religious upbringing in a Hegelian neighbourhood. As one might guess, from this description, Nietzschean human beings don't all turn out alike; and indeed most of them don't turn out very well at all (which is hardly surprising under the circumstances); although some have it in them to turn out very well indeed, and a few actually manage to do so, even if not for long.

My own version is most closely related to Nietzsche's, although a number of the others are up there in its family tree. (My version also has affinities with what I think would have been Wittgenstein's version if he had had one.) I now would like to suggest some of the things I think belong in the picture. I consider them to be a needed supplement to the neo-Hobbesian portrait that seems to be finding favour these days among some cognitive-science types and their philosophical fellow-travellers. According to them, the mental dimensions of human life are really just a disguised neuro-physiological subset of its physical dimensions. I do not doubt for a moment that everything that goes on in us has such dimensions. I do very much doubt, however, whether this will take us very far in the direction of making sense of human reality.

Hegel, I believe, had a better idea (so to speak). He may have talked strangely, but he was no idealist of the starry-eyed kind, and he was no mystical metaphysician either. For Hegel as for Nietzsche, this life in this world is all there is to us – but there is more to it than meets the natural-scientific eye. It also involves social and cultural phenomena, in which human experience finds objective expression and embodiment. To be sure, mental life goes on only when and where the appropriate sorts of neuro-physiological events are occurring; but that is not the whole story. The warp of its infrastructure may be neuro-physiological, but its woof is social and cultural. Its setting is not only the brain, but also human societies and institutions and their associated objectivities – from the languages spoken in them to the customs, practices, rules, laws and institutions established in them, to the artifacts fashioned and products produced and exchanged within them.

Indeed, human mentality is not only some subset of brain-states, but also is social, cultural, political, economic, religious, artistic, scientific, linguistic, and other such phenomena, in their living reality as intersubjective *forms of human life*. It has to do at once with their objectifications and with the varieties of experience made possible and structured by these objectifications. Our mental life can no more be adequately understood simply in terms of something going on inside our heads, abstracted from this context, than organic life can be adequately understood in terms of something going on within the individual organism, abstracted from its relations to its environing world.

By the same token, human mental life also cannot be adequately understood in terms of the various sorts of 'sensory inputs' our senses are biologically configured to be capable of receiving. And it is not enough to make further reference to the chemical and physical processes that occur from the moment our sensory receptors are impinged upon until the resulting neural ripplings subside. I take what goes on in our minds and lives to have a good deal more to do with the *significant content* that piggy-backs on these processes than with their nuts and bolts. What we 'take in', beyond the media of the messages, may be broadly characterized as *information*, which at least for the most part is conceptually schematized, and bound up with the interpretive and evaluative contexts within which its meaning is constituted. Information may be coded, expressed, conveyed and received in certain types of sensory images; but what is significant about these images is *the meanings they convey*, by virtue of the significance with which they have come to be endowed, as elements of conceptual, interpretive, evaluative *symbol-systems*.

We 'take in' both these systems themselves (as we learn them and continue to learn modifications and refinements of them), and also the rich variety of particular things they are used to convey. What goes on inside our heads and in our human lives is to a great extent a function of *the symbol-systems we internalize* and the interactions, transactions and other actions they make possible. We relate to each other by means of them; and our experience of environments and happenings is laden with them.

It would seem to be in our nature to operate at least for the most part by means of *representations*. And to whatever degree this is so, the representations by means of which we operate owe at least as much to the symbol-systems we internalize as to the sensory and neural apparatus with which we are endowed. Our neural system is the place in which such representations become effective; but it is the meaning-content of the representations that is of paramount importance in human life. And that content requires an entirely different sort of analysis, in terms reflecting its symbolic elaboration and its socio-cultural objectification.

It is not unreasonable to suppose that the human senses and brain have evolved in concert with the emergence and development in human social life of the phenomenon of symbolism – that is, in concert with the capacity to use, generate, teach and learn symbols, and to establish systems or orders of this composition. Indeed, it would seem that one of the primary evolved functions of our senses and brain is precisely to enable us to internalize, enter into, and participate in whatever social symbolic order might be at hand – the content of which then comes to loom large in what we go on to do.

Can naturalistic sense be made of this? Nietzsche thought so, and so do I. Let us suppose that, once upon a time, our proto-human ancestors were nothing more than Hobbesian beings – bodies with brains more or less like ours. It is not all that difficult to see how they might have turned into something more. (The story I am about to tell is indebted to the one Nietzsche tells in the fifth part of *The Gay Science* and in the Second Essay of his *On the Genealogy of Morals*.) Suppose that our Hobbesian beings are impelled by circumstances of a very practical nature to enter into group arrangements that place a premium on the development of their ability to communicate, and to coordinate their behaviour. Suppose further that a dialectic ensues, in which developments along these lines usher in more complex social arrangements, which in turn prompt further such developments.

Suppose that this results in the elaboration of systems of conventions and rules facilitating and regulating the ways these beings communicate and interact; and suppose that ways and means of fixing, teaching and learning them are devised and developed along with them. Our Hobbesian beings are turning Humean. Now suppose that the relations between elements of these systems begin to affect their use and function, and that various social dynamics likewise come to be reflected in them. Suppose that the sorts of things they make it possible to express feed back into them, further affecting the significance attaching to their elements. And suppose that the resulting conceptual, interpretive, evaluative and normative schemes come increasingly to structure the ways these beings encounter each other and their environing world, and frame and select the ways open to them to act in various situations.

By this point our 'Humean beings' have become more or less *human* beings. Their manner of existence has come to be mediated by socially generated and sustained domains of symbolic phenomena that exert a decisive influence upon the character and course of their experience and conduct. Their psychosomatic 'Humean nature' has not disappeared; but it has been transmogrified and so superseded. Their psycho-physiology has been transformed, from a configuration of features in terms of which their lives are *determined*, to but a part of what merely *conditions* their experience and conduct. While remaining a factor, it also serves as the means through which they are enabled to enter into socially and symbolically constructed *forms of life*, in terms of which the courses of their lives are now to a very significant extent to be understood. (If there is anything to the recent fuss about 'memes', I would say that this is what the kernel of truth in the 'meme theme' amounts to. 'Memes' are supposed to be sort of like genes, only they are cultural rather than biological. If you don't know what I am talking about, never mind. If you do, this is just to let you know that, while I think there is more to memetics than I think there is to sociobiology, I am no meme-maniac.)

Is this account plausible? Well, consider the obvious fact that we often do things because someone orders or asks us to do them, or tells us something, or because of what the directions we are following say, or because of some promise we have made, or because of some rule of a game we are playing, or because of some piece of etiquette, and so on, and on. In each case and in each action performed, the brain is certainly involved, and may be said to generate the movements in question; but the brain can hardly be said to be running the whole show. (On the other hand it is not really being run by whatever it is that we think of as 'the mind' either, in any complete sense, even though whatever it is that we've got along these lines is certainly involved as well.)

The significance of the brain in all of this is that it makes this remarkable manner of existence possible. Its significance is *not* that, of its own nature and in accordance with its own processes, it determines what forms these social and symbolic structures will take, and what courses of events will unfold within the contexts they set. Other animals have brains, and senses, and may (like our pets) live in the same environments we do; and yet they are quite oblivious to the things we respond to in the sorts of situations I have mentioned and countless others in our lives. There is an important difference; but what is it? To ask what they lack, and to answer that they lack 'minds', is only to offer a word where an account is needed. A better question is: what is it that occurs in our case that does not occur in theirs?

A clue to the answer may be found by asking what might be *needed to mediate* between symbol systems, on the one hand, and neural processes capable of engaging our organs of action and expression, on the other. Hand in hand with the elaboration of such systems, there must develop a way of internalizing them and representing their contents. In short, something on the order of *mental events* would seem to be required as an *intermediary* between an objectified symbolic order and the neural order. A long period of evolutionary development may have been required, during which this constellation of elements was increasingly strengthened, refined and elaborated, before human life as we know and live it emerged; but it could well have occurred, and very probably did.

This view of the matter opens the door to a conception of human *agency* that also makes conceivable the human possibility of a limited but nonetheless significant measure of individual *autonomy*, sufficient to enable us to make sense of those human phenomena seeming to require it. Our expressions and conduct may always be strongly *conditioned* by a combination of the way our senses and brain operate, and by our history of exposure to and interaction with our multi-dimensional and diverse social-symbolic as well as natural environing world. One does not have to buy into some robust version of free-will metaphysics, however, to salvage the idea that everything in our lives is not invariably and completely dictated by the details of this combination.

To rehabilitate this idea without having to venture beyond the naturalistic parameters of the conception of our human nature I am sketching, little more is necessary than, *first*, to acknowledge the relative autonomy of the elaboration of the contents of socially engendered symbolic orders in relation to neurological and all other merely natural processes; *second*, to take seriously the notion of individual mental life as provisioned through the internalization of these contents; and, *third*, to observe that, on the other hand, we also have an affective nature that is not strictly social, in which other forces are at work within us, and impinge upon what we internalize. It is this third consideration that may be the key to the possibility of a significant sort of human-personal autonomy transcending the effects of socialization and acculturation, even though by itself our affective nature is less than human.

What our minds have to work with, in all human cases, is derived from what might be called our social-symbolic education, and from the registering of the multitude of particular episodes of the kinds they make possible, in a manner conditioned by the deliverances of our senses and by the general character of our neural apparatus and its functioning. This would warrant the mind's characterization along the lines of the 'ensemble of social relations' of which Marx famously spoke in his eleventh 'Thesis on Feuerbach', contrasting his conception of human reality with Feuerbach's more simplistically naturalistic version.

But a human mind is a *dynamic* ensemble, rather than a mere inert result. Internalized elements and registering episodes are not merely recorded. They are drawn into interplay and interaction *both* by the meanings they carry in relation to each other *and* by the more fundamental psychological and physiological processes at work within us. Now suppose some distinctive and relatively persisting configuration of symbolically-informed and meaning-textured dispositions emerges, under the sway of which particular impulses can be mastered, responses controlled, and objectives formed and pursued through strategies devised. The result can be a human being to whom as much autonomy is attributable as the champions of choice, responsibility and creativity could reasonably desire and require. At the same time, this way of thinking of our nature also enables one to make good and important sense of the seemingly undeniable fact that human beings turn out very differently, and very frequently do not wind up attaining to anything like this sort of humanity, in any of its humanly possible realizations. What more could one want from such an account?

In conclusion: in dealing with our nature, there is a good deal of difference between truth and the *whole* truth. It is of the greatest importance to avoid making too much of certain things that may be true enough as far as they go – for example, that we are featherless bipeds, or naked apes – but that fall well short of doing justice to their purported object. Accounts of human nature, both philosophical and otherwise, have long been vulnerable to criticism along these lines. But that vulnerability is hardly fatal to the enterprise. We just have to keep on applying our intellectual consciences to our best efforts.

Even though I have been speaking with some assurance in the account I have been sketching, I am well aware that virtually nothing I have said is beyond dispute. I obviously think I am on the right track, or I would have talked about something else. In this business, however, the jury is always out, the final verdict is never in, the witnesses are always under cross-examination, and further testimony is always being taken. That's just the way it is. But we in the business don't mind. We've had 2500 years to get used to it. And this has its bright side: our work will be forever unfinished, and so we'll never put ourselves out of a job.

I hope that I have succeeded in making a convincing case that the idea of human nature does indeed have a future, and a philosophical one at that; and that a philosophical consideration of it is still possible, even after we have done our intellectual house-cleaning; and that it can be quite interesting. An enterprise of the sort I have been describing and displaying undoubtedly is, and will remain, a rather untidy and tentative affair. But then, the same is true with respect to human life itself; and so one could hardly expect matters to turn out any differently.

6

THE MIMETIC THEORY OF RELIGION

An outline

René Girard

Can archaic religion be regarded as a riddle with an answer? The late nineteenth- and early twentieth-century anthropologists never quite said so, but they vigorously attempted to solve that riddle. This enterprise failed, however, and the resulting discouragement, reinforced by the linguistic nihilism of many modern philosophers, has led to the anti-theoretical stance of our age.

The deconstructors derisively refer to religions as *grands récits*: pure fiction, in other words, unfit for scientific systematization. But the 'grand narrative' formula has no pertinence whatever. It harks back to Auguste Comte's misconception of religion as a first and naive attempt to do what only science can do, 'solve the mysteries of the universe'.

Archaic religions have more serious business than the mysteries of the universe: the survival of human communities. Actions in them are more important than words. Religiously significant actions are of two kinds: (1) the ones that must be avoided, the prohibited actions, and (2) the ones that must be performed, mostly *sacrificial immolations*. The narrative component of archaic cults, when they have one, is far from 'grand'. It consists in a *foundational myth* that deals exclusively with the specific cult of which it is a part.

The only researchers who still ask ambitious questions about religion as such, religion in general, are the sociobiologists. E. O. Wilson for instance, briefly inquired about the 'adaptive value' of religion. If it had none, he observed, it would not have survived very long. Quoting Durkheim, he concluded that religion must provide social 'cohesiveness'.[1]

This idea is true, I believe, but it has been around ever since people began to wonder if the etymology of 'religion' might not be *religare*, 'to

THE MIMETIC THEORY OF RELIGION

bind together'. How do religions bind societies together? Is it possible to give a precise answer to this question?

The real enemy of social harmony is internal conflict, rooted in rivalries for females, food, territory . . . In animal societies, these rivalries are of limited duration and intensity. As soon as the weaker antagonist perceives his disadvantage, he surrenders. The victor spares his life and becomes the dominant animal: he has first choice in everything. Dominance patterns still exist sporadically among us but they do not play a major role in our cultural and social organizations that always involve religion. At some point, dominance patterns must have broken down under the impact of internal violence, more intense among us than among other primates.

To attribute this intensity to some 'aggressive instinct', as many people do, leads to an impasse. A more fruitful path, in my opinion, is an investigation of the specifically human drive we call *desire*.

In addition to the needs and appetites we share with animals, we also possess a more problematic yearning that is exclusively ours, desire. Because desire often contaminates the biological needs and appetites human beings possess in common with animals, it is often confused with these. Most observers either reduce desire to appetites and needs, or they elevate it into some kind of metaphysical stratosphere that makes a down-to-earth analysis impossible. The specificity of desire is its lack of any instinctual object. From an early age on, we all desire intensely but we do not know exactly what. In order to find out, we turn to the people we admire; we *imitate* their desires in order to be like them without ceasing to be ourselves.

If human desires were not imitative, children would not learn the language and culture of their family and country. Our capacity to learn is one with our capacity to imitate. Mimetic desire is a most precious endowment, unquestionably, but it has one major drawback: it is responsible for much violence in human relations.

When we copy the desire of other people, we desire the objects already desired by the latter who, understandably, want to keep these objects for themselves. Models and imitators thus become rivals for the same objects. And *mimetic rivalry* triggers a circular process that intensifies – not one – but both desires, making them more and more similar as their reciprocal hostility increases. As the imitator becomes the model of his model, the model in turn becomes the imitator of his imitator. The two desires feed on one another and the good reciprocity of peace turns into the bad reciprocity of reprisals and vengeance.

The two rivals are annoyed by their reciprocity. They want to be 'different' but, whatever they do to assert this 'difference', their mimetic partner also does, and the reciprocity persists. This process is an insidious undoing of cultural differences, a paradoxical undifferentiation that proves contagious and tends to spread to originally uninvolved bystanders. Extreme individualism is little more, as a rule, than the comically impotent rebellion of mimetic rivals against the iron law of their bad reciprocity. The more they try to escape this law, the more it dominates their relationship.

At some point during the emergence of the human species, our ancestors must have become more and more mimetic and their rivalries must have intensified so much that the social system based on dominance patterns finally broke down. A specifically human system eventually replaced the animal system, but before this revolution succeeded there must have been many mimetic crises, many difficult transitions. Archaic cults must have emerged in the course of this difficult transition. During many thousands, perhaps millions, of years, there must have been many intermediate stages, many crises and many partial resolutions.

We cannot document this process directly of course: the archaic cults with which we are acquainted originated, without a doubt, long after the problem was solved. In these myths and rituals, however, a crisis-and-resolution pattern keeps recurring which is older, no doubt, than the oldest examples that have reached us. It can teach us a great deal, I believe, about the origin of religion and human culture.

At the beginning of many myths, the community is in trouble: it may be a famine, a flood, a drought, or some other natural disaster. The crisis may be also be defined in fantastic terms, as a battle of two giants, or the clash of two mountains, or of two celestial bodies, etc. It may be a supernatural monster who demands more and more sacrificial victims . . . An element of human conflict always seems to be present. The simplest and probably the best definition of this crisis is a conflict within the community. Whatever the case may be, the result is always the same: the community is dysfunctional; total destruction threatens.

Another frequent definition of this crisis is 'the plague'. Before modern medicine, the contagion of mimetic rivalry was often confused with pathological contagion. The total picture suggests that the initial crisis, even if it has a natural cause to start with, is essentially an epidemic of mimetic rivalry, a *mimetic crisis*.

THE MIMETIC THEORY OF RELIGION

In *Oedipus the King*, Sophocles alludes, no doubt, to the great Athenian plague of 430 BCE, but the essential manifestations of this epidemic are mimetic rather than pathological; they are the rivalry of Oedipus and Tiresias first, of Oedipus and Creon later. Greek tragedy is our greatest interpretation of mythology and it is implicitly, if not explicitly, mimetic. The tragic poets make it fairly obvious that Greek myths portray a crisis of mimetic rivalry unanimously, but ambiguously, resolved by the expulsion or death of an individual who may or may not be responsible for that crisis.

One more interesting symbol of mimetic rivalry in foundational myths, the most transparent of all, objectively, but the least understood in the modern world, is the battle of identical twins or twin-like brothers, cousins, etc. In both myths and tragedies, twins are more numerous than their statistical distribution in the human population warrants. The best known examples are Eteocles and Polynices, Dionysus and Pentheus, Romulus and Remus and, in some respects, Cain and Abel.

The twins are usually fighting for an object they both desire, a woman, a kingdom, a city, more generally the inheritance of their father over which they have identical claims. The twin-obsession of myths, just like the plague-obsession, points to the mimetic nature of the tragic conflict. The physical resemblance of twins is assimilated to the destruction of differences, to the production of reciprocity and identity, by the mimetic rivals.

Myths ascribe human conflict, not to too much difference, as most of us do, but to too little. The mythical obsession with twins combines a great insight into the structure of human violence with a dreadful confusion between biological and cultural 'undifferentiation'. Myths have no words for this process, and to signify it they often resort to twins. We moderns have the words but we have lost the insight.

The cultures that confused mimetic rivalry with the biological resemblance of twins greatly feared the birth of the latter. They regarded twins as germs of a mimetic crisis that would reproduce these twins uncontrollably and unravel the fragile pattern of differences of which every culture consists. The societies that held this view often killed both twins at birth or, sometimes, one in each pair only. This latter course clearly shows that the perceived danger was the simultaneous presence in the community of two perfectly identical beings. Each twin taken separately was regarded as harmless. To destroy twins was unjustified and cruel, no doubt, but it was not frivolous. From correct premises many archaic cults drew dreadfully mistaken conclusions. Many others did not.

In foundational myths, the main event is the climactic drama that puts an end to the mimetic crisis. Like this crisis itself, it may assume different forms and shapes. In the myths whose heroes are twins, for instance, one of the two finally kills the other, and this violence has foundational properties because it restores differences. Cain's murder of Abel *is* the foundation of the first human culture. Romulus's murder of Remus *is* the foundation of Rome. In the non-biblical world, all twins become gods, but the greater god is the murderer, the real founder of the community, Romulus rather than Remus. Since everything is identical to start with, one feels that, if the roles were reversed, if Remus killed Romulus, the result would be the same. The murder would still revive the differences lost in the crisis. Different versions of the same myth may resolve themselves in different dramas that are really interchangeable. This is the case with Romulus and Remus, for example. Livy has two versions of the scene. In the first, Romulus personally kills Remus and, in the other, Remus, we are told, died because he *fell into the crowd*. This phrase can only mean that Romulus was the crowd that lynched Remus.[2] The myth is both a twin myth and a *lynching myth*.

Lynching myths occur in all parts of the world. In order to minimize their importance in mythology generally, the old anthropologists often suggested that collective violence, as a theme, must be 'very archaic'. In many instances, they probably were right, in the case of Australian myths notably. Lynching, however, is prominent also in highly developed cultures, such as the Greek. All episodes of the Dionysiac cycle conclude with a lynching. Under the influence of some god, the people turn into a fierce mob and they rush madly at their victim whom they trample to death and tear to pieces, before devouring its raw flesh.

The Freud of *Totem and Taboo* is the only interpreter of archaic religion who acknowledged lynching as a central phenomenon around which all interpretation should revolve. His book was almost universally rejected. All authoritative voices in the philosophical, religious and even psychoanalytical establishments rose up as one man to discredit it.

Freud realized that behind archaic religion must lie the unanimous violence of entire communities. Unfortunately, he was so eager to plant the flag of psychoanalysis on this mountain peak of an insight that he himself destroyed its credibility. He suggested that there was only one real lynching at the dawn of history, whenever and wherever that was, and that its victim had to be a 'father' – who else? – the dreadful tyrant of the 'primitive horde'.

Many myths, of course, contain no lynching and even no individual murder. In the Sophoclean version of the Oedipus myth, for instance, the hero is 'merely' cast out, and in the Homeric version he is not punished at all. This lack of violence is not the overwhelming objection that it seems to be against the emphasis on lynching. Careful observation shows that among the minimally violent or totally non-violent myths, some at least contain traces of a lynching that must have been there in earlier versions and suppressed later *by the faithful themselves* who had become sophisticated enough to be shocked by the violence of their ancestors – just like our own contemporaries ...

These people initiated the practice of censoring or camouflaging the offending scenes, on the grounds, no doubt, that they could not authentically belong to their sacred scriptures. They convinced themselves that the lynching was an uninformed or malevolent tampering that they could legitimately suppress. This was done but their counter-tampering was so gingerly performed that, in some instances, the original lynching still shows through the final version. I have analysed examples of this revealing process in *The Scapegoat*.[3]

The censoring of collective violence has continued after archaic religions finally declined and disappeared. Plato's condemnation of the poets for representing religious violence is a new form of the same censorship. The absence of any serious debate around *Totem and Taboo* is another. This book may well be indirectly responsible as well for the tendency of mythological studies after the Second World War to retreat more and more into unreality. New interpretations are welcome only if they turn myths into purely imaginary constructs, pure literature, *grands récits*. The violence of mythology is hidden under thick layers of more and more convoluted concepts, the meaning of which can always be summed up in one sentence: 'all these lynchings are nothing to worry about – myths are pure fiction'.

Freud's explanatory scenario is intrinsically unbelievable and, moreover, it does not really fit the data. If all mythical representations of lynching patterned themselves on only one lynching, all of them would probably resemble that one model. Even if they did not, it is unlikely that they would vividly recall other well-known types of lynching too different to be patterned on the same model. This is what the record actually shows. This concrete diversity requires the many real models which the mimetic theory alone provides.

Why does the final lynching succeed in ending the crisis which nothing could end before? Why does the death of only one victim satisfy the universal appetite for violence which, during the mimetic disorder, numerous victims could not satisfy? The reason is that these victims were stirring up more desire for vengeance; they added more fuel to the fire of reprisals, because they never managed to unite the entire community against them. The final lynching alone is unanimous.

The fact that the myth itself believes in the justice of the lynching confirms the unanimity of the lynchers who are the authors of the myth, the entire community. The whole idea is absurd, of course. How could a single individual be responsible for a whole mimetic crisis? The crisis is a mortal peril for the community because its contagion makes more and more human interactions violent. It finally criss-crosses human communities with mimetic rivalries and no single individual can be responsible for all of them. The crisis necessarily involves, if not all members of the community, at least a great many.

If the single victims are innocent, however, what qualities, or what circumstances, make them acceptable, all of a sudden, to entire communities? To answer this question, we must find what happens after the community shatters into many separate fragments, many independent conflicts between twin-like rivals who all fight for the possession of mimetically desired objects.

As these rivalries further intensify, the reciprocal hatred becomes so intense that, finally, it extinguishes the desire for objects. Pushing all the disputed objects aside, the two rivals in each pair reach for each other's throats. They recall the infernal rivals in Dante's *Inferno* whose punishment consists in fighting each other for all eternity. This impression, however, is misleading. When the antagonists 'undifferentiate', for all practical (or, rather for all mimetic) purposes, they become interchangeable. Far from making substitutions impossible, intense hatred facilitates them.

Many rivals will now silently move away from their original rivals, and they will focus their hatred on someone else who seems more 'appealing' as an antagonist – or perhaps we should say more repulsive? What is the reason for the change?

Since all members of the community are equivalent, the selection of the victim, it seems, should be haphazard, completely random... This is sometimes true, no doubt, but not always. When it comes to polarizing an aggressive crowd against themselves, not all people are equivalent; some individuals have more drawing power than others, and they are more likely to end up as victims. All one can say about them is what the myths themselves say. Often the myths say nothing at all about their victims, but often also they mention one or more personal attributes that make their possessors more attractive *as victims* than other members of the crowd.

These attributes are disconcerting: since the single victims reappear after their lynching in the role of divine saviours and reconstructors of the community, one would expect their attributes to anticipate this reappearance and arouse respect and admiration. Not at all. These personal attributes are such, ordinarily, as to arouse our discomfort and even our disgust.

Among these attributes, the most frequent are physical blemishes, handicaps, infirmities. Many victims are lame, one-eyed, blind, hunchback, or otherwise impaired... Some have contagious illnesses. From others, a foul odour emanates, etc.

There are also cultural and social attributes with the same overall connotation, when viewed from the mob's standpoint. Many victims are located on the margins of society, either too high or too low, always from the perspective of the mob that provides the absolute yardstick. Kings and princes are often selected for lynching; so are beggars, vagabonds and homeless people. Any departure from the physical or social standards of the majority increase an individual's chances of being lynched.

Quite remarkable in this context is the large number of single victims designated simply as strangers or foreigners. It is easy to guess why. Archaic communities were often quite isolated, separated by great distances from their closest neighbours. When a stranger showed up, his or her appearance, speech and manners must have been matters of intense curiosity – friendly no doubt, at least initially – but the slightest intimation of trouble, an unexplained noise perhaps, or a rash gesture could trigger a panic so intense, I suppose, that, before the stranger had time to fear for his life, he had lost it.

All the physical and cultural attributes I mentioned, and many others, may be defined as victim marks or *stigmas*. Even in our own world, individuals who possess one such stigma are often protected by law from the discrimination and even persecution that always threaten them, just as it did, it seems, in the bygone worlds that produced foundational myths.

In a mimetic crisis, the people endowed with victim stigmas are more likely to be lynched than the people not so endowed, who attract less attention. As the number of people already mobilized against a potential victim increases, the mimetic fascination of other possible targets of exasperation will decrease and they are finally abandoned. A 'simplification' of the crisis occurs and it will proceed until only one centre of hostility remains, around which the entire community gathers.

When this happens, the community stands together, de facto reunited against the one last target that remains alone at the centre, the single victim who is about to be lynched.

Just like historical victims, the victims in foundational myths were often selected, it seems, because they belonged to some unpopular minority, or because they possessed some insignificant physical blemish which polarized the mob. They died for the same pathetically insignificant reasons that polarize mobs on the rampage always and everywhere.

If my reasoning is correct, not only should the single victim of a myth possess some victim stigmas but, logically, the individual finally selected as single victim should be the individual who possesses the most.

One must be careful, however, not to take the logic of victim stigmas too far. It is unquestionable, I believe, that crowds often select victims because of these victim stigmas and for no other reason; but not always. The association between the two is legitimate, even irrefutable, but it is not necessary. Or rather it is necessary only from a statistical viewpoint, which is enough for my purpose. I am trying to show that real phenomena of social persecution must lie behind foundational myths. I do not claim that the lynching is the 'effect' of a 'cause' that would be the victim stigma. The fact that an individual is endowed with such stigmas provides no certainty of persecution, only an enhanced possibility. If we assume that the victim with the most victim stigmas will be necessarily selected, we mistake the mimetic theory for a pseudo-science of positivistic explanations, which it is not. We expect some kind of mathematical rigour which cannot be there.

And yet, in many instances, the fit between the theory and the data is spectacular. The best known hero of Greek mythology, Oedipus, is a walking anthology of victim stigmas. His first is his apparent foreignness: he was born in Thebes, we are told, but he never lived there and, from a Theban viewpoint, he is foreign. This foreignness is his first stigma. His second is the royal throne upon which he sits. The third is his limp. To these three, he deliberately adds a most horrible fourth by blinding himself. Some of this must come from traditional sources, but how much comes from Sophocles himself? Quite a bit probably. This poet knows much more about the religious dimension than we can realize because we lack the knowledge ourselves.

THE MIMETIC THEORY OF RELIGION

Originally, the mimetic conflict is a rivalry for objects, rooted in ordinary mimetic desire, an *acquisitive rivalry* that divides and fragments the community more and more until it becomes so intense that it casts all objects aside and focuses on the antagonists themselves. Paradoxically, this *mimesis of violence* can do what nothing else has done before: reconcile the community. The same human beings who could not stop fighting when they all desired the same objects, as soon as they only hate, can join forces once again and form coalitions against the same enemy. This process accelerates until the community is once again united against one last victim, who becomes the victim of the unanimous lynching.

The same people who could not share the same desire, can, sad to say, share the same antagonist. The mimetic rivalry, which is divisive, makes the crisis worse and worse until it turns into a mimesis of violence which is cumulative and therefore can put Humpty Dumpty back together again. All this can happen, however, *only at the expense of one last victim*. From the viewpoint of the society, one single victim is a small price to pay in comparison with the price of the crisis.

Instead of festering forever inside the community, all resentment and anger converge against the last victim and the entire community feels 'cleansed' and purified of the bad passions which troubled the relations among its members. This metaphor of cleansing is universal; in Greek, the word is *catharsis*, which Aristotle, of course, used to designate what happens when the hero is finally cast into outer darkness at the end of a tragedy.

The community made dysfunctional by the mimetic crisis, becomes functional once again thanks to the lynching of the single victim. Since this phenomenon happens spontaneously and unconsciously, it has all the characteristics of a mechanism and there is no reason not to define it as such. I call it the *single victim* or *victimage mechanism*.

When, after a long mimetic crisis, a victimage mechanism unexpectedly operates, peace descends upon the ravaged community. The survivors are immensely relieved; their ordeal has convinced them that, by themselves, they cannot make peace. All they can achieve is more and more reprisals, more vengeance, more mimetic violence. This is perfectly true. Since these people are too honest to take credit for the miracle that saved them, they look for a saviour somewhere and they must identify him, or her – with the single victim, obviously.

The unanimous lynchers ultimately believe that the dreadful malefactor they all lynched did not really die, and did not even become angrier than before the community lynched him; on the contrary, he forgave everybody and turned into a wonderful benefactor.

This would be impossible, of course, if the victims were the mere human beings they seem to be at first. They must be transcendental beings, gods and goddesses. This is what all human communities ultimately come to believe, that the victims they unanimously lynch are superhuman, divine. This is *the birth of religion*.

Only with the advent of Christianity does it finally dawn on human beings that the divinities they always worshipped must be their own victims who suffered unjust violence. Christianity reveals an unpleasant truth that is not yet fully acknowledged.

In archaic religions, the divinization of the single victim was the beginning of a culturally creative reflection of the lynchers themselves. They wondered what their newly revealed divinity really intended to teach them. They came to the conclusion that he/she first caused the mimetic crisis to punish the community for its violence and indifference. And then, after submitting to the lynching, instead of punishing the lynchers most severely, that same divinity put an end to the mimetic crisis and saved the community.

What the saviour gods seem to demand of the renascent communities is that they should renounce all conduct that facilitated the mimetic crisis in the first place, all competitive and provocative attitudes – all mimetic rivalry in other words. These rules are the so-called *prohibitions*. All human cultures have them and they all think that some divinity has established them.

Human communities believed that the foundational divinity would punish all serious transgressions of the prohibitions, and they were right, since such transgressions are contagious and one cannot indulge in them without plunging once again into a mimetic crisis of human vengeance which is one and the same as the vengeance of the gods.

Some prohibitions are objectively misguided: the one against twins, for instance, which is rooted, as we earlier saw,[4] in an unfortunate confusion between the undifferentiating power of mimetic violence and the biological resemblance of twins. Contrary to the requirements of current demagoguery, absurd prohibitions are the exception and sensible ones are the rule.

Most of the time, prohibitions succeed in preventing new mimetic crises but not always. Human beings are so competitive that, even when they do their utmost to obey all prohibitions, sooner or later mimetic rivalries reappear, in a seemingly innocuous form at first, but the wiser people are worried. Remembering the past, they sense that a new mimetic crisis is afoot. The prospect is so frightening that they look everywhere for help. They find it in their own experience of the mimetic crisis and its resolution.

They meditate on the final lynching, the victimage mechanism. And they all conclude that the only possible reason for the malevolent demon to turn into a benevolent saviour *after the lynching* must be that he/she wanted to teach the people (1) how to render the proper cult to their saviour, and (2) how to protect them from mimetic crises in the future.

They wonder if they could not nip the forthcoming crisis in the bud by re-enacting the old one in an accelerated fashion, in order to reach as fast as possible the saving device, the unanimous lynching. *This is what sacrificial rites are.* Very often they begin with a mock mimetic crisis which is re-enacted too, because it was there the first time, and it does, indeed, facilitate the triggering of the victimage mechanism. And then comes the *sacrificial immolation* of a new victim, which is, of course, the heart of sacrifice.

The belief that divinities stage unanimous lynchings themselves in order to encourage human communities to repeat them and experiment in them is the reason why all archaic communities had their own sacrificial systems.

Many sacrifices resemble the foundational drama in the corresponding myths too much not to be the careful imitation of this drama. The typical Dionysiac sacrifice, for instance, or *diasparagmos*, consists in tearing some animal victim apart, trampling it to death and devouring it raw. This is precisely how the central drama is portrayed in Dionysiac mythology. The ritual repetition looks exactly like the original lynching. The only difference is that the victims are small animals instead of human beings. Without this difference, the sacrificers would be unable to perform the prescribed lynching.

Not all sacrifices, of course, are as similar to the original lynching as the *diasparagmos*. Here again, historical aspects must be taken into account. The moment comes in the life of many religious cults when the worshippers become scandalized by the requirements of their sacrificial system, and they replace the lynching with an individual immolation or even with no immolation at all. They suppress all visible violence and replace it with some vegetable offerings, or with libations, etc.

The modern observers who try to convince themselves that the non-violent forms of sacrifice are just as ancient and essential as the blood sacrifices that came before are mistaken, I believe. In exactly the same manner and for the same reasons as the people who did away with the lynching in the first place, and even with all forms of violence, they are participating in the universal cultural deception that consists in denying the true nature of sacrificial religions.

A careful examination of even the mildest rituals, from which violence seems completely absent, often reveals that, in reality, the violence is always present. This is the case with the Indian rituals studied by J. C. Heestermann in *The Inner Conflict of Tradition*.[5] The author's masterly genealogy of seemingly non-violent sacrifices brings to light revealing traces of a most violent origin. He does not interpret this origin exactly as I do but, as far as I am concerned, our two perspectives are easy to reconcile.

All human cultures try to *re-member* some past victimage mechanism as accurately as possible in order to *dis-member* new victims once again. They try to reactivate the mysterious power for peace that seems to originate in unanimous violence, the power that, at some indeterminate time in the past, saved the community from a previous mimetic crisis. It is the ever-present fear of a new crisis that keeps human communities sacrificing again and again.

When questioned about their sacrifices, archaic people always gave the same dual answer. Far from being a human invention, they claimed, sacrifices are gifts from the gods who established them as a cult of thanksgiving for themselves and as a protection from all dangers to the community, especially violent discord among its members.

Anthropologists have always dismissed these statements as insignificant. I believe they are true. Prohibitions and sacrifices are first and foremost a technique of peace-keeping. The two together provide the answer to the question posed at the beginning of this essay. How does religion make human societies more cohesive? Prohibitions and sacrifices protect human beings from the dreadful counterpart of their superior mimetic intelligence, their propensity to mimetic violence.

Religion is even more creative than it is 'adaptive'. Extremely simple modalities of the victimage mechanism must have appeared long before the birth of *homo sapiens* and they must have played an essential role in the development of our species. They must have protected from the violence of the males, for instance, small infants who remained helpless for a longer and longer time as they were becoming more human. Early forms of ritual sacrifice must have created, around the family, zones of non-violence without which the hominization process would have been impossible. Not only did religion bind communities together after they became fully human, but long before this happened, it must have played an even more decisive role. It made the sacrificial societies possible, the specifically human type of society, and humanity itself must be the child of sacrificial religions.

Many dramas in the Hebrew bible closely resemble the drama in foundational myths; so, of course, does Jesus' Passion in the gospels. Biblical accounts are more detailed and realistic than myths, but there is the same mimetic crisis, concluded by the same unanimous violence.

The first great scapegoat drama in the bible is the Joseph story. The hero is cast out by a whole host of envious siblings. His only offence is his great intelligence. His elder brothers resent Joseph's superiority so much that they sell him into slavery.

The book of Job is a scapegoat story as well: all the people in his community have long revered Job and blindly followed him. All of a sudden, they turn against their leader and methodically indict him in order to kill him legally.

A different and yet similar lynching threat is palpable in many Psalms: the narrator anxiously watches a violent mob encircle him; he loudly calls on Yahweh to destroy his enemies before they destroy him.

The most spectacular instance of scapegoating in the Hebrew bible is the lynching death of a meek and gentle prophet, the Suffering Servant (Isaiah 52–53). This pious man is devoted to everybody and hates nobody. Because he shies away from crowds, however, he is unpopular with them; he is one of those people who, as soon as something goes wrong, stands a good chance of being singled out as a scapegoat. No specific victim stigma is mentioned but the question of how such victims are selected is visibly present in the following lines:

> he had no form nor comeliness that we should look at him,
> and no beauty that we should desire him.
> He was despised and rejected by men; a man of sorrows,
> and acquainted with grief; and as one from whom men hide
> their faces he was despised, and we esteemed him not.
> (Isaiah 53: 2–3)

Just like the lynchings in myths, the Servant's lynching occurs in conjunction with the undifferentiation brought about by a great mimetic crisis. The mimetic undifferentiation is magnificently suggested at the beginning of the Second Isaiah: 'Every valley shall be exalted and every mountain and hill shall be made low; and the crooked shall be made straight and the rough places plain' (Is. 40: 4).

The gospels invite us to regard the violent death of the Servant and all similar sequences in the Hebrew bible as 'prophetic' of the crucifixion, which is, indeed, one more instance of the same collective violence, portrayed in even greater detail than all previous instances.

Jesus is as meek as the Servant and, at first, the crowds flock to him, just as they had flocked to the Servant, or to Job. In the end, however, they become hostile, just as in the other cases really, and Jesus undergoes the same fate as the Servant. His very kindness turns into an irritant that helps trigger the violence against him.

The crucifixion is not lynching *strictu sensu* but is certainly an example of unanimous violence. The power to kill belongs to Pilate alone but, in the Synoptic gospels especially, the pressure of the crowd plays a decisive role. Pilate fears a riot and his decision to crucify Jesus is his own way of joining the crowd and thus making it unanimous. Similarly, Peter's triple denial is the apostle's way of joining the same crowd. Earlier, similar crowds had made several attempts to stone Jesus. Stoning was the most frequent form of lynching in the ancient Near East, and the first Christian martyr, Stephen, will be stoned.

Like all foundational lynchings, the crucifixion occurs at the height of a great crisis. This one will culminate some years later in the fall of Jerusalem and the destruction of the semi-independent Jewish state. The historical reality of this particular crisis is unquestionable. Even historical exegetes are compelled to take it seriously. In the long run, Jesus' crucifixion does not resolve this crisis but inflames it further.

In his polemic against Christianity, the pagan Celsus resorts to the following argument: the pattern of many pagan cults and the pattern of the Christian story are too much the same not to discredit Christianity's claims of being unique.

This is the conclusion to which my own analysis might seem to lead: the pattern of many archaic cults and the pattern of Jesus' crucifixion are strikingly similar. In a world much better acquainted with archaic religions than Celsus was, these similarities seem more relevant than ever, and this relevance certainly plays a role in the ever-widening religious scepticism of our time.

Our world has no appetite for Christian literature, of course, but even though it often calls itself 'post-Christian' it still hungers for *anti-Christian* literature. Celsus is *more widely read* today (at least in France) than Origen's *Contra Celsum*, the source of our knowledge about Celsus. The Christian apologist quotes Celsus so abundantly that, a few years ago, an enterprising editor published a book under the name of Celsus, simply by assembling all these quotes together into a little book that completely disregards Origen, even though the entire material in it comes from the *Christian* apologist. Thanks to this publication, contemporary readers can *enjoy* their Celsus undiluted by Christian counter-arguments. Origen is completely ignored and forgotten.

At this very moment, more people are inclined to agree with Celsus, obviously, than at any previous time in Christian history. Even many Christians today are beginning to assimilate the lessons of 'comparative religion', and they suspect that Christianity must be a *death and resurrection myth* quite similar to all others in the archaic world.

Was Celsus, then, right after all? Is it not true that the similarities between the mythical and the biblical are too perfect not to ridicule all possible belief in the uniqueness of Christianity? My answer to this question is a resounding 'No!' Christianity seems equivalent to the mythical cults of death and resurrection only because our modern practitioners of comparative religion fail to notice a glaring and yet always ignored difference between the mythical religions and Christianity.

In all the dramas we have discussed, biblical as well as mythical, the victims are *scapegoats* in the modern and enlightened sense that recognizes the innocence of the victims against which mobs congregate for purely mimetic reasons. This definition seems to make the mythical and the biblical one and the same text; but in reality it does not. What mythical and biblical texts have in common is the scapegoat phenomenon which comes entirely from human beings, of course. This common feature, scapegoating, opens up the possibility of difference in the interpretation of it.

The first and most frequent interpretation of scapegoating is the mythical one which is provided by the archaic communities reunified and reconciled by this phenomenon. These communities sincerely believe that their scapegoat is guilty and they themselves act righteously when they try to lynch him, or her. Their violence seems just to the scapegoaters. They see it as legitimate self-defence against a real threat to their community.

This interpretation of scapegoating is no interpretation at all, really; it is a failure to identify the mimetic illusion that scapegoating really is. That is why the very idea of scapegoating, the idea that a unanimous community might be in the wrong, that it might gang up for no valid reason against a helpless victim, simply never occurs in an archaic society. Scapegoating remains unrecognized as scapegoating. That is the reason why for such a long time it provided an effective outlet for the potentially destructive rage of human communities.

Thus, for the myth-makers and their descendants, there is no such thing as scapegoating in our sense of the word. The collective violence in which the cult originates is always regarded as soundly motivated by the misdeeds of the victim. And when the persecutors, later on, ascribe the return of peace and order to this victim, they will divinize him/her but they will never forget that the new divinity can be a source of extreme violence as well as of peace.

In mythology, therefore, the phenomenon we call scapegoating is completely occulted, and this occultation is indispensable to the effectiveness of sacrificial cults. Unanimous scapegoating can generate archaic religions only insofar as their real nature is not apprehended.

Scapegoating is a collective self-deception so effective in archaic communities that the distorted view of the victim is interpreted, first as divine mischief, then as a divine protection for the community which includes, of course, sacrificial *rites*.

In the bible and gospels everything seems the same as in mythology, but in reality nothing is: instead of being regarded as guilty, the scapegoats are recognized as innocent. Instead of being regarded as innocent, the persecutors are regarded as guilty. The uniqueness of the bible and gospels is not a myth therefore, but a fact the importance of which cannot be exaggerated. The biblical tradition is genuinely unique, even from a purely anthropological viewpoint, because it demystifies the kind of scapegoating that the archaic world mistakes for the truth.

If the Hebrew bible were mythical, it would portray Joseph as guilty and his brothers as innocent. Similarly, it would portray the Suffering Servant as guilty and his lynchers as innocent. If the gospels were a myth, they would portray Jesus as guilty and the crucifiers as innocent. All myths are written from the point of view of the persecutors. Most biblical dramas, and the gospels in their entirety, are, however, written from the point of view of a small dissenting minority – Jesus' disciples after the resurrection – that never arises anywhere else. The presence of these dissenters destroys the unanimity indispensable to the religious effectiveness of scapegoating.

All archaic religions are founded upon blindfolded scapegoating, and they uncritically agree with the violent mobs. They are totally dependent upon their foundational illusion from which they derive all their themes.

It is the bible and Christianity most decisively that finally discredit mythical scapegoating and make it intelligible by proclaiming the innocence of its victims. For the *first time in human history*, scapegoating is universally acknowledged as the collective self-delusion that it could not be in archaic cultures.

In addition to being supremely original, therefore, the bible and the gospels are supremely *truthful*: they demystify or de-mythify or, if you prefer, they deconstruct the self-delusion of scapegoating. The increased realism of biblical and gospel descriptions is an aspect of this new truthfulness.

The biblical de-mythification has been effective in the last two thousand years since, as it spread to the entire world, archaic religions have disappeared from the face of the earth. It has been a slow process, however, and in recent times, neo-pagan and neo-mythical thinkers such as Nietzsche and Heidegger *have* had a certain success in their attempt to re-mythologize the world. Their hostility to representation, to realism, to scientific knowledge and many other precious by-products of the biblical religions is an essential part of their message.

The gospels proclaim the innocence of Jesus in a thousand different ways. One of the most revealing, from the perspective of the present essay, is *'the lamb of God'*, an expression which suggests that Jesus is a completely innocent victim who was sacrificed, not because he deserved such a fate, but because of an unjust violence that does not come from God but from man.

Another powerful phrase that comes originally from the Hebrew bible is *'the stone that the builders rejected has become the keystone* (or *cornerstone)'*. This formula can be read in two manners. First, it defines mythical and sacrificial systems that are rooted in scapegoating but never become aware of it. In archaic religions, the divinity is really an unrecognized scapegoat, a formerly rejected stone that has become the keystone.

When Jesus applies this formula to himself, it still means the same thing, of course, but a radically new dimension is added. Jesus consents to become the scapegoat knowingly in order to reveal the entire religious system of the past as the delusion that it is, and thus make it inoperative. He himself, therefore, becomes the keystone, not of one more archaic religion, but of a new world in which scapegoating will be no more. Jesus sacrifices himself for the purpose of saving from their violence human beings who, even after two thousand years, still manage to elude this revelation. In spite of its lack of understanding, our world is clearly moving, albeit with local backslidings, relentlessly forward towards the whole truth.

7

SECOND COMINGS

Neo-Protestant ethics and millennial capitalism in Africa, and elsewhere

Jean and John Comaroff

Prolegomenon

Herewith three glimpses of the future in a present-just-past. Each conjures with Christianity at a critical moment in the Common Era;[1] all are culled from the bulging notebook of the global anthropologist, from the virtual archive that we are increasingly compelled to keep as our subject-matter becomes ever more mobile, ever more liable to migrate across space and time.

The *first* comes in the form of an announcement. The messiah has arrived. He is to be found, by his own account, in East Siberia, wherein lies 'the Promised Land of the Future'. More prosaically, he lives in a compound near Minusinsk. Sergei Torop by name, he prefers to be called Vissarion.

He has his own webpage,[2] of course, on which he explains that 'Vissarion – also the name of Stalin's father – means "giving the life" in "the language of the Universe".' In the event that that language is not understood by ordinary mortals, seven more conventional vernaculars convey his cyber-message, which promises that his Word will soon spread across the World. The 38-year-old, ethereal-looking saviour established the Last Testament Church in 1991, after the repressed memory of two millennia flooded back to him, after he came to realize that he was not the child of Siberian construction workers but the Son of God, after he learned that 'all religions are inserted in him'; the origin myth of the movement, significantly, dates these revelations roughly to the fall of the USSR. Vissarion has acquired a substantial following, the Vissariontsi, composed largely of 'disenchanted [former] Soviet intellectuals and idealists'. While their exact number is uncertain, they have attracted the attention of the Orthodox Church, which is monitoring them carefully; also of the state, which has ignored them thus far, largely because the arrival of the church has breathed life into a dying local economy. The movement, which is rooted in agribusiness, has a strong green orientation, seeing itself as 'A Siberian Global Experiment Targeting Human Survival under Circumstances of Social and Natural Cataclysm'. Vissarion himself was a traffic warden until he turned messiah, persuaded his disciples to hand over their earthly wealth to him, and took up residence in the City of Sun, which is what he calls his rural dominion. This dominion is reminiscent of a Soviet collective – although it has formed a joint stock company, Tabrat Ltd, to bankroll its material existence. In short, the Second Coming here envisages a future in the past, a hereafter (or there-before?) that revivifies the glories of a socialist commune by lodging it securely in the global capitalist economy. Vissarion has not escaped scepticism: he has been portrayed as an enchanted entrepreneur who earns a lucrative income from service delivery in the God business, a business flourishing anew in these turbulent times,[3] a business, suggests Tom Whitehouse, that often yields high profits to its High Priests: Torop, he goes on to note, lives in *very* lavish circumstances. No wonder that Orthodox clergy see him as an 'evil pyramid schemer', an image which we shall have cause to revisit. Whether or not he is a charlatan, a con man with a Christ-like appearance and a creative line in income redistribution, is beside our present point. The various features of his religious movement – its corporate scaffolding, its entry into the world of the joint stock venture, its presence on the web, its global outreach, its appeal to technical solutions for planetary problems, its promise of instant redemption at a price in hard currency, its well-requited head of operations – are all of a piece. They tell a story at once very old and very new.

So, too, does a rather different religious movement, one which gives us a *second* glimpse into the future-perfect. We first encountered the New Life Church in Mafeking, South Africa, in the late 1990s. While it originated before the fall of apartheid, it typifies a brand of upbeat, technically-hyped Pentecostalism that is aspiring to fill the moral void left by a withering of revolutionary ideals and civic norms in the postcolony. While New Life is the creation of a talented pair of pastors, a husband and wife who have shaped it independently of denominational oversight, their community belongs to the International Federation of Christian Churches; this is a global network of congregations, all of which combine a lively charismatic realism with a frank materiality, the latter embodied in a religious subject quite comfortable with this-worldly desire. Congregants pay a tithe, and are encouraged to expect that their investment, both spiritual and monetary, will yield tangible empowerment. They are offered a range of services, from marriage guidance to financial counselling, that recast the pastoral in a distinctly service-oriented, therapeutic key. As in many such movements, the stress on divine manifestation is accompanied by a preoccupation with cutting-edge media: 'It might sound heretical', notes the founding pastor, 'but we strive above all to make our services exciting, affecting. Our competition, after all, is the video arcade, the movie house, and the casino.' (Remember the casino. We shall return to it as well.) In New Life's sparkling suburban sanctuary a sophisticated sound stage replaces the altar. Services are punctuated by lilting hymns and love songs to Jesus, crooned by a modishly dressed, youthful band – or 'worship team' – equipped with electronic instruments. Overhead, a large karaoke screen flashes the lyrics; in a booth to the rear, a technician monitors the acoustics. Meetings draw large crowds that span a wide spectrum of race, age and class. They centre on the repetition of stylized personal testimonies that narrate, in psychologically inflected terms, a self reborn into an individualized world of transparency, purpose and prosperity.

The *third* glimpse is somewhat more mundane. In Columbus, Indiana, a small town some four hours drive from Chicago on Highway 64, there is an extraordinary array of churches. Columbus is known for its public architecture; this because the local captains of industry came to a decision, at some point in the past, to make their town into a shrine to the built form. And so many internationally famous 'names' erected buildings across the flatlands of this otherwise unprepossessing corner of the midwest. One of them is a profoundly beautiful, profoundly spiritual edifice. Designed by Eero Saarinen, the North Christian Church houses a congregation of Disciples of Christ, whose journal, *Cutting Edge*, is indeed incisive. Volume 29 no. 2 of year 2000 is dedicated to the topic of 'Buildings for the Post-Christendom Church'. 'Christendom', it declares, 'is dying'.[4] What began in the fourth century of the common era is over, a new reformation is under way.

But what, precisely, are its signs? Among other things, 'the adoption of market-driven planning to replace tradition', thus appealing to a generation that wants 'choices, convenience, quality, and specialized services' in religion as in everything else.[5] By extension, church facilities, like prayer itself, require 'above all [to be] useful, adaptable, and marketable'. And so, in one of the most conservative crannies of Christian America, the church enters the new millennium by making common cause not with a capitalist ethos grounded in virtuous work, not in the production of the self through the production of value, but with a world of convenience and consumption, of free choice and flexibility; a world in which the provision of services, religious services like other customer services, is paramount.

Each of these vignettes evokes the ghost of Max Weber. Each speaks of a new moment in the history of capitalism, of its Second Coming, this time in neoliberal guise, this time on an even more global scale than before. They also speak of a new religious spirit to go with that moment, a spirit which, as we shall see, is rampant in Africa. But not only in Africa. Note that our three instances come from what used to be called, respectively, the second, third and first worlds.

All of which raises a number of conundrums for our understanding of economy and society, culture and history, faith and identity at the start of the new century. Some of the corollaries of the Second Coming of which we speak – 'plagues of the new world order', Derrida calls them[6] – have occasioned heated debate. Thus, for example, populist polemics have dwelt on the planetary conjuncture, for good or ill, of 'homogenization and difference';[7] on the simultaneous, synergistic spiralling of wealth and poverty; on the rise of a 'new medievalism'.[8] For its part, scholarly debate has focused on the confounding effects of rampant liberalization: on whether it engenders truly transnational flows of capital or drains it off to a few major sites;[9] on whether it weakens, sustains or reinvents the nation-state;[10] on whether it frees up, curbs or compartmentalizes the movement of labour; on whether the current fixation with democracy, its resurrection in so many places, betokens a measure of mass empowerment or an 'emptying out of [its] meaning'.[11] Equally in question is why the present infatuation with civil society has been accompanied by alarming increases in civil strife; also by reports of the palpable rise in many countries of domestic violence, rape, child abuse, prison populations and, most dramatically of all, criminal 'phantom-states'.[12] Why, in like vein, the politics of consumerism, human rights and entitlement coincides with puzzling new patterns of exclusion, patterns that refract long-established lines of gender, sexuality, race and class.[13]

Other features of our present predicament are less remarked. Among them are the odd coupling of the legalistic with the libertarian, constitutionality with deregulation, and – at the core of our concerns here – of hyper-rationalization with the exuberant spread of innovative occult practices and money magic, pyramid schemes and prosperity gospels; the enchantments, that is, of a decidedly *neo*liberal economy, whose ever more inscrutable speculations seem to call up fresh spectres in their wake. Note that, unlike others who have discussed the 'new spectral reality' of that economy,[14] we do not talk here in metaphorical terms. We seek, instead, to draw attention to the distinctly pragmatic qualities of the messianic and the millennial; not merely in the tenor of organized religion, of which we shall have a lot to say, but of capitalism itself as a gospel of salvation. As this suggests, in speaking of millennial capitalism we intend not merely capitalism at the Millennium, but also capitalism in its messianic, salvific, even magical manifestations; capitalism as a cultural and moral economy with the capacity, if harnessed properly, to enrich the poor (and further enrich the wealthy), to solve social problems, to heal the sick, to elicit divine favour, to add material value to the commonweal.

The question, patently, is why? Why has capitalism taken on these features? What is new about them? And how, exactly, have they reconfigured the religious world in their wake? We have sought to address the first two questions elsewhere. Here it is on the third that we focus.

Let us, then, cut to the heart of the matter. If we are to understand the spirits of our age, the place to begin, as Marx noted for another historical juncture, is with epochal shifts in the constitutive relationship of production to consumption. This is *not* to say that the essence of neoliberal capitalism is reducible purely to that relationship. Quite the opposite: there is now a large literature on the various dimensions of the new global economy – from the workings of the electronic commons and transnational corporations; through the changing, labile character of work and labour, its mobility and its transience, its gendered and generational inflections; to the impact of space–time compression, of flexible accumulation, and of the planetary flow of signs, styles and commodities upon old sovereignties, old loyalties, old identities. All of these things are crucially important in understanding the shape of the world we live in.[15] For now, however, we have perforce to take them for granted. In any case, we would suggest, it is specifically by interrogating the shifting articulation of production to consumption, of the *pro* to the *con* in capitalist economics, that we might make sense of the emergence of new forms of enchantment – and of the kinds of neo-Protestantism to which they appear to be giving rise in postcolonial Africa. And elsewhere.

I Capitalism at the Millennium, millennial capitalism

Consumption, recall, was the hallmark disease of the eighteenth and nineteenth centuries. Of the First Coming of Industrial Capitalism. Of a time when the ecological conditions of production, its consuming passions, ate up the bodies of producers. Now, at the beginning of the twenty-first, semiotically transposed, it is often said to be the 'hallmark of modernity', the measure of its wealth, health and vitality. An overgeneralization? Maybe. Yet the claim *does* capture popular imaginings. It also resonates with the growing Eurocultural truism that the (post)modern person is a subject made with objects. Nor is this surprising. Consumption, in its ideological guise – as 'consumer*ism*' – refers to a material sensibility actively cultivated, for the common good, by Western states and commercial interests, particularly since the Second World War. Also by some noncapitalist regimes: in the early 1990s, even Deng Xiaoping advocated 'consumption as a motor force of production'.[16]

In social theory, as well, consumption has become a prime mover.[17] Increasingly, it is *the* factor, *the* principle, held to determine definitions of value and the construction of identities. As such, tellingly, it is the invisible hand that animates the political and material imperatives, and the social forms, of the Second Coming of Capitalism. Note the image. The invisible hand. Gone is the *deus ex machina*, a figure altogether too concrete for the so-called 'post-industrial' era.

As consumption became the *Zeitgeist* of the late twentieth century, so there was a concomitant eclipse of production; an eclipse, at least, of its *perceived* salience for the wealth of nations. This has heralded a shift, across the world, in ordinary understandings of the nature of capitalism. The workplace and labour, especially work-and-place securely rooted in a stable local context, are no longer prime sites for the creation of value or identity.[18] The factory and the shop, far from being secure centres of fabrication and family income, are increasingly experienced by virtue of their replacement at the hands of non-human or 'non-standard' means of manufacture. Or by their removal to an elsewhere – where labour is cheaper, less assertive, less taxed, more feminized, less protected by states and unions. Hence the paradox, in many economies, of high official employment rates amidst stark de-industrialization and joblessness; note that the Dow Jones index tends to rise when employment rates drop. In the upshot, primary production appears to have been superseded, as the *ur*-source of wealth, by less tangible ways of generating value: by control over intellectual property, copyrights, franchises and licences; by owning the means of communication and the conveyancing of people and things; by the provision of services; and, above all, by the capacity to direct the flow of finance capital.

Symptomatic, in this respect, are the changing historical fortunes of gambling. Risk has always been crucial to the growth of 'modern' economies. But, removed from the dignifying nexus of the market, games of chance (give or take the occasional parish raffle or Bingo night) were deemed morally dubious, both by Protestant ethics and by populist morality. Casinos were set apart from the workaday world. They were situated at resorts, in reservations and on river boats; liminal places of leisure rather than sites of honest toil. Living off the proceeds of this form of speculation was, normatively speaking, the epitome of immoral accumulation: the wager stood to the wage as sin to virtue. There have, self-evidently, always been different cultures of betting. *Sui generis*, however, this species of activity falls outside the domain of work-and-earning; often in the murky, nether space between the normative and the transgressive. Over a generation, gambling, in its marked form, has changed moral valence and invaded everyday existence almost everywhere, being routinized in a widespread infatuation with high risk dealings in stocks, bonds and funds whose fortunes are governed largely by chance. It also expresses itself in a fascination with 'futures' and their downmarket counterpart, the lottery. Here the mundane meets the millennial: 'Not a lotto tomaro' ['Not a lot of tomorrow'], proclaims an ironic, inner-city mural in Chicago, large hands grasping a pile of casino chips, beside which nestles a motherless newborn babe.[19] The future *futures*, as bitter parody. This comes at a moment when 'gambling [is] the fastest growing industry in the US', when it is 'tightly woven into the national fabric', when it is increasingly 'operated and promoted' by government.[20] Indeed, life itself has become the object of bookmaking; it is no longer the sole preserve of the 'respectable' insurance industry. Herewith a recent report in *Newsweek*:[21]

> In America's . . . casino culture, no wager is *outré*. So how about betting on how long a stranger is likely to live? You can buy part or all of his or her insurance policy, becoming a beneficiary. Your gamble: that death will come soon enough to

yield a high return on the money you put up. The Viatical Association[22] of America says that $1 billion worth of coverage went into play last year.

In the era of 'casino capitalism', securing instant returns *is* often a matter of life and death. In 1999, for example, the *India Tribune* reported that one of the biggest central Indian States, Madya Pradesh, was 'caught in the vortex of lottery mania', which had led to several suicides.[23] Witnesses described 'extreme enthusiasm among the jobless youth towards trying their luck to make a fast buck', precisely the kind of fatal ecstasy classically associated with chiliastic movements. More mundanely, efforts to enlist divine help in tipping the odds, from rural Taiwan to the Kalahari fringe, have become a regular feature of 'fee for service' or 'roadside' religions.[24] These are locally nuanced fantasies of beating capitalism at its own game by drawing a winning number at the behest of unseen forces. Once again that invisible hand.

The change in the moral valence of gambling also has a public dimension. In a neoliberal climate, where taxes are anathema to the political centre, lotteries have become a favoured means of filling national coffers and generating cultural capital. The defunct machinery of a growing number of welfare states, to be sure, is being turned by the wheel of fortune. With more and more governments depending on this source for quick revenue fixes, says George Will, a well-known conservative commentator in the US, betting has 'been transformed from a social disease' – subjected, not so long ago, to scrutiny at the hands of Harvard Medical School[25] – 'into social policy'.[26] Once a dangerous sign of moral turpitude, 'it is now marketed almost as a "patriotic duty"'.[27]

And yet crisis after crisis in the global economy, and growing income disparities on a planetary scale, make it painfully plain that there is no such thing as capitalism without production. Apart from all else, Fordist manufacture has *not* disappeared. It has been transformed, melded with other kinds of productive arrangement, dispersed and reorganized – with the effect that sites of fabrication have been removed from sites of consumption in such a way as to give the appearance, in many parts of the world, that proletariats, *sensu stricto*, are a thing of the past. This displacement, this rendering absent of visible production, has convinced the likes of Derrida[28] that we have reached the end of 'the world of work' as we know it; the end of the epoch of *homo faber*, of class consciousness, of the modernist idea of self-construction through virtuous labour. All identities seem to be contrived through self-fashioning, all wealth by means of the entrepreneurial. All of which affirms the putative primacy of consumption. And makes the operations of capital appear arcane, quixotic, magical. If Western scholars have been somewhat slow to reflect on why this is so, their 'others' have not; especially those others who live in places where there has been a sudden infusion of commodities, an explosion of new forms of wealth, and a simultaneous shrinking of the labour market. Many, to be sure, have been quick to give voice to their perplexity at the secret of this wealth: of its sources and the capriciousness of its distribution, of the mysterious forms it takes, of its slipperiness, of the opaque relations between means and ends embodied in it. Our concern here grows directly out of these perplexities: out of worldwide speculation, in both senses of the term, provoked by the shifting conditions of material existence at the end of the twentieth century.

The increasing legitimacy of speculation, we have argued elsewhere, is itself a corollary of the *experiential* paradox, the doubling, at the core of neoliberal capitalism, of capitalism in its millennial manifestation: the fact that it appears to produce desire on a global scale yet to decrease the certainty of work and the security of persons; that it appears to magnify class differences but to undercut class consciousness; that it appears to contrive a world in which consumption takes precedence over production in the construction of personhood and identity; above all, that it appears to offer up vast, almost instantaneous riches to those who master its spectral technologies – and, simultaneously, to threaten the very being of those who do not. This doubling is most visible in postcolonies; especially in those, set free by the events of 1989 and their aftermath, that entered the global arena with distinct structural disadvantages. A good deal is to be learned about the historical implications of the current moment by eavesdropping on the popular anxieties to be heard in such places: on the mounting disenchantment with liberty under libertarian conditions; on the nostalgia for past regimes, some of them immeasurably repressive; on moral panics occasioned by rapidly rising suicide rates; on the upsurge of assertions of identity and autochthony; on the widespread fears, in many parts of Africa, Asia and Central Europe alike, concerning the apparently preternatural production of wealth.

The close of the Cold War – and, in its wake, the death of apartheid in South Africa and democratization movements elsewhere on the continent – fired utopian imaginations. But liberation under neoliberal conditions has been marred by a disconcerting upsurge of violence, crime and disorder. The quest for democracy, the rule of law, prosperity and civility threatens to dissolve into strife and recrimination, even political chaos. Conspiracy theories burgeon on all sides. Everywhere there is evidence of an uneasy fusion of enfranchisement and exclusion; of xenophobia at the prospect of world citizenship without the old protectionisms of nationhood; of the effort to realize modern utopias by decidedly postmodern means; of the fetishization of human rights, the rule of law and civil society, a construct whose populist appeal seems everywhere to have risen in rough proportion to its intangibility as a principle of praxis. Gone is any officialspeak of egalitarian futures, work-for-all, or the paternal government envisioned by the freedom movements of yore. Gone, too, is the modernist nation-state as we once knew it; radically transformed, its hyphenation is being ruptured under the impact of global economic and electronic integration, amidst unprecedented flows of people, commodities, currencies, amidst changes in the very nature of citizenship and the construction of identity. These transformations have expressed themselves increasingly in a spirit of deregulation, with its taunting mix of emancipation and limitation. As those citizens not fortunate enough to win the lottery of life try to find salvation in enterprise, they find themselves battling against the eccentric currents of the 'new' world order, which short-circuit received sovereignties, received means and ends, received connections between personhood and place. And as the great containers of modern social order have been strained and fractured, so have the cultural, ethical and spiritual coordinates on which they were founded; coordinates that charted concepts and institutions long taken for granted in classic Western (for which read Judaeo-Protestant) ideology: among them, the dichotomy between the sacred and the secular, the transcendent and the temporal, the material and the moral, the pious and the pecuniary – and, most of all, modernity and enchantment.

Which, by turn, focuses our gaze on occult economies and new religious movements.

II Occult economies and new religious movements

A striking corollary of the dawning Age of Millennial Capitalism has been the global proliferation of 'occult economies'. These economies have two dimensions: a material aspect founded on the sustained effort to conjure wealth – or to account for its accumulation – by appeal to techniques that defy what had commonly been taken to be practical reason; and an ethical aspect, sparked by a seeming increase in the disconcerting manufacture of value by arcane, 'magical' means.

Magic, of course, is very much in the eye of the beholder; it is difficult to quantify the presence of the occult – and, therefore, to make any claim to its increase. As we have already noted, finance capital has always had its spectral enchantments, its modes of speculation based on less than honest toil, less than rational connections between means and ends. Both its underside (the pariah forms of gambling of which we spoke a moment ago) and its upper side (a fiscal industry, embracing everything from insurance to stock markets) have been rooted, from the first, in two inscrutables: a faith in probability, itself a notoriously poor way of predicting the future from the past, and a monetary system which depends for its existence on 'confidence', a chimera knowable, tautologically, only by its effects. Wherein, then, lies the claim that occult economies are presently on the rise?

In the specific context of South Africa, we have argued[29] that there has been a marked increase of occult-related activity – arising out of accusations of ritual killing, witchcraft and zombie conjuring – since the late apartheid years; also of fantastic pyramid schemes, of the sale of body parts for 'magical' purposes, of allegations of satanic practice, of tourism based on the sighting of fabulous monsters, and the like. Here popular magazines run 'dial-a-diviner' advertisements, national papers carry headline articles on medicine murders, television broadcasts dramas of sorcery, and more than one 'witchcraft summit' has been held. Whether or not the brute quantum of occult activity exceeds that of times past, it *is* clear is that their reported incidence, written about by the mainstream press in more prosaic terms than ever before[30] has forced itself upon the public sphere, rupturing the flow of mediated 'news'. It is this rupture – this focus of popular attention on the place of the arcane in everyday production – to which we refer when we speak of a global proliferation of occult economies.

It is not difficult to catalogue the presence of these economies in different parts of the planet. In West Africa, for example, Geschiere has shown how zombie-making is an endemic feature of everyday life, how sorcery and witchcraft have entered into postcolonial political economy as an integral element of a thriving alternative modernity, how magic has become as much an acknowledged aspect of mundane survival strategies as it is indispensable to the ambitions and machinations of the powerful.[31] Nor is all of this based in rural situations or among poor people. In Nigeria's lively national press, Bastian shows, witchcraft is a frequent topic, both in quality broadsheets and in tabloids.[32] Far from falling into the domain of the 'customary' or the 'exotic', it is a vital idiom for understanding the mysteries of contemporary life – urban and rural, political and personal. One might add, parenthetically, that accounts of West African supernaturalism are frequently recycled in the popular American press, where they have an avid readership, both black and white. The video films which Nigerian sociologist Asonzeh Ukah terms 'perhaps the most vibrant media phenomena' on the continent draw heavily on idioms from Pentecostal mass culture, and centre on 'issues of melodrama and excess, of accumulation, betrayal and witchcraft'.[33]

Occult economies thrive in various parts of Asia, too, as Rosalind Morris indicates.[34] In Thailand – where fortune telling has been transformed by global technology and e-mail divination has taken off – one 'traditional' seer, auspiciously named Madam Luk, reports that her clients nowadays ask three questions to the exclusion of all others: 'Is my company going broke?' 'Am I going to lose my job?' and 'Will I find other employment?'[35] Here, as well, the fallout of neoliberal capitalism is having a profound impact on magical practice, a process splendidly captured in Morris's account of the career of one of Thailand's most renowned spirit mediums, who recently staged a dramatic, mass-mediated confession: he declared himself a fake. This, no less, so that he might take up a career as a distributor for Amway, a global pyramid scheme run by two Christian patriarchs in a small rural town in Michigan. Such schemes, says Morris, are the economic counterpart of mediumship: they 'occult' the production of value with a disarmingly personalized, hyper-real directness. The verb is hers, after Žižek;[36] of the point itself, more in a moment.

Sometimes dealings in the occult take on a more visceral, darker form. Throughout Latin America in the 1990s, as in Africa and Asia, there have been mass panics about the clandestine theft and sale of the organs of young people, usually by unscrupulous expatriates;[37] violence against children has become metonymic of threats to social reproduction in many ethnic and national contexts, the dead (or missing) child having emerged as the standardized nightmare of a world out of control.[38] There, and in other parts of the globe, this commerce – like international adoptions, mail-order marriage and indentured domestic labour – is seen as a new form of imperialism, the affluent North siphoning off the essence of poorer 'others' by mysterious means for nefarious, often ritual ends. All of which gives evidence, to those at the nether end of the global distribution of wealth, of the workings of insidious forces, of potent magical technologies and modes of accumulation.

That evidence reaches into the heart of Europe itself: hence the recent scares, in several countries, about the sexual and satanic abuse of children;[39] also about the theft and abuse of human tissue and genetic material by an unholy alliance of Godless scientists and corporate vampires. An extreme instance is the urban myth that traversed the internet in 1997 about the secret excision of kidneys, by apparently incredible means, from business travellers waylaid at international airports. Several major police departments, moral commentators and mass media in the USA took these stories seriously enough to investigate them.[40]

Note a persistent theme in all this. The anxiety that has come to surround transformations in the everyday economic world is occasioned by two things: firstly, by the opening up of new *kinds* of translocal markets, of an inscrutable traffic, in people, labour, services, images and things; and, secondly, by the explosion of new forms of financial speculation and e-investment which are at once seductive and dangerous. If the former is epitomized by the sale of persons and their bodies, part or whole, the latter reaches its apex in the extraordinary intensification, lately, of pyramid schemes, many of them tied to the electronic media. These schemes, and a host of scams allied with them – a few legal, many illegal, some alegal – are hardly new. But their recent mushrooming across the world has drawn a great deal of attention; this partly because of their sheer scale and partly because, by crossing national borders and registering at addresses far from the site of their local operation, they insinuate themselves into the slipstream of global capital, thereby escaping control. Recall those whose crash sparked the Albanian revolution early in 1997, several of which took on almost miraculous dimensions for poor investors; one pyramid manager in Albania was 'a gypsy fortune teller, complete with crystal ball, who claimed to know the future'.[41] Even in the tightly regulated stock markets of the USA, there has been a huge rise in illicit operations that owe their logic, if not their precise operation, to similar scams; this because investors have become ever more 'disposed to throw dollars at get-rich-quick schemes'. $6 billion, in fact, was lost to such schemes on the New York Stock Exchange in 1996.[42] Voodoo economics is alive and well at the financial centre of the Western World.

These scams also bring to mind others, different yet similar, that arise from a promiscuous mix of scarcity and deregulation. Frequently, the space of speculation is a place of enchantment, mystery, even salvation. This was the case with the Foundation for New Era Philanthropy, a US pyramid created 'to change the world for the glory of God'. On the basis of a promise to double their money in six months, its founder, John Bennett, persuaded 500 nonprofit organizations, Christian colleges and Ivy League universities to invest $354 million.⁴³ Miracle 2000, a South African 'empowerment' scheme that promised a 220 per cent return on investments in 42 days, also had a strongly millennial side to it. So popular did it become that it drew crowds from across the land to the East Rand home of its 39-year-old founder, Sibusiso Radebe – crowds that would wait days to make their deposits. When an elite crime-busting unit of the South African Police Services cracked down on the scheme in the winter of 2000, arresting Radebe, hundreds of outraged investors marched on the Directorate of Public Prosecutions in Pretoria, carrying placards that proclaimed him as their 'Messiah'. He was, they said, 'doing more to alleviate poverty than the government'.⁴⁴ In something akin to a 'memorial service', these protestors sung hymns and prayed for the return of both their saviour and their savings.⁴⁵ When Radebe was eventually released on bail, 'ululating investors carried [him] shoulder-high and described him as a biblical Moses, who had delivered the downtrodden Israelites to God's promised land'.⁴⁶ During his subsequent trial in the Pretoria High court, faithful followers kept vigil outside, bearing placards that declared, with deliberate *double entendre*, 'Do My Prophet No Harm'.⁴⁷

All of these things have a single common denominator: the allure of conjuring wealth from nothing. In this respect, while they recall older magicalities, they are the offspring of the same animating spirit as casino capitalism; indeed, perhaps they *are* casino capitalism for those who lack the fiscal or cultural capital – or who, for one or another reason, are reluctant – to gamble on more conventional markets. Like the wizardry that made straw into gold in an earlier moment of economic transition,⁴⁸ these alchemic techniques defy reason in promising to return unnaturally large profits on small investments, to yield wealth without work, to produce value without effort. Here, again, is the spectre, the distinctive spirit, of neoliberalism in its triumphal hour. In its shadowy penumbra, the line between pyramid schemes and prosperity gospels is very thin indeed.

Which brings us, then, to the spread of new religious movements across the planet.

These, we suggest, may be seen as the apotheosis of the occult economies of which we have been speaking; their holy-owned subsidiaries, if we may be forgiven the pun. Such movements take on a wide variety of guises. Some, like the Vissariontsi with which we began, sound perennial themes of apocalypse and utopian communitarianism, albeit tuned to a distinctively local key. But the followers of Vissarion also share a good deal with other neo-Protestant denominations elsewhere, among them the New Life Church in South Africa:

the tendency to view congregations as joint stock companies, offering the faithful a tangible return on their investments; a fascination with commodities of all kinds, especially with new technologies and media that seem to condense the numinous magic of global enterprise; an eclipse of the ideal of patient toil and paradise postponed by the promise of prompt reward; the fusing of a millennial spirit with the speculative force of finance capital, so that the instant accumulation of wealth becomes synonymous with the unmediated power of God; a tendency, because of all this, to be viewed by more orthodox believers as being mercenary, Satanic, magic-ridden.

These features are even more palpable in the so-called 'fee-for-service' faiths, those consumer cults alluded to above, which are challenging more established Christian denominations in Africa and elsewhere. Typical of them is the Brazilian movement, the Universal Church of the Kingdom of God (*Igreja Universal do Reino de Deus*), which, since 1994, has grown rapidly all over southern Africa. Controversial in its country of origin, this church is reforming the Protestant ethic with enterprise and urbanity. It has an elaborate website and owns a major television network in Brazil that sponsors its high-profile religious rock groups and soap operas, as well as its own candidates in secular elections.[49] Above all, it promises swift payback to those who embrace Christ, denounce Satan, and 'make their faith practical' by 'sacrificing' all they can to the movement.[50] Here Pentecostalism meets neoliberal enterprise head on; here the theological waxes psychotherapeutic. In its African churches, most of them – literally – storefronts in town centres, prayer meetings respond to candidly material motives, offering everything from cures for depression, through financial advice, to remedies for unemployment; the movement has regular members, but much of its business is with itinerant passers-by – clients and customers really – who select the services they require. Even the smallest churches have elaborate electronic sound systems; pounding music, indistinguishable from any other rock music to all but the best trained ear, beats out a distinctly this-worldly tempo. A collage of advertisements for BMWs and lottery winnings adorns the altar in one such church, beneath the heading: 'Delight Yourself in the Lord and He Will Give You the Desires of Your Heart (Psalms 37: 4)'. Tabloids stuck to walls and windows carry stories, told in the first person, about those whose rebirth in the fold was rewarded by a rush of wealth or an astonishing recovery of health.

The ability to deliver in the here-and-now, itself a potent form of space–time compression, is offered as the measure of a genuinely global God, just as it is taken to explain the lively power of satanism; both have the instant efficacy of the magical and the milleniary. As Kramer says of Brazilian Neo-Pentecostals, 'inner-worldly asceticism has been replaced with a concern for the pragmatics of material gain and the immediacy of desire . . . [T]he return on capital has suddenly become more spiritually compelling and imminent . . . than the return of Christ.'[51] This shift is endemic to many new religious movements at the end of the twentieth century. For them, and for their many millions of members, the Second Coming evokes not a Jesus who saves, but one who pays dividends. Or, more accurately, one who promises a miraculous return on spiritual venture capital.

It might be argued that, as neoliberal forces have eroded the capacity of liberal democratic states to provide education, health and welfare, religious movements – above all, those flexible 'prosperity' movements that mimic the workings of business – have expanded their institutional reach into formerly 'secular', public domains. In South Africa, for instance, where a rising sense of entitlement runs up against the reality of privatization and dwindling public resources, churches have invested ever more heavily in building schools, clinics and sports centres. They have expanded their ministry in time and content, offering a host of special services, from exorcism and electronic entertainment to personal financial counselling, services which are on offer to members and non-members alike. In the process, religious transactions have been commercialized as never before: in Nigerian Pentecostalism, as Ukah notes, the dynamic intersection of mass media, religion and consumerism has generated a new economy in religious material culture; here, as in comparable West African Muslim circles, videos, cassettes and posters extend the influence of charismatic leaders over ever larger distances, marking out new diasporas of sacral consumption. As their enterprises take them ever further into 'civil society', these denominations also involve themselves actively in politics, both local and national. As a consequence, notions of the sacred and profane, of membership and congregation, of the calendar and of the institutional scope of organized religion, are all being radically reshaped. So, too, are the means of mediating and manifesting divine power.

Why? How – to put the matter more generally – are we to account for the current spread and impact of occult economies and prosperity cults? In framing the problem as we have, we have already pointed in the direction of some answers.

III Towards a privatized millennium

To the degree that millennial capitalism fuses the modern and the postmodern, hope and hopelessness, utility and futility, the world created in its image presents itself as a mass of contradictions: as a world, simultaneously, of possibility and impossibility. This is precisely the juxtaposition associated with cargo cults and milleniary movements in other times and places.[52] But, as the growth of prosperity gospels and fee-for-service movements illustrates, in a neoliberal age, the chiliastic urge emphasizes a privatized millennium, a personalized rather than a communal sense of rebirth. In this, the messianic meets the magical. At the beginning of the twenty-first century, the cargo, glimpsed in large part through translocal media (above all TV), takes the form of huge concentrations of wealth accruing, legitimately or otherwise, to the rich of the new planetary economy. It often appears to be enigmatic wealth, derived mysteriously, as we said earlier, from financial investment and management, from intellectual property and other rights, from electronics and cyberspace, from transport and its cognate operations, and from the supply of various sorts of post-Fordist services. All of which points to the fact that the covert mechanisms of a changing market, not to mention abstruse technological and informational expertise, hold the key to hitherto unimaginable fortunes; to capital amassed by the ever more rapid flow of value, across time and space, into the fluid coordinates of the local and the global.

Herein, of course, lies the other side of the coin: the sense of impossibility, even despair, that comes from being left out of the promise of prosperity; from having to look in on the global economy of desire, on its quixotic technologies, from the outside. Whether it be in post-Soviet Central Europe or postcolonial Africa, in post-Thatcherite Britain or the neoliberal USA, in a China edging towards capitalism or in Neo-Pentecostal Latin America, the world-historical process which came to be symbolized by the events of 1989 held out the prospect that everyone would be set free to accumulate and speculate, to consume, and to indulge repressed cravings in a universe of less government, greater privatization, more opulence, infinite enterprise. For the vast majority, however, the millennial moment passed without visible enrichment. The citadels of power and privilege seem as impregnable as ever.

The implication? That, in these times – the late modernist age when, according to Weber and Marx, enchantment would wither away – more and more ordinary people see arcane forces intervening in the production of value, diverting its flow toward a new elect. They also attribute to these arcane forces their feelings of erasure and loss: an erasure, in many places, of community and family; a loss of human integrity, experienced in the spreading commodification of persons and their bodies, in the unyoking of the market value from the social value of objects and relations, in the substitution of quantities for quality, abstraction for substance. None of these perceptions is new, as we have said; Balzac described them for France in the 1840s,[53] as did Conrad for pre-revolutionary Russia,[54] and neither was alone; Gluckman spoke of the 'magic of despair' which arose in similarly dislocated colonial situations in Africa.[55]

Nonetheless, to reiterate, such disruptions are widely *experienced* throughout the world as intensifying at a frightening rate at present. Which is why the ethical dimensions of occult economies are so prominent; why the mass panics of our times tend to be moral in tone; why they so often express themselves in religious movements, movements that pursue instant material returns and yet condemn those who enrich themselves in unGodly ways; why, more generally, occult economies consist, at one level, in the constant quest for new, magical means for otherwise unattainable ends, and yet, at another, voice a desire to sanction, even eradicate, people held to have accumulated assets by those very means. Satan and salvation, it seems, remain the conditions of each other's possibility.

In sum, occult economies in general, and neo-Protestant religious movements in particular – in Africa and elsewhere – are a response to the perception of an epochal shift in the constitution of the lived world: a world in which the most promising way to create real wealth seems to lie in forms of power/knowledge that transgress the conventional, the rational, the moral – thus to multiply available techniques of producing value, fair or foul. In their cultural aspect, these economies bespeak a resolute effort to come to terms with that power/knowledge, to account for the inexplicable phenomena to which it gives rise, to plumb its secrets – a byproduct of which is the invention of new realist spectres. Thus, for example, the unprecedented manifestation of zombies in some parts of the South African countryside has grown in direct proportion to the shrinking labour market for young men.[56] For some at least, the former provide a partial explanation for the latter: the living dead are commonly said to be killed and raised up by older people, by witches of wealth, to toil for them, thereby rendering rural youth jobless. There are, in this era of flexitime employment, even part-time zombies, a virtual working class – of pure, abstract labour power – that slaves away at night for its masters.

In this context, moreover, the angry dramas through which ritual murderers are identified often become sites of public divination. As they unfold, the accusers discuss, attribute cause, and speak out their understanding of the forces that make the postcolony such an inhospitable place for them. This is an extreme situation, obviously. But in less stark circumstances, too, changing moral and material economies tend to spawn simultaneous strivings to garner wealth *and* to make transparent the means by which that wealth may be produced.

As all this suggests, appeals to the occult in pursuit of the secrets of capital generally rely on local cultural technologies: on vernacular modes of divination and oracular consultation, on spirit possession and ancestral invocation, on sorcery busting and forensic legal procedures, on witch beliefs and prayer. We stress, though, that the use of these technologies does not imply a repetition of, a retreat into, 'tradition'. *Per contra*, their deployment in such circumstances is frequently a means of fashioning new techniques to preserve older values, of retooling culturally familiar signs and practices. As in cargo cults of yore, this typically involves the mimicking of what appear to be powerful new means of producing wealth.[57]

The rise of occult economies – amidst and alongside more conventional modes of economic practice, shading into the murky domains of crime and corruption – seems overdetermined at the start of the twenty-first century. This, after all, is an age in which the extravagant optimism of millennial capitalism runs up against an increasingly nihilistic, thoroughly postmodern pessimism. As the connections between means and ends become more opaque, the occult provides ever more suggestive metaphors for our times. Note how commonplace it has become to pepper media-parlance, science-speak, new age psychobabble, and technologese – even the law[58] – with the language of enchantment. But, we insist, occult economies are not reducible to the symbolic, the figurative or the allegorical alone. Magic is, everywhere, the science of the concrete, aimed at making sense of and acting upon the world – particularly, but not only, among those who feel themselves disempowered, emasculated, disadvantaged. The fact that the turn to enchantment is not unprecedented, that it has precursors in earlier times, makes it no less significant to those for whom it has become an integral part of everyday reality. Maybe, too, all this describes a fleeting phase in the long, unfinished history of capitalism. But that makes it no less momentous either. Especially in the white heat of the millennial moment.

IV Towards a beginning

However we wish to characterize this Uncommon Age – as an epoch of death (of ideology, politics, the subject) or rebirth (of the spirit of Marx, Weber, the Adams, Ferguson and Smith) – ours are perplexing times; times caught uneasily between Derrida's 'end of work' and Žižek's 'plague of fantasies';[59] times in which the conjuncture of the strange and the familiar, of stasis and metamorphosis, plays tricks on our perceptions, our positions, our praxis. This conjuncture appears at once to endorse and to erode our understanding of the lineaments of modernity. And its post-ponements. Here, plainly, we have tried to do no more than offer some preliminary observations about the passage from the apocalyptic perplexities of the present to the mundane realities of the future, interrogating, with due respect to Max Weber, the elective affinity between the spirit of a rising millennial capitalism, the occult economies which are growing up in its penumbra, and the neo-Protestant religious movements that give voice to its ethos.

Of course, the inscription of materiality in moral economy, of the pursuit of this-worldly wealth in other-wordly religious faith, is hardly new. In the *Protestant Ethic*, Weber himself italicizes a passage from John Wesley that says: *'we must exhort all Christians to gain all they can, and to save all they can; that is, in effect, to grow rich'*.[60] What, then, *is* new? We have suggested that the answer lies in an historically concrete conjuncture. One one side of that conjuncture is a postmodern, post-industrial, salvific form of capitalism, a capitalism that no longer waits for the messiah – with due respect to Vissarion – but acts like one. It is a form of capitalism that is experienced, to invoke Marx's *camera obscura*, upside down; that appears to have done away with production, and productive labour, as its fundamental source of property, personhood, family, identity, community, moral order, even 'society'; that has altered the sovereignty of the nation-state and displaced its traditional public institutions; that has reconstituted space and time, expanding their virtual and global coordinates; that has, conversely, elevated consumption into a prime mover, into the foundation of being in the world, into an epistemic act that makes the legal, psychotherapeutic, self-contracting individual of the 'new' world order into a stakeholder, itself a trope that fuses gambling with corporate citizenship.

On the other side of the conjuncture is the religion of the Vissariontsi in Siberia, of the New Life Church in South Africa, of those Disciples of Christ in Indiana, and many others besides. It is a religion of free choice and a flexible architecture, of instant materialities and deals with the divine, of radically voluntarist subjects and repressed memories, of mass-mediations, global imaginings and enchanted investments. Old-time religion, it seems, is, at least in its neo-Protestant manifestation, being compressed into space–time religion. Thus it is that, as the past becomes the future, new spiritual movements seek to harness the numinous magic of global enterprise, to fuse a messianic spirit with the speculative force of finance capital, thereby 'taking the waiting out of wanting', thereby separating salvation from saving and/or this-wordly ascetism. This is not to say that the Auld Protestantism is dead and gone. Quite the contrary: there are many contexts in which it is putting up animated resistance, where the first incarnation of Max Weber is alive and well. However, a Second Coming seems imminent in more and more places across the planet. It is a Second Coming that heralds a new Protestant Ethic, a new Spirit of Capitalism, and a new historical anthropology to make sense of both.

Postscript

This past summer, as we were walking on a crowded street in Cambridge, Massachusetts, we were given what looked like a cheque by an eager, clean-cut young man. It *was* a cheque. Issued by the 'Jesus Christ Bank of Unlimited Resources (Matthew 6: 33)', dated 'Now', and made out to 'Whomsoever will (John 1: 12)' for the sum of 'Eternal and Abundant Life (Romans 6: 23)', it bore the signature of 'The Blood of Jesus Christ (Matthew 26: 28)'. The account number, in the name of Love, Grace and Faith – which sounds rather like a combination of a 1960s rock group and a law firm – is 'Romans 5: 8/Ephesians 2: 8, 9'. On the back are instructions for 'cashing the check'. 'Secure in your heavenly passport and visa today', they advise, 'cash this check daily for your every need as you strive to stay away from sin . . . And if you need prayer and counseling, contact Pastor S@prodigy.com'. We share this promissory note in the spirit of its final message: 'Please pass this tract on.'

8

CAN A PREMODERN BIBLE ADDRESS A POSTMODERN WORLD?

Anthony C. Thiselton

I

I shall try to set out a positive answer to what may seem *prima facie* to demand a necessarily negative response; and in five sections of argument. First, postmodern writers are deeply suspicious of truth-claims which relate to universals, or to trans-contextual criteria of truth which claim to operate outside the prior interests of fragmented peer-groups, or (in Rorty's terms) 'local' or ethnocentric interests. Yet biblical writers speak not only of a creation and end which concern 'universal' world-history, but also of a gospel which explicitly transcends the ethnocentric interests and truth-claims of Jew and Gentile, male and female, slave and free. Can such an ambitious agenda rest on anything more than pre-Kantian, pre-Nietzschean innocence?

Second, clearly the very term 'postmodern' seems to presuppose a sequential following of a period of 'modernity', in relation to which it is variously construed as a reaction, critique, modification or degeneration. Jürgen Moltmann has expressed a preference for the use of the term 'sub-modernity' for what many describe as postmodernity.[1] Richard Bernstein calls postmodernity 'a rage against humanism and the Enlightenment legacy'.[2] In my second section I shall argue that postmodernity does not primarily or only represent a sequential advance or decline in relation to modernity, but what some have already described as a 'mood', attitude or ethos. In more specific terms, I shall argue that it describes a mood widespread in ancient Roman Corinth which leads Paul the Apostle to draw a conscious, critical, contrast between a socially constructed value-system based on 'recognition' and virtual realities created by rhetoric, consumerism, peer-group competition, and self-promotion, and broader non-instrumental, non-pragmatic, truth-claims conveyed by the givenness of grace from beyond local communities. Indeed, 'local' construals of truth go back to pre-Socratic philosophy concerning which Nietzsche and the later Heidegger propose some rehabilitation for more recent times.

Third, I recognize and accept the need to focus more sharply on the level of critical self-awareness which might have been possible for premodern biblical writers in appearing to participate in such sophisticated debate. Those who hold a progressivist and broadly developmental view of the history of human thought may more readily identify themselves with Hegel's claim that until his own times 'religions' tended to use uncritical imagery or representation (*Vorstellung*) rather than the critical concept (*Begriff*) made possible with the advent of historical reason in Hegel's philosophy. Such an assumption lies behind the work of Strauss, Feuerbach, and in effect more recently, in the mid-twentieth century the proposals of Rudolf Bultmann about myth in the New Testament. In my third section I shall argue (i) that if this assumption is valid, Bultmann cannot claim that demythologizing begins within the New Testament, or that he is merely following the path already begun by Paul and John; and (ii) that the subtle and complex use of such rhetorical and logical phenomena as code-switching, persuasive definition, an awareness of logical grammar, and use of sophisticated devices of Graeco-Roman rhetoric would hardly have been open to Paul and to the writer of the Epistle to the Hebrews, not to mention subtle uses of narrative time, flashbacks, strategies of reader-response and so forth regularly attributed today to the 'simple' Gospel of Mark, with its colloquial Greek which invited 'improvements' from Matthew-Luke – such subtleties serve in any case to make such a sweeping assumption entirely problematic.

Fourth, postmodern writers often have an overtly political agenda which is regularly aimed at deconstructing the norms and boundaries presupposed as 'truths' by an Establishment into instrumental constructs of social power-interests. The incisive demolitions and reformulations of Barthes and especially Foucault relate closely to issues of power and marginality within the pages of the bible. Jesus of Nazareth exposed some of the supposed boundaries imposed by pharisaic or scribal piety as social constructions that embodied inconsistencies generated by interests of privilege rather than by authentic truth, even in terms of Old Testament traditions (cf. for example Mark 7: 11 on *corban*; 13.52). Nevertheless neither Jesus nor the writers of the epistles see all differentiation as social construction. Indeed, accounts of creation (Genesis 1: 1–2: 4), of gender (1 Corinthians 11: 2–16), and of 'order' even in the eschatological consummation (1 Cor. 15: 20–58), presuppose that distinctions of role or nature may in many cases depend on the givenness of divine decree, not on the power-interests of social construction. To be sure, debate is needed concerning whether the very notion of divine decree is itself a device of social control and construction, but here we are beginning to raise the very contrast between theistic and anti-theistic world-views. What is at stake is now no longer postmodernity but the validity of theism.

A fifth cluster of issues, addressed in my final section, concerns claims about linguistic indeterminacy and the correlative problem of the role of human and perhaps also divine agency in communicative linguistic acts. I shall argue that to subsume theories of linguistic indeterminacy and an anti-representational view of language into a comprehensive theory of language is as untenable and as one-sided as the opposite error of regarding all language as deriving its meaning from a single determinate referential relation to states of affairs within the extra-linguistic world. Both of these views fail to take account of the multifunctional and multidimensional nature of language and meaning. The biblical writings function consciously to perform a variety of linguistic functions. Paul Ricœur, for example, convincingly underlines the diverse hermeneutical and linguistic or semiotic dimensions which are called into play when specific biblical genres function explicitly as *narrative* discourse (fictive or fictional), *prophetic* verdict (declarative or intersubjective), *prescriptive* law (contextually constrained or potentially trans-contextual), *hymnic* expression (psalms of praise, lament, accusation or other modes of address), *didactic* communication (relating to states of affairs, conduct, in persons), and *wisdom* modes (undertaking exploration in the face of what is largely but not wholly hidden).[3] To try to impose on all these modes of discourse a postmodern doctrine of indeterminacy and radical plurality or 'erasure' (on one side), or the early modern notion of a single determinate meaning derived from simple extralinguistic reference and representation (on the other), becomes exposed as an absurdity in the face of the particularities and contingencies of diverse biblical language-functions and varied textual performances.

II

I return to my contention that postmodernity does not depend for its currency or its appeal primarily or solely on being a reaction against, or modification of, 'modernity' in the Western tradition of philosophical, scientific and social thought. This is not to deny Bernstein's point (cited above) that it is very often fired and inspired by a 'rage' against the presumptuous illusions of high modernity as expressed in secular Enlightenment thought. Its optimistic progressivism, its individualism, and its claim to universality often based on abstract rationalism and on a disregard for historical reason and historical situatedness do indeed invite and provoke many of the most characteristic negations and reactions of postmodernity. In practice the Christian gospel also and equally rejects these claims of high modernity as presumptuous and as based on illusion, as well as on overextending the legitimate scope of scientific method to include, in effect, a world-view or comprehensive account of all that is. Nevertheless within the New Testament the 'postmodern mood' of social construction has more in common with the culture of first-century Roman Corinth, which Paul opposes, than with apostolic faith and apostolic preaching.

Paul has a respect for rational argument which presupposes a shared notion of reasonable entitlement for this or that belief-system that refuses to collapse belief into the product of mere causal persuasion or rhetoric, or into socially habituated patterns of assumptions or into the power-interests of socially defined peer groups. The whole of 1 Corinthians constitutes a plea for coherent, 'centred', belief and conduct – against the fragmented interests of specific socio-religious groups whose main self-justification was the construction of a 'reality' within which they perceived themselves as 'spiritual people'.[4]

In universities of our times, Christian theology at its best seeks to hold together two poles: on one side the particularities and social contingencies which mark serious hermeneutical and historical awareness, and on the other side a retention of epistemological courage and nerve to consider, to put forward, and to test, truth-claims which transcend the limits of specific local contexts. As Pannenberg convincingly observes, whereas Nietzsche and Freud locate the grounding of faith in 'God' in such limited contexts as that of the experience of a guilty conscience, 'God' confronts us with 'the one totality of reality'; it is 'a key word for awareness of the totality of the world in human life'.[5] Pannenberg also alludes to Karl Rahner's formulation of this point, and earlier speaks of the intellectual obligation entailed in speech about God to address the problem of universals, since God is creator of all.[6] Because Christian theists perceive the action of God in and through 'the non-exchangeable individuality and contingency' of events in history, above all in the historically conditioned event of the incarnate life and work of Jesus Christ, and yet also in transcendent patterns of action and meaning such as eschatological promise, newness and the resurrection, a dialectic of the particular or contingent and the universal or trans-contextual is set up.[7]

In my own University of Nottingham this dialectic finds expression in the possibility of genuine dialogue between the Department of Theology, and Critical Theory on one side, and Philosophy on the other. With one it shares a sense of the importance of ideological suspicion and, at times, of deconstruction (surely a method reflected here and there perhaps in Ecclesiastes and most certainly in Job), and with the other it shares a deep concern for the validity of rational truth-claims made on behalf of given logical arguments and systems of thought, within the constraints of constructive questions about human rationality, responsibility and active agency. While my doctoral candidates have engaged in debate with their peers in both of these other Departments or Schools, I should be surprised if the same kind of dialogue proved to be possible between Critical Theory and Philosophy. The former tends to accuse the latter of failure to take historicality and historical situatedness seriously; while the latter tends to view the former as reducing ideas and rational thought to mere socio-historical forces. A leaning towards one side or the other can be detected within the Faculty of Arts. The Inaugural Lecture of a Professor of Hispanic Studies, for example, explicitly promoted deconstruction as a political, rather than literary, tool, to expose an ideology of North American domination over the economics and cultures of Latin Americans. By contrast, humanist accounts of historical causality tend to find more ready hospitality in the School of History and Art History.

Our University also has lively inter-Faculty debates on the ethical, social and legal implications of genetic research. Here, on one side, those from Theology, Law and Social Sciences tend to focus on issues of personhood in contrast to more mechanistic approaches to this area. On the other hand, some geneticists welcomed social scientists into their laboratories with delight, to underline that genetic 'givens' could not be reduced to the mere constructs of social constructionism: delight shared by those from Theology.

In these contexts a balance-sheet emerges with sympathies on both sides. Positively, David Harvey sees postmodernity as a reaction against 'positivist technocratic and rationalistic universal modernism' and against 'the standardization of knowledge' which characterizes a naive privileging of science and technology as a world-view in high modernity.[8] From the standpoint of Christian theology, the negative corollary is what Harvey identifies as 'fragmentation, indeterminacy, and intense distrust of all universal or "totalizing" discourses: characteristics which constitute 'the hallmark of postmodernist thought'.[9] If we place the two sides of the balance sheet in closer contrast, the spirit of (secular) modernity gives priority and privilege to the development of 'objective science', and gives privilege also to 'autonomy' (as exemplified in Kant); but on the other side modernity retains a respect for universal moral law. On one side, (with Christian theology) postmodernity challenges the progressive optimism of modernity with its illusory faith in the natural sciences to solve almost all human problems, and underlines the limits and illusions of autonomous individualism. On the other side (in contrast to Christian theology) postmodernity feeds on a culture of suspicion rather than trust, replaces truth-claims and argument by pragmatism and rhetoric, disengages meaning from human agency to reduce it to an unstable product of changing textual forces, and in the context of Derrida's thought perceives 'signatures' as having 'more to do with absence than presence', as against the promissory function of named discourse in much biblical material.[10]

Even the postmodern critique of the privileging of the natural sciences as offering world-views rather than 'local' methods of discovery reveals a deep ambivalence in relation to values and attitudes which Christian theology derives ultimately from the bible. David Harvey rightly attributes this disillusion with progressivism and universal science to 'the re-discovery of pragmatism in philosophy (e.g. Rorty[11]), the shift of ideas about Foucault's (1975) emphasis upon discontinuity and difference in history . . . new developments in mathematics emphasising indeterminacy (catastrophe and chaos theory, fractal geometry . . .)'[12] These movements or moods remain ambivalent in relation to the bible and to theology because on one side, they underline the radical historical finitude of human agents and their discoveries and 'advances' as heavily conditioned by their location or situatedness in the contingencies of space (local geographical resources) and time (what has gone before); nevertheless on the other side they overextend the borrowed metaphor of 'incommensurable' paradigms (on which Kuhn modifies his earlier work of 1962), and, worse, with Lyotard, they undermine and reject the very notion of a 'grand narrative', a providential design or purpose in tradition and history, or 'meta-narrative'. In a very widely quoted comment Jean-François Lyotard offers what is probably the most frequently used definition of postmodernity when he observes: 'Simplifying to the extreme, I define *postmodern* as incredulity towards metanarratives.'[13]

One of Lyotard's interpreters, Bill Readings, defines 'grand narrative' as a story that 'claims the status of universal metanarrative, capable of accounting for all other stories in order to reveal their true meaning'.[14] Traditionally Christian theologians, however, have claimed to perceive the bible as a wide and contextualizing narrative of God's purposive and covenantal dealings with the world, with nations, with communities, and with individuals in ways which bring to light the meanings of these smaller stories within this overarching frame. Yet, with the challenge of postmodernity, many theologians have generated the irony of seeking to escape an ontological 'foundationalism' precisely by elevating the status of narrative. Unless, however, we remain at the level of individual, congregational, or local story, such a manoeuvre can suggest little more than a misunderstanding of what is at stake in a three-cornered encounter between modernity, postmodernity and biblical Christian theology. If we return from Lyotard's metanarrative to Derrida's erasure of meaning and Barthes's radical plurality of meaning, Kevin Vanhoozer's suggestion that these are 'counter-theological' also remains convincing: 'To refuse to halt meaning is finally to refuse God', as Barthes explicitly concedes.[15] Vanhoozer concludes: 'Derrida's deconstruction of the author is a more or less direct consequence of Nietzsche's announcement of the death of God.'[16]

We are not yet ready to anticipate our fuller discussion of biblical material and the issue of the level of its self-awareness and critical consciousness. Nevertheless it is worth drawing attention to Paul's conscious rejection of hidden meanings and manipulative strategies of persuasion, and his urging of transparency in matters of truth (e.g. 1 Corinthians 2: 1–5; 2 Corinthians 3: 12–14: 6). He alludes to the practice of Moses (2 Cor. 3: 13; cf. Exodus 34: 29–35) in hiding the fading nature of the glory which shone from his face after encounter with God, by the strategy of hiding his face behind a veil. Paul draws a contrast between such a strategy and that of 'boldness', 'openness', and transparent statements of truth-claims which he himself consciously chooses to adopt with an integrity in which word and deed are matched. Covenant promise presupposes a substantial degree of continuity and stability which Paul expounds and adopts. David Harvey underlines, by contrast, the 'virtual reality' of postmodern construction; that which in due course we shall identify with the obsessive desire for a self-perception and status defined by how peer-groups 'recognize' themselves or others. In contrast to 'representation', Harvey observes, the postmodern condition confronts us with 'illusion, myth, aspiration', projection, and 'signs chasing signs'.[17] It projects 'diverse networks' which, I argue, reflect the 'status inconsistency' generated by competing 'multidimensional' recognition-systems, status-systems, and value-systems in the Roman Corinth of AD 50–55, in the period of Paul's visit and writing.[18]

All of this resonates with party politics and with popular Western culture today. 'Reality' becomes the plaything of the media, of political spin, of chatshow hosts, of manipulative journalists and politicians; the atheistic aphorisms of Nietzsche appear as duly fulfilled prophecy: 'Truth is that kind of error without which a certain kind of person cannot live.'[19] 'All that exists consists of interpretations.'[20] 'Knowledge works as an instrument of power.'[21] '"The salvation of the soul" means "The world revolves round me".'[22] Paul and other New Testament writers, however, profoundly and emphatically reject the notion of 'religion' or 'salvation' as a vehicle of self-affirmation, peer-group self-promotion, or triumphalism, together with a notion of 'God' that amounts to a projection of human desires and interests. This claim constitutes the central thesis of my published lectures sponsored by the *Scottish Journal of Theology*, delivered in the University of Aberdeen and revised as a coherent book.[23] Paul continues his exposition of integrity and transparency in 2 Corinthians 3: 12–14: 6 with the comment that, far from offering a self-affirming human construct, Paul proclaims what has been 'given' at huge personal cost for the sake of the flourishing of others (2 Cor. 4: 7–15). I shall argue in due course that a critical self-awareness of the role of self-deception concerning these issues was virtually forced upon Paul by the transparently instrumental use of religious slogans for self-promotion and 'recognition' in Corinth. Margaret Mitchell, L. L. Welborn, and many other specialists have argued convincingly and in great detail that the 'splits' (*schismata*) in the church of Corinth instantiated notably in 1 Cor. 1: 10–12 utilized the language of politics (Mitchell); indeed, the language of power-play (Welborn).[24]

The biblical writers, especially Paul, not only reject the reduction of truth-claims about acts of God or salvation to instrumental power-play, but also more especially reject what have now become postmodern assumptions that truth-claims have no 'hard' currency beyond the 'soft' currency of local groups and interests largely determined by social class, race, gender, cultural conditioning, peer-group interests and correlative 'recognition' within a guild. Thus Richard Rorty accepts that 'relativism' has become an exhausted term, but substitutes in its place 'ethnocentric' or 'local' for the soft currencies of neo-pragmatism which he views with approval.[25] Truth is little more than intersubjective agreement among given persons at given times. He endorses the claims of Foucault that, for example, 'human rights' and 'homosexuality' are concepts which resist such questions as 'whether there really are human rights'; these are 'recent social constructions'.[26]

From the standpoint of Christian theism and biblical faith, this looks very like a re-run of A. J. Ayer's doctrinaire dismissal of religious and ethical language as expressing no more than non-cognitive, emotive, expressions of approval or preference which, in the absence of universal scientific empirical verifiability, were to be regarded as 'non-sense'. Ayer's category of 'non-sense' runs closely parallel with Rorty's project of 'rubbish disposal'.[27] In Rorty's view 'the true' is simply what proves itself to be useful and acceptable in relation to the projects of particular persons or groups. He approves the maxim of William James that '"The true" . . . is only the expedient in the way of our thinking . . .'.[28] 'Truth' is no more than 'justification', and 'justification is always relative to an audience'.[29] For the theist, however, consigning to the 'rubbish' bin everything except pragmatic preference (backed in some cases by tanks, nuclear weapons and dollars) is as irrational and as downright narrow and blind as Ayer's attempt to label as 'non-sense' everything except a quantifiable world of empirical observation. Ayer's view took about ten years to collapse under its internal self-contradictions which exposed it as sheer positivism disguised as a theory of language. The self-contradiction in Rorty is the pretence of offering a 'local', modest, unassuming, pragmatism, while elevating it at the same time into a sweeping reductionism of all serious epistemology and ontology, and dubbing these as 'rubbish'. As Kierkegaard might have observed, how can such a finite, situated, human being assume such a quasi-omniscient trans-local view? Rorty insists: 'There is no Way the World is.'[30] Clearly, by contrast, the biblical writings include assertions and confessions about the way the world is, as well as laws about how the world should be, and promises about how the world will be. In my 1999 Presidential Paper to the Society for the Study of Theology (University of Edinburgh) I have argued that American pragmatic postmodernity constitutes a more insidious influence upon Christian theology than the more pessimistic iconoclastic postmodernity of France, Germany and Italy, which at least serves to deconstruct idolatrous religion.[31]

III

Does 'postmodernity' presuppose a sequential relation to modernity, whether it is described as a reaction against it, modification to it, or degeneration from it? Enough has been said already to indicate that postmodernity reflects a mind-set, attitude, ethos, or *mood*, which does not depend on a conscious comparison with, or sequential relation to, modernity to discuss its main features. Admittedly the use of comparisons with high modernity helps both to explain its historical origins and to trace its contours. Thus Rex Ambler perceives as its major theme a sense of disillusion that 'the typically modern relation to the self can no longer be sustained'.[32] Jameson insists that postmodern aesthetics and politics are 'necessarily linked' with issues of classical or high modernism.[33] Seyla Benhabib speaks of 'skepticism... towards continuing the "project of modernity" based on disillusionment'.[34] Elizabeth Ermarth argues that since postmodernity may be seen as a kind of sequel to modernity, the term and its mood depend on how we understand 'modernity' for its currency of meaning.[35]

Most of these writers, however, set postmodernity in relation to modernity in order to focus on some particular philosophical or political feature. Although these claims are not false, it remains no less true that, with Thomas Docherty, we may also characterize postmodernity as *'a mood, and not a period'* (my italics).[36] A number of theological writers rightly also disengage postmodernity from a sequential stage in the supposed advancement or development of human thought. Richard Roberts insists that the premodern, the modern, and the postmodern respectively do not represent three neatly sequential stages but rather three sources of co-existent cross-currents often in conflict, drawing us in different directions.[37] Thus in the same essay Roberts proposes that the church today should include among its combined resources 'residual tradition' (in part, the premodern), processes of education (in part the modern), and an awareness of consumerist market-forces (largely the neo-pragmatic or postmodern). Dan Hardy endorses the view that premodern, modern and postmodern forces 'co-exist' (i.e. are not sequential), but advocates a stronger emphasis upon unity and coherence than is fully compatible with most postmodern thought.[38]

I have argued in my commentary on 1 Corinthians that a historical, archaeological and socio-cultural reconstruction of mid-first-century Roman Corinth identifies precisely this *postmodern mood* with the Corinth of Paul's day.[39] We have already noted above the research of Wayne Meeks to the effect that in their obsessive sense of insecurity and search for 'status' and 'recognition', the Corinthians operated with a radically pluralist diversity of scales and types of recognition. Status was viewed not in terms of any 'single thing', but in terms of a 'multidimensional phenomenon [in which] ... one must attempt to measure their rank along *each* of the relevant dimensions' (Meeks's italics).[40] 'Status-indicators' included at different levels 'occupational prestige, income or wealth, education and knowledge, religious and moral purity, family and ethnic-group position, and local community status (evaluation within some sub-group independent of the larger society . . .)'.[41] The second important point is not merely the radical plurality of this 'local' diversity but still more fundamentally that 'the weight of each dimension [of evaluation or recognition] depends upon who is doing the weighing'.[42] Both of these two aspects resonate entirely with the approach of Rorty: radical pluralism of the local or ethnocentric, and the transposition of truth about states of affairs into 'recognition' by some persons or group as the criterion of evaluation (see above).

The emphasis placed upon evaluation and recognition by the audience in rhetoric runs parallel with the mind-set in which consumers determine the value and importance of production by market forces. Archaeological research on ancient Corinth confirms the claims of Donald Engels that Corinth was a commercial centre in which competitive market forces determined huge variations in the amassing of business wealth and international trade.[43] Its very geographical position on the isthmus between its eastern harbour of Cenchraea, which faced across the Saronic Gulf to Asia and Ephesus, and its western harbour of Lechaeum, which faced across the Corinthian Gulf to Italy and Rome, joined by a paved roadway, the *diolkos* of only some six kilometres, placed it at the intersection of trade between East and West, and North and South. Light ships and cargo could be transported over the *diolkos* and sailors were eager to avoid the often treacherous voyage around the Southern Cape of Malea.[44] Archaeological discoveries of coinage witness to abundant trade of a cosmopolitan nature, published in successive volumes of *Hesperia*, the official journal of the American School of Classical Studies at Athens.[45]

Most striking for today's visitor to the site of ancient Corinth are the remains of the monument erected by Gnaeus Babbius Philinus, which records twice that as '*aedile* and *pontifex* he had this monument erected at his own expense' and adds that in his office as *duovir* he also approved its construction. This typifies the way in which a *nouveau riche* man of influence could not only rise to high office, but commission the construction of monuments and no doubt also rhetoricians to ensure 'media recognition' of his new-found status as an admired city benefactor. This illustrates 'the ideas of self-promotion, publicity and recommendations written in stone'.[46] It is important to recall that the Greek city of Corinth was largely destroyed when it rebelled against Rome in 146 BC and was refounded as a Roman colony in 44 BC by Julius Caesar, when its core population was made of Roman veterans,

Roman freedpersons, and probably also slaves and those seeking to succeed in manufacture and trade.[47] Ben Witherington admirably sums up the cultural mood of simultaneous insecurity and ambition within competing value-systems when he observes: 'for Paul's time many in Corinth were already suffering from a self-made-person-escapes-humble-origins syndrome'.[48]

The Apostle Paul was *critically aware* of the huge gulf which separated the givenness of divine grace and the givenness of the *kerygma* of a crucified Christ on one side and the socio-rhetorical expectations of a message designed to match the specified self-affirmations of a variety of groups. Bruce Winter convincingly demonstrates that in contrast to the truth-seeking rhetoric of rational argument advocated by Cicero and by Quintilian, 'in Alexandria and Corinth there was a high-profile sophistic movement in the first century ... the "Second Sophistic".'[49] 'Truth' was generated not by rationality and coherence, but by pragmatic rhetorical effect and audience applause. The sophists anticipate entirely Richard Rorty's 'postmodernity'. There is no such task as 'getting reality right ... because there is no Way the World is'.[50] 'Justification is always relative to an audience.'[51] Yet this is what Paul *consciously and critically rejects*. To the Second Sophistic, to first-century Corinth, and to Rorty's pragmatism, the cross cannot be other than an *affront* (1 Cor. 1: 18–25). For Paul the issue is whether the Christian proclamation has to accord with the pre-given criterion of the cross, or whether 'the cross', 'Christ', and 'being people of the Spirit' become constructs shaped by what affirms and pleases consumer-audiences. Hence Schrage perceptively entitles 1 Cor. 1: 18–2: 5 *'Das "Wort vom Kreuz" als Grund und Kriterium von Gemeinde und Apostel'* ('The "word of the cross" as basis and criterion of [both] church and apostle').[52]

Together with Winter, Stephen Pogoloff, Andrew Clarke and John Moores have contributed greatly to our appreciation of Paul's necessary awareness of this gulf. Pogoloff cites the rhetorical competitions concerning which Cicero, Quintilian and Seneca lament the applause-seeking, audience-orientated criteria presupposed in such provincial centres as Corinth and Alexandria as against the traditional truth-seeking arguments of classical rhetoric in Rome. Truth (with Richard Rorty and the later Stanley Fish) becomes the property of 'winners'. The rhetoricist, Seneca the Elder, Cicero and Quintilian complain, thinks more of himself and of audience approval than of the case and its merits: 'Every effusion is greeted with a storm of ready-made applause ... The result is variety and empty self-sufficiency.'[53] The genius of Pogoloff's research on Corinth is his recognition of how closely Corinthian attitudes anticipate the mind-set of so-called anti-foundationalism, and of the collapse of epistemology into causally, psychologically, or politically persuasive pragmatic rhetoric.[54] This is precisely why Paul makes a firm decision (1 Cor. 2: 2) to reject methods of pleasing speech shaped by audience approval-ratings and manipulative 'cleverness', but to declare the *kerygma* of a Christ crucified, 'so that your faith might rest not on human "wisdom", but on the power [what is solid and effective] of God' (1 Cor. 2: 5; cf. 2: 1–5). The 'criterion of the cross' (Schrage) brings *all people* under judgment and grace. As Pogoloff shows, audience-constituted rhetoric is bound to divide wider communities into local or ethnocentric groups.[55]

Andrew Clarke explicates this contrast in terms of differences between secular and Christian patterns of leadership in Corinth. In contrast to the secular style of leadership that seeks 'recognition' and the high status accorded by rhetoric, social standing, professional expertise, or the influence of patrons and reciprocal favours, Paul is content with 'weakness': to pin everything on the gospel which entails identification with a crucified Christ who is regarded by many as a shameful affront. He therefore dissociates himself from the path of those 'who sought personal advancement ... the pursuit of esteem and praise'.[56] He does not seek to use such manipulative power-tools as patronage or benefaction.[57] Apostolicity meant the very opposite of 'leadership ... on show', but points to the 'given' of the grace of Christ crucified and raised.[58] Paul rejects the manipulative strategy that seems to have functioned in the church of civil litigation where financial and social influences could prove decisive.

Finally John Moores vigorously relates Paul's strategy to issues today. He writes: Paul does not think 'the identity of a message ... is in any sense determined by what it means for those at the receiving end. For him it is rather *their* identity than that of the message which is determined by their response. To subject him to the criteria of present-day ... reader-response theory would be to turn *his* ideas on the subject upside down' (his italics).[59] This is all the more convincing because Moores writes as one fully familiar with the work of Umberto Eco, C. Perelman, enthymemic logic and semiotic theory. The Corinthians' postmodern *mood* well resonates with Stanley Fish's 'Rhetorical Man', in contrast with the transformative, transcontextual, power of the proclamation of the cross, which Fish's 'Serious Man' could perceive as transformative. When he advocates the stance of rhetorical man, Fish describes precisely what much Corinthian culture admired and what Paul rejected: 'Rhetorical man is trained not to discover reality but to manipulate it.' 'Serious man ... can be characterized by sincerity, faithfulness to the self', while rhetorical man necessarily remains 'an actor'.[60]

IV

Can we imagine that if Paul sees the cross as, in Schrage's words, 'the ground and criterion' of what is at issue here, it would be anachronistic to speak of his awareness of all that is at stake as less than one of 'critical consciousness'? After all, even if he uses a touch of irony in his choice of words, Fish is right to say that [This] 'contrast ... can hardly be exaggerated ... The ground is itself foundational.'[61]

The word 'critical' may well set us off track by three historical contexts which influence its application. First, it need not imply any opposition between doubt and tradition which many associate with Descartes. Gadamer, among others, has exposed the shallow inadequacy of this supposed opposition. Second, it need not imply endorsement of the critical or transcendental philosophy of Kant. Kant's attempts to define the limits of reason and the role of mental construction in the perception of order remain at very least controversial, and those who question Kant are not thereby 'uncritical' thinkers. Third, Hegel's comparison between the uncritical use of *Vorstellung*, representation, in religion, as against *Begriff* [critical] concept in philosophy addresses the issue more closely, but did critical thought await Hegel's formulation of historical reason, and is the contrast as clear-cut as Hegel and D. F. Strauss maintained?

It is noteworthy that the later Heidegger, for all his earlier emphasis on radical historical situatedness and finitude, returned not to Hegel, who (Heidegger maintained) still elevated *Geist* or Spirit in quasi-dualist terms, but to the pre-Socratic philosophers of premodernity. The Milesian School of the sixth century BC acknowledged the instability of change, but nevertheless allowed for a continuity in terms of that which underwent change. Heraclitus, by contrast, tended to undermine the notion of continuity 'behind' change ('You cannot step twice into the same river, for fresh waters are ever flowing in upon you'). Yet even Heraclitus allowed for a stability of the constitutive principles that govern change. Zeno of Elea formulated his paradoxes to seek to undermine Heraclitus and the Pythagoreans, but it was left to Gilbert Ryle to show the logical consequences of differences between the logic of an observer and the logic of participants. Ironically, the arch-ontologist Parmenides in effect promoted scepticism by arguing that change itself was illusory, while Protagoras (c. 490–420

BCE) came nearest to the mind-set of postmodernity by urging notions of truth and of virtue rested in general on sheer norms of convention in human behaviour. Even if Aristophanes overdraws the picture in *The Clouds* to provide fun at his expense, the dictum of Protagoras 'Man is the measure of all things' means *either* (1) that 'true' means only what given people *believe* to be true; or (2) that whatever a person believes is 'true' *for that person*. Either interpretation, but especially the first, paves the way for Foucault's scepticism about 'norms' and for social constructivism.

Is all of this premodern thinking, then, entirely 'uncritical'? To be sure, as J. B. Skemp urges, most first-century Christian writers were not Greek philosophers.[62] Nevertheless Skemp's work (1964) on the 'Ordinary Greek' still tends to presuppose the agenda of Adolf Deissmann which sought to underplay the level of education and conceptual sophistication that marked the earliest Christian communities and the New Testament writers.[63] The debates since set up by E. A. Judge, Wayne Meeks, Gerd Theissen and Bruce Winter serve to redress the balance, even if Meggitt still emphasizes the economic poverty of many.[64] We noted Winter's convincing arguments above, coupled with those of Pogoloff, Clarke and Moores, that a replay of all the issues about the collapse of 'truth' as given into 'recognition' as constructed by rhetoric and social power-interests took place in mid-first-century Corinth.

It is not the case that Paul could have held an 'uncritical' conceptual awareness of these high stakes on both sides. It was the case, however, that a transformative proclamation of a Christ crucified presented a *theological critique*, not a philosophical one. The gospel could not be marketed as a package shaped and defined by the interests of consumers or by market forces. This is why Paul explicitly describes it as an *affront* (Greek *skandalon*) to those who have this horizon of expectation (1 Cor. 1: 18–25), and why he insists on proclaiming what is 'given' (1 Cor. 2: 1–5; cf. 11: 17–23, 15: 3–6). Indeed, this very point brings us to note the level of *critical rigour and sophistication* with which Paul uses the patterns and devices of classical Graeco-Roman rhetoric to put forward *rational argument on the basis of shared premises*.

Anders Eriksson provides a masterly study of Paul's rigorous methods of argumentation in 1 Corinthians, usually on the basis of shared premises. Paul consciously uses rhetorical strategies with a high level of sophistication. The treatise on the resurrection, for example, which is the most carefully polished rhetorical argument, embodies shared tradition in the *exordium* (15: 1–2), in the *narratio* (15: 3–11), the first *refutatio* (15: 12–19), the first *confirmatio* (15: 20–34), a second *refutatio* (15: 35–49 and *confirmatio* (15: 50–57) and the *peroratio* (15: 58).[65] But this strategy is not confined to chapter 15. Traditions constitute premises in 8: 6, 11; 10: 16; 11: 17–34; 12: 3; 16: 22 and elsewhere. Throughout several of his epistles Paul uses assonance, chiasmus, *insinuatio*, irony, *narratio*, *propositio* and antithesis.[66] M. Bünker demonstrates Paul's knowledge of contemporary rhetorical theories in 1 Cor. 1: 10–4: 21 as well as in 15: 1–58.[67] We have already noted the significant contributions of Margaret Mitchell and John Moores (above). In particular Moores examines the phenomenon of 'code-switching', in which the logical currency of a term such as 'spiritual persons' is drawn from a communicative code presupposed by the readers and 'switched' into a decisively different conceptual currency by the writer.[68] This assumes a high degree of critical conceptual awareness and rigour, but I have traced numerous examples of such code-switching and re-definition in 1 Corinthians.[69]

Even Paul, however, does not embody the most sophisticated rhetorical style in the New Testament. The Epistle to the Hebrews, which is agreed by specialists to be non-Pauline, opens as a brilliant homily which employs alliteration, rhythm, elegance, force and careful, conscious artistry, with many intra-textual allusions and resonances.[70] At what was once regarded as the other end of the spectrum in terms of lack of linguistic polish, the Gospel of Mark is nowadays widely credited with a highly sophisticated narrative strategy, including a conscious differentiation between 'clock-time' and narrative-time. Thus Mark begins the narrative of Jesus at a rapid pace; slows down the tempo following Peter's confession of the Messiahship of Jesus at Caesarea Philippi; and finally projects the events of the Passion in slow motion.[71] This focuses attention on the dominance of the cross as the purposive goal of the life of Jesus. More controversially, Frank Kermode attributes to Mark a conscious strategy of puzzlement which invites readers to look to 'church' or apostolic interpretation for the clue to the meaning of the story.[72] If Kermode's account of Mark were convincing (and I do not find it so) Mark would not only be critically aware of the strategies of postmodernity, but also be seen to be employing them.

A further argument about the degree of critical self-consciousness shown by the New Testament writers arises, probably surprisingly, from the debate which followed Rudolf Bultmann's proposals about demythologizing the New Testament. His definitions of myth have been widely recognized to be inconsistent and even contradictory.[73] Although he attributes to 'myth' an uncritical premodern view of the world as a 'three-decker' universe, Bultmann more emphatically insists that the programme of demythologizing, especially in its second and third senses relating to analogy and to de-objectification both exposes metaphor or analogy *as* metaphor or analogy, and perceives objectification as a process *begun within the New Testament itself*. Both, he insists, constitute demands of the New Testament itself rather than of 'modern man'.[74] He writes: 'Very soon the process of demythologizing began, partly with Paul, and radically with John.'[75] However, if the difference between pre-critical embodiments of myth and critical awareness of when analogy is analogy and of when de-objectification relates to attitudes, participation and self-involvement (as well as presupposing often also states of affairs), this *'waking out of a pre-critical sleep'* is fundamental to Bultmann's understanding of the level of conceptual awareness that he attributes to biblical writers. For again and again he claims that his proposals follow their example, and are not imposed either by a liberal theology or by a modern philosophy.[76]

In addition to these *conceptual* considerations, we may return finally to *theological* factors which enhance this critical self-awareness. Paul not only struggles with a 'postmodern mood' at Corinth; he is also fully aware of *the capacity of the human heart for self-deception*. This biblical theme goes back to Jeremiah and to the Psalms, and is internally entailed in the notion of 'hidden depths' below the surface of the human heart (Hebrew, *lebh*; Greek, *kardia*). The fullest modern exposition of the importance of this motif for Paul is found in Theissen's *Psychological Aspects of Pauline Theology*. Paul concedes that such are the hidden depths of the heart that he cannot, and should not, pronounce verdicts on himself (1 Cor. 4: 1–5): 'Paul does allow for unconscious intentions that could stand in tension with his consciousness'.[77] Paul speaks elsewhere of human secrets hidden from the conscious mind (Romans 2: 29), and of secret motivations which prophetic preaching may expose to consciousness (1 Cor. 14: 20–25). Only the realities of the last judgment can reveal the true nature of human motivations and achievement (1 Cor. 3: 5–17). Self-perception grows from the work of the Holy Spirit (Rom. 8: 26–27) who 'searches the heart', and the Johannine sphere of 'darkness' underlines the deceptiveness of what only God's Spirit can bring to light (John 16: 8–13; cf. 14: 17). We cannot claim with any degree of credibility that biblical writers were unaware of the problem so sharply focused later by Nietzsche and by Foucault that truth-claims about the self, about others, or about God could be put forward as disguised ways of promoting power, self-interest or strategies of manipulation.

V

We may conclude by summarizing, by way of contrast, some points at which the biblical writings address postmodernity by way of support and endorsement, even if there is also critique. First, we may take up the issue of self-deception. Nietzsche, Barthes, Foucault and Derrida have exposed the 'mythologies' which serve as mechanisms of disguise to promote truth-claims on behalf of the power-interests of persons or groups. On one side, Theissen and other biblical scholars have identified a self-awareness of the seductions of self-deception within the pages of the bible, especially in Paul, but not exclusively so. Elsewhere I have argued in detail that in the Pastoral Epistles and other biblical writings there is a subtle awareness that 'true' and 'false' is not only a matter of the correspondence of propositions to what is the case, or coherence between them, but a relation of integrity and disengagement of self-interest in matters of life and conduct.[78] The logic of 'All Cretans are liars' put onto the lips of a Cretan serves to bring out the self-contradictory notion of first-person utterances in which their truth-value is undermined by the character and conduct of the speaker.[79] On the other side, the theological understanding of the consequences of *corporate* self-deception is brilliantly exposed long before it was thought to be a distinctively 'postmodern' insight by Reinhold Niebuhr in his *Moral Man and Immoral Society*, published as long ago as 1932. People will commit the most unethical acts, he argued, if they can deceive themselves into claiming that these are 'for my family', 'for my country', or even 'for my social class or my race'. Already a *theological* critique, at least in embryo, is anticipated in advance of Rorty's neo-pragmatic ethnocentrism. However, Niebuhr is simply explicating in his own context a critical principle that is also reflected in the biblical writings.

We also noted in our Introduction some common ground between Jesus and the New Testament on one side and Foucault and postmodern deconstructionism on the other concerning 'marginality' and 'boundaries'. Jesus, we earlier noted, rejected the arbitrary fencing off of degrees of religious and ethical purity in such a way that some were branded as 'outsiders' whatever their attitude of heart. Such scribal or pharisaic traditions placed obstacles in the path, and burdens on the backs, of those very outsiders whom the host of the wedding feast in Luke insists are welcome at what clearly represents the divine and Messianic banquet (Luke 14: 15–24, where the emphasis falls upon urging outsiders to come and be welcome; cf. the more allegorical version of the royal wedding in Matthew 22: 1–14, where the emphasis falls upon judgment for 'insiders' who remain content with their self-sufficiency).

Nevertheless, Jesus and the biblical writers do not deconstruct all differentiation as mere social construction in defence of interests. Creation is diverse because God decreed 'differences' of order which give rise to what Thomas Aquinas associates with the principle of plenitude. He cites Genesis 1: 4, 'And God divided the light from the darkness', and comments, 'Distinction and variety in the world is intended by the first cause . . . He makes creatures many and diverse . . . Divine wisdom is the cause why things are distinct; also why they are unequal. It would be an unfinished world were it all on one level of goodness.'[80] Similarly, even the events of the end-times are characterized by differentiated order (1 Cor. 15: 23–28), while boundary-distinctions in service and ministry, while neither absolute nor inflexible, are related to divine decree which reflects the 'ordered differentiation' within the Godhead (1 Cor. 12: 4–11, 27–30).

To be sure, the metaphor of the body, with its unity and diversity of members, is drawn from Roman and Greek literature; but whereas in Livy it is applied on behalf of the elite to dissuade slaves from revolt, in Paul it is turned upside down. The supposedly 'less honourable' are to be honoured as indispensable to the welfare of the whole (1 Cor. 12: 21–25).[81] Distinctions of roles and boundaries of identity are not merely social constructions to be deconstructed in the interests of the weak; Paul defends the weak and the marginalized by a more subtle and lasting route. Respect for the otherness of the other, mutuality and reciprocity provide a more constructive strategy than an egalitarian politics of 'sameness' or 'interchangeability', whether we are speaking of parents and children, church polity and gender, the gift of diverse 'somatic' modes of being at the resurrection, or of God as Father, Son and Spirit.

The controversial issue of indeterminacy in language also reveals similarities and dissimilarities with the varied genres employed within the biblical texts, and once again demonstrates the genuineness of address and engagement between the bible and postmodernity. The wisdom literature and the parables of Jesus (in contrast to similitudes, similes and allegories) reflect the open-endedness of exploration in which hearers or readers are invited to 'complete' a meaning, but with ever-new reappraisals and discoveries. On the other hand, shared kerygmatic traditions, embryonic creeds and confessional formulae, and above all promissory language, demand a stability and degree of specificity that give them operative currency. The biblical canon includes both traditions and iconoclasm. Sacred texts which offer only iconoclasm would be as self-defeating as the so-called paradox of scepticism. Most significantly, as Vanhoozer and Wolterstorff among others urge with passion, a bible which addresses humankind with words of renewal, promise, hope and love, is a text which presupposes agency.[82] It is not the mere product of textual forces, even if it draws on language-systems that remain potential until they are actualized by speakers, writers and specific texts.

In the end, the question of 'givens' may ultimately turn on the contrast between a theistic and a non-theistic world-view. At the heart of the bible and of Christian faith stands the divine sovereign initiative of giving the gift of Godself in sheer grace. As I noted in 1980, in Romans 11: 6 Paul expounds a piece of logical or conceptual grammar: if 'grace' is a consumer product even in part constructed by the recipient or by the church, 'grace is not grace'.[83] If this is not a conscious address to challenge the scope of human or social construction, it is difficult to see what might count as such.

CONCLUSION
Dialogue on the 'Common Era'

The Editors

Paul Gifford[1] There's an irradiating dialogue to be pursued around these texts. We shan't manage more than a tiny fraction of it, but let's see how far we can get . . . I thought Moltmann got us off to a racing start by his way of looking backwards and forwards. Real hope for the future springs from an authentic redemption of the past. That's a striking pattern of sense, recapitulating the Judaeo-Christian inheritance. It retraces the *shape* of the CE matrix – but it also has pretty universal applicability too.

Could we perhaps consider this shape alongside Ricœur's theory of 'narrative identity'?[2] For Ricœur, remember, we tell our story – individual or collective – so as to get a purchase on our own continuity in time and a sense of that elusive principle of subject-identity – the *ipse* – which has no name and no handle in objective science. This allows us to open up the space of creative imaginings, modellings, configurations – sketching the space of ourselves still-to-be. Subject-identity, whether personal or collective, is always a certain articulation of *project* and of *memory*. 'I' am, 'we' are, at the point where a projected future is articulated in terms of a narrativized past. That's a very useful basic model of how human identities work. It's the way we all stand in relation to the 'Common Era', however old we think it is . . .

How do our contributors relate to these two patterns? And let's not forget: some of the most interesting issues arise in the spaces in-between – the comparisons, the gaps and the margins.

Nigel Rapport Are we in a position to be hopeful? Where does hope lie? It lies in value pluralism (for John Gray). Or in narrative hospitality[3] – giving room in our personal and social practice to other traditions of memory, their eras, their identities (Ricœur). I take those to be post-Enlightenment and 'postmodern' perspectives. Or it lies in some kind of singular transcendence which might be biblical (revelation), as for Moltmann and Thiselton and perhaps Girard, or anti-biblical (Nietzsche's revaluation of values) in the case of Richard Schacht. Both of these latter forms of hopefulness can be seen to maintain some notion of a singular transcendence overcoming the circumstances of the present. The notion of the Overman, even though it's *anti*-theological, is still a form of existential transcendence.

Trevor A. Hart I'd personally go with Moltmann on the roots of hope. Yes, they are tied to Judaeo-Christian revelation, but his characteristic emphasis is that hope does not lie in a historical future, it's hope for a future which lies beyond history – and which is hope *for the whole of history*. In your terms of 'transcendence', he's articulating not just the notion of God doing something from outside the system – the something which is done comes from beyond the limits of the historical process, yes, but in a way that interrupts it and sets it up afresh . . .

NR You mean Heaven?

TH Heaven's OK by Moltmann! But no, not a lingering afterlife of pale shades, not even a postscript of blissful pie-in-the-sky: we're talking about the biblical idea of a 'new creation', of a final transfiguration *of the here-and-now*, anticipated *already* in the here-and-now. That refers of course to the first or original creation. God who creates things in the first place is the One capable of bringing about the radical novelty or newness which Moltmann thinks of as the only answer to the state the world is in. The analogy he draws on for this is the compound event of crucifixion-resurrection. Good Friday, the crucifixion, is not just a historical event; it's a theological symbol of all that history, given its own momentum and direction, finally comes to – i.e. it's a sign of the radical evil, or the potential for radical evil, in the world. Resurrection, precisely because it's not rooted in something immanent in crucifixion itself, is a symbol of the fact that, if there finally is to be hope, it has to rest in a radical recreative activity of God, not in the realization of some aptitude for perfection of human beings or of something latent within the historical process. That's a very radical, entirely particular notion of 'transcendence' (I'm not sure even John Gray, for instance, takes the measure of it).

NR A messianic notion?

TH Yes, certainly. Apocalyptic, too, if you want to distinguish those things. Messianic strands within biblical tradition tend to relate to things that happen within history, in the future, but in continuity with currents of history – the hope for a coming King whose reign will be 'like' that of David – whereas 'apocalyptic' tradition tends to be about an interruption of historical process. The Son of Man 'coming on the clouds'[4] is coming 'from above'. Coming from beyond, from outside, and breaking into the system of historical cause and effect. It's definitely an interruptive thing. And that's interesting, too, because it draws attention to something within the mainstream eschatological tradition of Christianity: this religion is actually capable, in terms of its own logic – its *own* identity-matrix given out of revelation – of taking radically seriously the darkness and despair and hopelessness of history, of the way the world is; and, on the other hand, not despairing finally, because there is a hope that lies beyond. Yet it can do this, without collapsing into 'other-worldliness', without abandoning this world – allowing it to 'go to hell' – because its hope is invested in the recreation *of this world*. That's the very high value in Moltmann of this world. We are called to live in accordance with this hope *in the midst of* the here-and-now as we experience it. An ethical imperative is rooted in the hope.

PG 'Behold, I make all things new.'[5] Yes, and isn't it the 'new creation' that really makes sense of the 'redemptive' bit of the Judaeo-Christian matrix? But then, don't Christians also have to come clean and admit that one of the costs to Christianity of Christendom was that it did substantially lose the *cosmic plot* of its own – theological – narrativization of the Common Era? You do have to say: this is a twentieth-century recovery or rediscovery of the logic of the matrix, don't you?

I'm thinking, you see, of French writers like Saint-Exupéry, who opens his *Terre des hommes* (1937) with the sentence: 'Genesis is not over' – but he is throwing that assertion *in the face of* his received French Catholic culture, and claiming that the 'earth of men' – let's now say 'of humankind'! – is *taking over from religion* the challenge of making all things new (he'd read Nietzsche, of course!). So had Paul Valéry, who writes a parodic remake of the story of creation and fall in 'Genesis' (1922).[6] There, God destroys his perfection by creating and withdraws into absence. His breath upon the clay is a 'sigh of despair'. It's the serpent – the figure of human consciousness, dynamic, reflexive, full of desirous self-love – who writes, and narrates, the epic story of the human adventure in history. In this 'narrativization', creation is closed, finished; it doesn't move: only the unquiet dynamic of human dreams does. That's the immanent 'nothingness' of human consciousness 'lifted up towards Being'. Behind that model, which Valéry is objecting to in parody, there's a Greek-inspired ontotheology *with which Judaeo-Christianity is identified* – and with which it perhaps partially *identified itself* . . .

Or Camus: remember the figure of the Jesuit priest Paneloux in his novel about the plague (1947)? Camus's idea on the 'ethical imperative' is that Christians are ambiguous allies of humanists in their struggle to succour human ills and afflictions, because they are in secretly fatalistic complicity with an *unjust order of creation* behind which lurks an inscrutable – *and entirely inactive!* – Deity. Nothing interruptive at work; no sense of divine creativity originally, on-goingly new . . .[7]

You really can't blame these French writers for bringing down the shutters on 'religion' if that's what they thought they were rejecting. I wonder, too, if Nietzsche had seen what Moltmann sees, he could have said that Christianity is a 'Platonism for the people'? He really was talking about something else, wasn't he? A shrunken, individualistic, idealist pietism of Protestant antecedence . . . and he despised the Jewish-Christian 'slave morality', the 'nuzzling and pawing' of God. Infantile, almost animal! Overman is the antithesis to *that* 'thesis', in a very nineteenth-century sort of dialectic . . .

NR Nietzsche's writing on Judaism and the Jews is instructive for what it reveals about the notion of the Overman: in the ideology of Judaism, the obeisance to Jehovah, there are the roots of a slave- or herd-morality; but in the practice of Jews is that overcoming of the conditions of the present through strength which will epitomize the Overman. Nietzsche wrote: 'The Jews [. . .] are beyond all doubt the strongest, toughest and purest race at present living in Europe', with a 'genius crafted in a long school of suffering', for 'money and patience', 'mind and spirituality'.[8] It was almost inevitable that, 'within the herd-thinking of other races and national-social groupings of Europe', the Jews' 'energy and higher intelligence, their capital in will and spirit', would arouse 'envy and hatred, and [. . .] sacrificial slaughter'; 'one should not be afraid', however, Nietzsche concluded, to follow the Jews' example and to 'proclaim oneself simply a good European and actively work for the amalgamation of nations'.[9]

PG Very interesting: justice done by Nietzsche to an indeed remarkable people. What ironies, though, in respect of Nazi appropriations of Overman! But also in relation to modern Israel, which de Gaulle – who had read his Nietzsche – described at the time of the Six Day War as

CONCLUSION

'an elite people, self-assured and dominating'. I even have a Palestinian colleague who thinks *his* people have 'drawn the shortest straw in history', because they are wrestling not so much with the State of Israel, but with the giant shadow of Western guilt about the Jews...

But 'sacrificial slaughter' must be some sort of cue to bring in René Girard. Hope in Girard has to do with Moltmann's 'abyss'. It's about recognizing and tackling the shadow side of the human psyche, individual and collective: so we're talking 'redemption' again, but this time in anthropological, not in theological categories. Violence is always linked to 'religion', yes – but what does Girard mean by 'religion'? He means, in a thousand disguised forms, ancient and modern, the sacralizing tendencies of the deep psyche of desire – the *archaic sacred* in all of us. That's singular: Girard is saying religion in *this* sense isn't something woefully superimposed on sound pagan nature by Jewish and Christian culture (as post-Enlightenment optimism fondly imagines when it indicts fanaticism and sectarianism as 'religious'): it's natural, primary, in some sense 'always-already-there' – co-extensive with culture, and, really, *at the root of all cultures*. You could say, on his theory, that it's the commonest common denominator in anyone's Common Era. That's because mimetic desire is everywhere; and, consequently, violence also. Emissary victimization – scapegoating – is the age-old common way of dealing with mimetic desire and the socially destructive violence it breeds.

The developmental model of the origin of religions which Girard offers (and he told us his theory links increasingly now to current biological-evolutionary thinking) is that the blow-which-kills also *divinizes* this dark force or 'god': men sacralize the victim, by whom, apparently, is purged or exorcized the impending crisis of competing and conflicting desires within the social group – thus relieving *them* of responsibility and allowing them to be 'innocent'. That's how religion comes to be the basis of civilization; and that's why civilization, founded on a 'divinely sanctioned morality' is always, in the ultimate, based spiritually and ethically on a *deep-seated conspiracy of evasion*. We divinize what establishes or restores order, morality, civilization – thereby *discharging us*, apparently, of the real problem – *which is ourselves* (our own mimetic desire, our own propensity to violence, our own sacralizing of both, hence our own scapegoating). Until the crisis recurs. And that's true everywhere, in all common eras, until you get to the Judaeo-Christian scriptures...

So Girard does give, in non-theological terms, from the direction of cultural anthropology, a real sense – albeit, as he would be the first to say, a partial one – of what's particular and original in the

CONCLUSION

Judaeo-Christian tradition. Given that the crucifixion of Jesus is seen to realize in *perfectly inverse symmetry* the figure of the scapegoating mechanism – the one act that designates it *as such* and blows the gaff *in principle and forever* – Girard really is offering to explain what's special in the start-date of *our* Common Era. From that point, a new sort of community, a new sort of hope is open and possible . . .

NR Is he saying our society is an exception? 'In all cultures except our own there are references to violent human sacrifice or substitutionary animal sacrifice.' Really?

PG In the context of his chapter, he means that, in the Common Era, we have begun not to use the mechanism of sacrifice (i.e. in its literal, overt, archaic form) as a way of releasing the socially destructive tensions of mimetic desire. And, yes, that is one of the effects – among others – of the novelty in manners and morals which, gradually and imperfectly, did begin to spread thanks to the cultural ascendancy of Christianity. That's perhaps worth saying: our postmodern mind-set tends to sweep this sort of progress grandly away, and concentrate instead, with lynx-eyed suspicion, on what Christianized Europe didn't do, or did imperfectly and 'too late' for our taste – not to mention the particular evils it introduced, and its particular hypocrisies . . . No doubt there's room enough for that! Girard certainly thinks that the old thrusts of the archaic sacred, the old temptations of mimetic desire and emissary victimization are *all still there* underneath our faith-culture – *and* our post-Enlightenment rationality *and* our 'postmodern' Western liberalism! Those are the archaic *eruptions* we all fear and exorcize still. Our own 'politically correct' culture, he says, has the dubious honour of being the first to 'scapegoat scapegoaters'. And, yes, of course they can happen *also* in culturally Christianized Europe; that's what crusades and religious wars and witch-burnings and pogroms are all about. They can even erupt, locally, in the church itself (anathemas, persecutions, inquisitions). And in Christian theology itself – think of certain 'penal' and 'substitutionary' theories of the atonement!

Of course, we're all very good at sitting in the great armchair of historical judgment. We're bound to be on Girard's theory. But the armchair wouldn't be there for us to sit in if there had been no progress, no refinement of conscience, no new norms set . . .

David Archard How does Girard think of progress?

CONCLUSION

PG He's often not tender to post-Enlightenment moral optimism in the manner of Rousseau. *Candide* too is a no-no (although he's convinced that the defender of Calas[10] grasped more of true Christianity than its established interpreters and defenders!). But, in his seminar, he is quite forthcoming on progress actually realized in the Common Era. He responds to the question: 'Evil is ever-present; violence and scapegoating are still in evidence now. Yet you said we had a better society now?'

René Girard Well, it's easy enough to show that we are 'worse' – we kill more people now. But we also save more. The hospitals of Paris and London – the hospital as house of God, the notion of care of the sick without identification papers – that's an invention of the Christian Middle Ages (even if the idea of hospitalization as such goes back to Hippocrates). The idea of recognizing all men, rather than one's actual group or tribe only – is a direct inspiration of Christianity. This also has wider, more ambiguous effects, both good and bad: the ability to take care of people enables the concentration of a labour force – hence, the modern technical transformation of the world, which really begins in the Middle Ages – with the cathedrals, actually (even if the Egyptians built pyramids, the Romans aqueducts, the Incas temples and the Chinese walls). A similar influence is at work in the creation of a one-world culture. Today, it's not 'politically correct' to say we are unique, it's considered ' mean' to other cultures. But I think we are so obviously unique that it's forbidden to say so! Ex-colonial peoples say rightly: you have been unjust to us; but they can only really say that from a Western, biblical viewpoint. Before Christianity, conquerors do whatever they want. Look at the empire of the Athenians after the Persian wars, or the Romans, or any number of oriental empires – they were much more power-led, much more cruelly exploitative.

Yes, there is an ongoing economy of violence – and it is still operative in the modern world (although we must add: firing someone unjustly isn't the same as killing them). Nevertheless, our society is certainly also more humane. The ideal of social justice is barely 200 years old as expectation, as cultural norm. Our inventions: elections – amazing! Or the notion that the world is responsible for disaster relief in Bangladesh. No doubt with a morally advantageous posture in view. But show me any previous time when nations got credit for helping each other out in the form of humanitarian assistance! We are not grateful enough for this. There is more violence than there should be – of which we are all now the spectators. But no one before talked about the world being 'violent' – they accepted that it just was! The mediaeval church first limited violence – it said with moral realism: you won't stop people fighting – but not on saints days, please; thus limiting the 'natural right' of all soldiers, the masters of the universe. Torture? – yes, of course – but it was limited. The amazing thing is that it was ever suppressed. Witchcraft? But no one sees or says that the fifteenth and early sixteenth century is the last age in Europe to have had witchcraft! All ages everywhere else have believed in witchcraft. Yes, there is a goodness unperceived, and a real singularity, in 'the modern world'.

NR But still I come back to this business of exceptionalism: the crucifixion, the start date, the direct inspiration of Christianity, etc. Is all that really justified? What about Gandhi – isn't he a paradigm of nonviolence too? 'Might is right, because God says it is' – that's the line of Muslim fundamentalists: 'Whatever might be your liberal notions of rectitude, we know what must be right because it's in the Qu'ran.' You must see this is crucial for the time of global encounter, multi-faiths and plural values . . . Isn't Christian particularity in this context actually offensive, scandalous?

PG Well, yes . . . and no . . . It depends whether or not we're talking about a particularity so radical, so comprehensive in kind, that – paradoxically – it can be one of open inclusion, potentially all-inclusive. Are we looking at a particularized *cultural* identity, merely? Or, somewhere beneath that, very frequently obscured by it, at a transcultural sketch of human identity *as such*? That's really the question. Girard said a good deal about the Christian particular, and its 'scandal', in his seminar. I'd better let him explain himself in a series of extracts. He wasn't here directly envisaging the context you mention, but still . . . see how far you think he answers you:

> **RG** *Skandalon*: from limping (in Greek) and stumbling-block (in Hebrew). It's often abysmally translated in modern bibles by euphemistic expressions which really disintegrate the word ('occasion of sin' etc.). Translators see some kind of

CONCLUSION

sexual symbolism in it; but I think they're wrong. The essence of the thing is this: it's the stone against which, the more you stumble, the more you want to stumble; it's what attracts at the same time as it repels. What is meant is that the mimetic rivals desire the same thing – and run into each other – the more they desire the same 'goods' – and the more mimetically they desire them – so the more they run into each other; there's a demonic thing which both horrifies and draws you on. Shakespeare knows this mechanism (e.g. Valentine and Proteus in *Two Gentlemen of Verona*). The more they run into the obstacle, the more they desire the object and wish to deprive the rival of it. So the best friends in the world can become the worst enemies: it's a super-Shakespearean theme. I think this is the *skandalon*. You're caught in a vicious circle and can't get out of it; and it moves towards death. All ambiguous aspects of mimetic desire, I would say, are to be referred to the *skandalon*, and not to Freud. Freud will bring in castrating Oedipal fathers etc., not seeing that families are the only places you *can* brag of your success without fear of this reaction of mimetic rivalry.

The crisis of mimetic rivalry is everywhere; it's the mainstay of the human situation. It's not present in animals [in the sense that animals have needs and appetites, but not desires, so that their conflicts are limited – Ed.]. And it describes what leads to the crucifixion. The devil and the *skandalon* are pretty much the same thing. Jesus even says to Peter: 'Get thou behind me, Satan' – 'move behind me, because you are the obstacle in front of me'. 'You're the devil because you are a *skandalon* to me; your thought is that of man, not of God.' The *skandalon* can be the thought of man, too, you see [. . .] Think, if you like, of Satan as the subject of the structure (Lacan's term) – of the bad mimetic structure functioning in spite of ourselves.

The killing of Christ was a very ordinary thing – but with a difference. [. . .] Jesus is precisely not a mimetic rival; he comes 'from above', to enable human beings to change their lives, and give up their violent ways; and this is the offer of the kingdom of God. I think this is clear in Matthew. The gospel is: 'do not retaliate', for that is merely vengeance. Remember: you can see the 'natural' idea of the 'divinity' of violence in the fact that it does not end with a generation; it's something transcending space and time. But men reject this call; at which point, they go back to the scapegoat, and they don't have to choose one, since they have before them the man who has challenged the system – in theological terms, the kingdom of Satan i.e. of violence and sacralized power. Satan is portrayed as seducer and adversary. He is the obstacle, the *skandalon* which keeps attracting as it repels. [. . .] Jesus says to his disciples: even you will be scandalized by me, i.e. happy are those who will not take Satan's part (as Peter does), who will not participate in the Passion and will realize I'm here to establish peace and nothing else. 'Satan' has very specific reason to go after the scapegoat who has challenged the system. [. . .]

And yet, the crucifixion is the work of the Paraclete, the Holy Spirit: in Greek, the lawyer for the defence, the advocate for the victims: it reveals the innocence of Jesus – and the relative innocence of all other emissary victims. It shows the mythic accounts of violence presenting the scapegoat as guilty are not to be believed, are untrue. That's why I see the bible, and Judaeo-Christianity as a whole – as the most radical critique imaginable of mythology and of religion. [. . .]

Q And yet this death is still a 'sacrifice' as defined by the institutional church?

RG I'm not speaking anti-theologically here; not against theologies derived from the first seven ecumenical councils of the church. The way I spoke about sacrifice in my early works derived from the fact that my approach from anthropology naturally designated 'sacrifice' as an act of violence appeasing the community. I began from the Alpha; but in good biblical logic, we should start from the Omega. In a text in German, I have 'recanted my errors' on the word 'sacrifice'[11] [. . .]

Now, I would even say: sacrifice (in its new, Judaeo-Christian acceptance) is part of the relation of God to us: part of human reality. Death itself has a purpose – God could make himself known to us only through-and-beyond death. I'd be inclined to reject many naturalistic views of the incorporation of the entire universe into schemes of death and rebirth, even if life-out-of-death does work pretty well all over the place. [. . .] But I do see a genuine cosmic inclusive-

CONCLUSION

ness in the gospel: the 'Lamb slain from the foundation of the world', the 'grain of wheat' that has to die that there may be life for the whole world. That's part of the structure of God's relation to us, you see. The Creator withdraws into himself, dies to himself, that the world may live autonomously. Biologists show this; they say – half-jokingly – that they are doing natural theology . . .

Q Isn't the very singular 'sacrifice' of the gospels an activity, indeed a 'work'? Jesus isn't passive. 'I lay down my life'.[12] Nobody takes it from me.

RG Yes, especially in John. 'He came unto his own and his own did not receive him.' 'The light shines on in the darkness and the darkness did not comprehend it . . .'[13] And here's the difference from the Greek *logos*, with which the Christian particular has been massively confused in the West: the function of this 'work' is to expel the expulsion of God, which makes it impossible for Him to be here with us. Heidegger, who claimed the Greek *logos* for his own neo-paganism, already said the two forms of *logos* have nothing to do with each other. The Greek *logos* keeps opposites together 'with violence'; it is a form of violence. Of course, Christ is seen by Heidegger only as a messenger. Yet Heidegger, in his own way, does end the confusion which, in my view – I say this tentatively – is the great mistake of Christian theology (though it's not too present in the first seven councils of the church) – taking on board too much of the concepts and logic of Greek thought, and neglecting the logic specific to the bible. So, really, I'm not a gnostic, as French theologians, reacting to my early books, imagined.

The Father and the Son know that the Son will run into this death. The crucifixion is inevitable. The Son goes voluntarily. But, as a human being, he doesn't want to die; and does his best to persuade people. His action is designed to persuade men to choose. The question isn't posed to them radically before Gethsemane. The active nature of the 'sacrifice', the concept of voluntary self-sacrifice – there's the deep discontinuity with the archaic-mythic tradition of sacrifice. [. . .]

Few churches today think of this 'sacrifice' in terms of an expiation made to a wrathful God. God is separate, apart from this world, because man doesn't understand and God couldn't 'explain'! Throughout the bible, He attempts to explain – but men still don't understand. [. . .] Hence the death of Jesus. That's the beginning of the dismantling of a world patterned by archaic religion and built ultimately on violence. It's extremely slow; after 2000 years, we're perhaps just beginning to get there. Jesus gives thanks that this thing is shown to the non-wise, the children. Conceptually, of course, we're hard put to say what the crucifixion does. [. . .] Anselm, for instance: the Father, conceived as a super-Man, demands expiation from a pure Victim. Much better say: Satan is 'duped' by the cross (as St Paul does in Corinthians): 'If the Powers, the kings of this world, had known, they would not have crucified the King of Glory',[14] since this puts an end to their power, built ultimately on the founding murder. The emissary transaction, designated as such, *no longer works*. Pilate expects it will, and at first it does (he avoids a riot); but finally, and in the ultimate, it brings the death of our conspiracy of evasion, and of this disorder itself.

But, careful: not without struggle and division. In the Synoptics, the question is asked: does the Christ come to bring peace? No – 'I am come to bring a sword'. This 'apocalyptic' motif is sometimes said to be absent in John – but look at the omnipresent theme of clash and division – 'and the Jews were divided'. Look also at the ending of this gospel, which is to be read more 'apocalyptically' than most people do. Instead of uniting, rebuilding the national culture, this new fact divides, divides, divides. 'Division' is not a catastrophe providing – this is an awesome proviso, little heeded, little met, easily travestied – it's a sign the Kingdom is on its way.

The modern objection is often: 'This religion promised us peace, but we didn't get harmony and world peace out of Christianity. We are entitled to peace.' I say: 'Have you ever read the gospels?' But they haven't: they have ready-made objections which are used automatically instead.

NR I'm not objecting, necessarily; but I find it difficult to enter into this particular radicality, and to accept this point of absolute reference. I would begin to approach the problem of harmonizing conflicting 'identities' of culture, civilization and faith, and of bringing peace, from a quite different direction – in terms of the 'ironism', which Richard Rorty considers as characteristic of liberal democracy.

Rorty describes ironism as 'a reaction against the absoluteness of final vocabularies'; and ironists as those who recognize the relativity of their own consciences, their most central values, beliefs and desires. Ironists recognize that the vocabulary in which they state their highest hopes does not refer to a reality beyond the reach of time and chance: that today's truth was yesterday's heresy and will be tomorrow's superstition. And yet, Rorty goes on to say, recognition of this contingency would be his definition of freedom. Furthermore, such recognition is the chief virtue of which the members of a liberal society can boast; the major aim of liberal society may be the substitution of contingency for what Isaiah Berlin identified as the barbarism, the 'moral and political immaturity', of absolutism.[15]

Ironism is also the key to liberal societies; for here are social groupings recognized as ideological constructs. However much communities may present an essential (and essentialized) singular face to the outside world – and to themselves – they are nonetheless composed of and constituted by a multiplicity of individuals who work to accommodate their diverse meanings and motivations in the form of common symbols and equivalent behaviours. The social commentator should not confuse the rhetoric of metaphysical homogeneity with the reality of individual diversity – any more than should community members themselves.

Within the *ironism* of a liberal democracy, communities are 'safe' for individuals because here people may make and inhabit such social groupings (ethnic, religious, local, occupational) as they wish while at the same time recognizing their constructed, ideological nature: the contingency of community identity. The community in a liberal society does not value itself, its culture, over and above the lives of its individual members; the 'liberal community' is an ironic community which ultimately denies itself. Rorty would claim an awareness of such a liberal society to be of global appropriateness, and argue that the idea of such a state should be globally advocated and vindicated . . .

DA There's a very simple meliorist view of history: human nature is improving – look how much better we are than we were 100, 200 years ago, etc. That seems to me a very weak version of the meliorist position. There's a much stronger version: history has unity, an end – teleology. Hope can be grounded in the weaker or the stronger version. In the stronger version, history reveals itself to us. It's interesting that in all the chapters, the strong view has its source and analogue in Judaeo-Christian eschatology: the idea of humankind fulfilling its created purpose. If that actually goes – disappears – it's

CONCLUSION

harder to see how you have the resources for that vision, which was certainly there in the nineteenth century.

PG If we follow Moltmann's 'take' on what you call the 'analogy', the thrust of post-Renaissance thought – of the whole period dominated by an increasingly anthropocentric Western humanism – is to offprint from Judaeo-Christian eschatology a series of appropriated 'absolutes' imported into, and exclusively relocated within, history. The great nineteenth-century idealisms and spiritualisms are the epitome of that process at work. Michelet's *History of France* (for instance): the entire work is a transposed theological epic. 'Humanity had to recognize Christ in itself, become aware in itself of the perpetuity of the incarnation and the passion.'[16] The Revolution is the new revelation. 'God' has his 'second epoch', now secular and without mediation. The new incarnation of the divine is . . . France! In the name of humanity, she takes up the challenge of realizing this telos in history. (John Gray speaks in similar vein of the Enlightenment ideal of universal emancipation as 'a mystical theodicy, emptied of its transcendental content and turned into a doctrine of secular salvation'.)

The result is that 'history' becomes swollen with all the absolutes, all the horizontal projections of transcendence, which are imported into it. The line of Michelet's ideological narrativization of the Common Era, though it didn't mean to – it intended to be the all-inclusive, universal projection of liberty, equality, fraternity – led pretty directly to the rise of competing imperial nationalisms and the First World War . . . From transcendence appropriated and reinvested in the here-and-now comes a new principle and dimension of violence . . . It's something which has always challenged the admirable invention of liberal democracy . . . and, surely, ironized its ironists!

TH Yes, Moltmann jumps heavily on the idea of progress for just that sort of reason. But there's an ambiguity, too. He will say happily, with Girard, that the ideals that sprang out of the Enlightenment were in themselves no bad thing. Postmodern reaction to the Enlightenment is misplaced, because these are not bad things to hope for in human life. The problem he sees is that when you divorce the moral ideals and the hopes from the transcendent basis, you collapse the metaphysical basis for hope down into the historical process, and then you end up with no resources to realize the hopes; then you end up with disillusion, despair and . . . Nietzsche, i.e. the overbid of the Overman. Meanwhile, as our Western societies register the shock of huge political, social, economic and technical change, we (in

CONCLUSION

Europe anyway) come to doubt the overbid. Meanwhile, the mighty deconstruction-machine of twentieth-century critical reflexivity dissects the entire inheritance of the Common Era, so that you end up with a kind of fragmentation and polarization: lots of micro-hopings proper to groups and interests and 'communities', but no bonding hope which is truly common and genuinely communal.

Thiselton, too, makes a good, complementary point here: fragmentary and plural value systems characterize the ancient world, in which Christianity took its rise, just as much as the late twentieth-century value-pluralist society. In the latter case, a function of the collapse of universality, of a common frame of self-understanding, of project – and of hope.

NR I thought that was a very interesting point of Thiselton's. But I'd like to put a question to you on the 'radical interruption' in Moltmann: that's our hope, he says, but at the same time we've got to like or appreciate or respect the present world as it stands?

TH For Moltmann, there is a sort of other-wordliness which is inappropriate, certainly. 'It doesn't matter what we do in this world, we can let it go its own way, because sooner or later we're going be out of it.' A 'pie in the sky by and by' type of view. Other people, the ecosystem, they are, on that view of things, just part of the transience of history. His view is 'other-worldly' in a different sense: he sees the source of transformation as coming from 'outside' or 'above'. He sees the resources for transformation as coming, in terms of temporal sequence, 'from the future' (i.e. as distinct from a potential for the future coming from the accumulated events of the past). It's actually from outside that this potential comes, from the God who draws us into the future. The other key point to see is what and whom he's drawing into this future It's us, it's history as process. He actually wants to say that the whole of history will, in some sense, be taken up in this 'new creation', and not just that which happens to find itself at the temporal 'end' of history.

One of the problems with certain utopian notions of progress, clearly, is that lots of eggs get broken to make the omelette. That's fine for those who happen to be there for the omelette – good for them! But what about us, and what about the victims? What Moltmann is saying is that the whole of the historical process, all that is good and worthwhile in it, will actually be restored to the fullness of its created potential, raised up in its 'newness'. The Marxist E. Bloch was attracted by the transmigration of souls, you know, precisely because he thought it would be unfair if all the people who had died were not there in this Marxist utopia – so everyone ought to be able to pass from one existence to another in order to get there. With Moltmann, all that is good in this world will be taken up and redeemed in the 'utopia'. That means that there's an intrinsic connection between the here-and-now and that future. The good in this world is the paradigm for our imagining of the future that is to come. But there is also a discontinuity: it relates to all that should be shunned, and got rid of – and which indeed passes away. So that for Moltmann we are called to live respectfully towards other people and towards the created world because it's this world that is the focus of God's promise; it's the stuff out of which the new creation will be generated . . .

NR But presumably, this world is also his creation? So irrespective of the discontinuity, this interruption, it could be said that there's an overriding continuity because this is God's creation, that's going be God's creation; there's not going to be a radical reinvention insomuch as all the good stuff from this world is going to be there?

TH Something of it is going to be there in some sense, certainly. This is where Moltmann relies heavily on the logic of metaphor and analogy. He's not saying everything in this world as we know it will be there . . .

NR 'Souls', I suppose?

TH I suspect Moltmann might prefer the term 'persons' to 'souls'. We certainly shouldn't exclude physicality. All the things which in this world we place value on, which God places value on, will in some analagous version, be there. There are also things about this world that will not be there; that's the point about the logic of hope. An eternal validation of misery and suffering and hatred – that wouldn't be much to hope for. So something is going to be absent – but that which is good will be taken up and, in some sense, be present, even though we can't know in what form it will be present. Now that means there's a very strong validation for the claim that hope provides us not only with an ethical imperative but also a pattern by which to live. Even if we can only express it in positive and negative metaphors such as: 'there will be no suffering, no war, no injustice'; 'life in all its fullness', 'weapons reforged into the instruments of stable and harmonious community'. What we believe about what will be the case in the future at least gives us some paradigm for ways of

CONCLUSION

living and acting in the present. So we should live as if we were *already* citizens of this world in which there will be no more X, Y and Z. The patterns of our living now should reflect what we imagine will be the case. The logic of imagination is vital at this point – we can't *know*; but neither are we 'agnostic' about the matter.

NR And why does he think all this?

TH Well, that's his interpretation of what the bible teaches us about God, basically. In dialogue with modern thought forms, modern concerns . . . But it is always-already-there in the 'live', recreating matrix of Judaeo-Christian revelation. There is a given story to be told about God's dealings with the world . . .

PG In a '2000 year' perspective, you could even do some more imagining and envision the Common Era itself as the ordinary *cultural-historical time* in which we 'don't know' in the ultimate, but in which that sort of hoping has 'come to the ears of humankind' as a datum present and abroad: to be responded to. It's the era 'interrupted' – interpenetrated, mobilized, energized – by *another duration*, an inner time which carries us forward or draws us on, transforming the quality of being of the common, historical-cultural time etc. Very variably so, of course, with complex local and global relativities of cultural acceptance, ethical embodiment and social effect: mediaeval Europe's 'Christendom' being one such (not necessarily privileged), our own contemporary 'rump-of-organized-religion', liberal value-pluralist thing being another (not necessarily disgraced). If God is even-handed, I suspect that all ages of human (cultural-historical) time at least start, in some sense, equidistant from, or equi-proximate to, this coming future. 'Future', of course, in relation to *our* historicity only . . . That's of course the last anthropocentrism our postmodernity clings to: we do insist on a stable, unequivocal, decently chronolinear, properly narrativizable 'time', even if our post-Enlightenment appropriation of transcendence can't well imagine any new 'grand narratives' capable of taking it forward.

And that *is* a problem: no story, no hold on one's own identity. Hence: no confident articulation of past and future, no basis of hope or of community. We do lack the 'assurance of things hoped for, the conviction of things not seen'.[17]

DA Secularists can't offer anything like the vision of hope that's available in a theological perspective. We can't reconcile the past, there's no reconciliation for those who are its victims... the detritus left behind – the secularist has got to think that it's just *tough* on those people. But all those who have complained about this thought they were standing in a twilight, that the owl of Minerva was about to fly away anyway...

PG John Gray is certainly putting a heavy caution on the idea that liberal humanism can for long be travelling companion to a transcendentally inspired hope such as you find in Judaeo-Christian tradition. His is the argument of the 'excluded third', isn't it? If Christian belief declines, liberal humanism, declaring its unacknowledged debt, will sink into insignificance; reciprocally, only Christian belief can ensure a future for Enlightenment humanism... So really, the choice is between a 'postmodern' value pluralism and a renewed Christian belief...

DA Gray certainly feels he's breaking with the Enlightenment project as well as with Christianity. But the Enlightenment is still going to be the one for the determined secularist: the project is that truth, justice, reason, beauty, can be pursued using only human powers. And if you believe, as Gray does, in value pluralism, then that's a direct attack on the Enlightenment project. He doesn't think there is a single answer to the question what is good, what is true, what is beautiful. It's hard, from that point on, to see how value pluralism comes up with any basis for common hope as distinct from a tolerant and tolerable co-existence of a tenuous kind.

NR Well, I've referred to Richard Rorty; and he's no twilight owl. Nor, I must say, does tolerable co-existence sound to me such a bad deal. It just needs a framework for managing diversity in the here-and-now, which liberal democracy supplies.

In his essay 'On Ethnocentrism' (1986),[18] Rorty explains the *global appropriateness* of liberal democracy and says how his claim can be distinguished from the project of the religious missionary. He describes the society of liberal democracy as having a certain characteristic form: legal-constitutional procedures underlying substantive beliefs. Here is a meeting of a diversity of individuals and communities, world-views, values and traditions, under the aegis of universalistic procedural rules – but without insistence on a necessarily closer substantive meeting than this. It's a procedural umbrella, under which a veritable bazaar of private diversity may maintain itself and flourish; it offers a universalistic procedural justice and a compromise: a

CONCLUSION

curtailing of the final end of absolute liberty of each individual and each social grouping so as to make room for that of others.

It's also a curtailing of expectations concerning the everyday reach of *deep understanding* (outwith the procedural) or *love*. It accepts that while justice must be the public face of the polity, love might remain something of a private face only: a compromise which allows for a societal synthesis while championing freedom of conscience. There's a firm distinction between public and private.

The procedures over which a liberal polity calls for consensus, and which a liberal polity would advocate other parts of the world adopting, are also procedural, entailing little substantive agreement: value pluralism within a procedural environment which makes institutional but not substantive assumptions of a meeting of difference. On this basis, liberal beliefs are *morally exportable*: worth pinning one's highest hopes to, worth fighting for. Even though today's liberals may possess a 'postmodern', ironic attitude to all beliefs – including their own – they recognize their contingency, recognize that liberal beliefs pertain to no 'necessary rationality', no 'absolute truth', and recognize that these beliefs are recent, local and unusual Western cultural developments, the manifestation of one particular form of life, which most other cultures, past and present, might abhor – still they believe that practically they provide 'the best hope for the species'.[19]

So liberals are prepared to assert their superiority in a language they recognize inevitably to be a situated human creation, in terms of arguments which are circular and by reference to standards which are relative. They are prepared to accept, as Rorty puts it, that 'in the process of arranging things so that relatively fewer people get hurt', some will get hurt – Nazis, religious fundamentalists, cultural traditionalists.[20] The way to substantive diversity passes through a procedural singularity – even an overweening one.

PG Hmm! Two cheers for overweening liberal democacy! Three, if 'we', the collective subject of the system 'liberal democracy', can genuinely and in fact avoid picking up the nineteenth-century mantle of revolutionary – and 'missionary'! – France (*inter alios*) i.e. the temptation of 'transcendence from below', and of 'hegemony by the back door'. That would be a genuine historical first, though, wouldn't it?

It seems to me also that culture is something that transcends – and *links* – your public and private spheres, which the sociologist and the political theorist, each for his or her own special purposes, are anxious to disjoin; and the same is true, more radically, of time. Collective *identities* do involve both *culture* and *time*, don't they?

CONCLUSION

And there's a deeper issue still. Of the different authors in this volume, it does seem that all except our American-based contributors, Richard Schacht and perhaps the Comaroffs, have an acute sense that it is the Enlightenment project that is truly in crisis. Gray, who assuredly holds no candle for Christianity, speaks of a contemporary wake for a now deceased Enlightenment. Schacht disagrees: he's the interesting exception (just as he was in that entertaining account of his formative years, but here in a different sense). He does believe implicitly that this project is fully sustainable as a linear projection. The fount and origin is Hume (who takes us out of the God-shadows). The articulating hinge-to-the-future is Nietzsche (who redefines the problem of identity as that of the self-configuring potential of creative moral will). And the future is a new phase of evolutionary psychobiology in dialogue with the human sciences ... Out of knowledge, control. Progress without shadow, really. It's that almost Comtian 'narrativization' which, as Gray points out acutely, is the mind-set which still, perceived or unperceived, subtends most secularisms.[21]

For Schacht, the Common Era is henceforth truly *post-Christian* (as opposed to being merely *post-Christendom*), having genuinely and legitimately sloughed off its contingent Judaeo-Christian matrix. But I do wonder whether this certitude isn't due to a deficient identification of the matrix itself. 'The Christian view of human nature', he says briefly, is 'either Platonic or Aristotelian, according to the philosophical model borrowed.' That's certainly harmonic with Nietzsche, who thought of the new religion as founding the common era upon a hellenized Judaism, i.e. on the foundation of a theistic idealism underwriting a slave morality. The matrix, on this account, has no original specificity of its own beyond the delusory wish holding these disparates together ...

I guess 'God is dead' is a literally true, fully realized proposition in Schacht. It doesn't rate discussion, really. One can almost hear Girard murmuring 'vulgar atheism': the idea that God dies of senescence.[22] What about the true and awesome Nietzschean 'we have killed him'? The violence, the torment, of the prophetic madman who proclaims this – and of Nietzsche himself? To my ear, Schacht sounds like a robustly self-confident, sanitized, democratic New World transposition of this awesome European prophet and of his flaming indictment of European decadence.

My basic question, I suppose. would be: is the future of Hume and Nietzsche *enough of a future*? Enough, let's say, to rethink *in hope* a post-September 11 world?

CONCLUSION

NR I agree that Nietzsche is awesome, prophetic. But he's always tied to the negative side of the twentieth century. Unfairly, I think. Another way of looking at him is to say the twentieth century shows precisely the kind of freedom Nieztsche said that we had: the Nazi Revolution, the Soviet Revolution, the Velvet Revolution – and, yes, the terrible and apocalyptic 11 September. Not good things, terrible things – but exemplifying the radicality of the human imagination. Scientific advance rewrites the possibilities of our culture and civilization; but it isn't always put in the hands of good men. Freedom means risk. There's always a dialectic going on of scientific and technological advance and the way we frame it philosophically and limit or direct it socially.

PG You're saying systems need moral subjects . . . and that the problem is indeed ourselves. But the sources and the resources of those subjects? The reach-in-hope of this value-framing and directing? How are they to be *shared* in a pluri-faith, multicultural world with every possible sort of disparity and difference, including those of culturally transmitted value-programming? What hope of fully human, fully inclusive community out of these? Except as a function of what Gray calls 'the Christian inheritance to the Enlightenment': hope of salvation belonging to all humans; the salvation of the species being worked out in history (if not *within* history).

NR What's wonderful about Nietzsche is the notion of the Overman and of the constant rewriting of the self. The revaluation of values and the possibility of the *individual* doing that from an existential standpoint. He's a prophetic ex-Protestant. If the pattern works for the individual, why not for the collective which is an aggregation of individuals?

DA But with Nietzsche, you're talking about the radical *impossibility* of morality. Hume thinks that morality is possible in the absence of God. That's his greatness. He has a straight post-Enlightenment rationalistic, materialistic, scientistic view of the possibility of morality, and within that, of shared values. Nietzsche is the most radical critic of the possibility of shared values, shared morality. I really don't see how the future can be *both* Hume and Nietzsche.

NR Well, Nietzsche also says it's important to set the conditions within which a certain kind of Overman can be inculcated. That Overman must be nourished and protected. That's an ethical and social vision. There isn't a type of person all should become. We must provide the conditions whereby you can 'become yourself', fulfil yourself. It's the ethical impulse in its pure creativity, liberated from that deforming and restrictively coded set of inferior values that Nietzsche called decadent . . . Religion, Judaeo-Christianity, for Nietzsche, is slave morality; it's a binding, not a bonding . . . Isn't that true of other religions too? Doesn't he sketch the form of a universal future which is imaginable, both scientific and spiritually free? I'd recall Shacht here: the next evolutionary phase . . .

DA That may or may not be right as a narrative of the past. But it's not a vision for the future which present humanity can easily share *qua* humanity.

NR Hmm . . . what about Ricœur?

PG He doesn't address the question of hope directly, of course. *Rigueur et pudeur*: he's not a thinker who allows personal convictions to wander lightly into professional texts – it's the absolute condition of his mastery in his particular field. He even set aside from his book *Soi-même comme un autre* the last two lectures of the original Gifford Lecture series, the ones treating his theme of selfhood and otherness in the Judaeo-Christian scriptures. The postscript of his present text is actually a generous concession to our project.

His key insight is perhaps that there is a fundamental crisis of both historiography and of memory which is crucial to how we tell the CE story from now on. It turns on a hermeneutic choice offered to us. Historians who invoke, in a vein of postmodern relativism, a Saussurian model of the arbitrary relation of signifier and signified in the verbal sign – a model producing, at its extreme point, in the French-Jewish deconstructionist Derrida, an infinite play of non-referential signs – are impotent to refute negationism about the Holocaust, i.e. impotent to have any grip whatever on history-in-the-making. Is there any exit from this postmodern palace of mirrors? What models are there of the – imperfect, ever-rewritten – *correspondence* of memory, and of history-writing, to a *truth* of things in respect of the past? The hermeneutic problem raises a strategic crisis of self-understanding – which in turn sends us back to the foundational perspectives of the Common Era.

Ricœur said in his remarkable seminar: 'I keep being surprised by the misuse of the so-called Saussurian model. It concerns only the realm of lexical signs (*langue*) and not at all that of discourse (*parole*). Nobody can ignore this more accurate reading if they read the whole

CONCLUSION

of Saussure. As to the use of the term "postmodern" as describing a new era, I take it as a dubious "philosophy of history".'

Other seminar answers of his are also highly relevant to our debate. He first answers the question from Professor Daphne Hampson of our School of Divinity: 'Aren't the ancient sources of our culture hopelessly archaic? Why should biblical positions be relevant to us now?'

> **Paul Ricœur** When the bible is relegated to the past, a break is introduced into the living tradition of collective memory, and into the writing of history. The social bond is also profoundly modified – there is no longer what Northrop Frye called a 'common code'[23] for imaginative self-representation (although I would point out that Frye himself, in our conversations at Chicago, seemed to me to understand the bible merely as a play of the imaginary . . .)

> **Daphne Hampson** Don't you actually underestimate the break in culture represented by modernity and postmodernity? We cannot simply return to Plato, surely, still less to Judaeo-Christianity? Isn't it time to think anew?

> **PR** It is still possible to return to these sources, because they are still eminently capable of structuring our imaginary self-representation, modelling our paradigms of self-understanding: our memory, our promising, our hoping . . . Our cultural situation is that of people returning to these texts from the outside, without being committed to them. But read the bible just like a Buddhist text, if you like – you can't help noticing its originality, its sheer contemporary pertinence. One of the great services rendered by René Girard is to have shown that. Judaism, then more decisively, Christianity, steps outside the narrative of archaic religion, introduces a break: 'Nobody takes my life' – ' I give it up' . . . Girard makes an opening, by showing non-believers in a non-religious language the pertinence of the Jewish-Christian paradigm – and that we are all champions of the sacrificial system of 'archaic' religion . . . Hostility towards Girard's theses corresponds often to a secularist vulnerability or defensiveness here . . .

> **DH** But the Judaeo-Christian tradition deals with male solutions to male problems, doesn't it – aren't we moving beyond all that?

CONCLUSION

PR Well, certainly, the Oedipus complex is going out of fashion now as a model, having dominated intellectual debate in three or four decades of the middle-late twentieth century. (Anyway, it isn't Oedipus who's guilty – but his father . . .)[24] In that sense we're moving on. But our current neurosis is one of depression, of abandonment. Melancholy isn't just a psychiatric disease, though. In Lacan's language, it bears an effigy of the 'lost object of desire'. Our memory is unfinished, unachieved. What Christianity brings first of all – even before hope – is a reconciliation in respect of our loss. Think, by way of analogy and of contrast, of the lost body of the risen Jesus ('They have taken my Lord away, and I know not where they have laid him').[25] The dilemma of the disciples, as we read it, is: how to be reconciled to a living friend no longer physically with them (*'mais je m'avance, peut-être?'*). The quest or search in memory, for memory, for what to remember, rejoins the problematic of desire – and of the sources of courage and of hope, which are not sexually oriented or limited as the concern for 'gender' tries to claim. Why are we interested in the past? Because of the lost object: there is the intuition of a promise not kept, of a potential to be fulfilled. Cf. the obsession of our time with infancy, childhood, going back to the Romantics, really – this refers to a promise associated with life itself and with birth – and it reacts to the other great preoccupation of our time with a being-towards-death (Heidegger). So that to remember is to seek to give a content to our hope. If we dream of utopias – if we keep dreaming of them – it's because, in the past, the hope didn't happen . . .

Q Is there a positive function of forgetting?

PR Yes. Sometimes forgetting is a blessing: it preserves us from the hell of total recall. We need to drop things in order to keep things, and, especially, in order to create an identity-forming story-line. We must select in order to write history. We recognize all traces can be rubbed out. And yet: where do the rules of a once-learned, but now forgotten, foreign language go to? Are they lost? No, modern psychology shows they are simply unavailable. So forgetting has the double function of destruction and of preservation. Bergson speaks of *la durée* – the silent inner constitution of the treasure of our own identity at the level of our unconscious (memory is unconscious, fundamentally – is, perhaps, the unconscious?). The existential dimension of our past is there; we are under its protection and it can be recovered.

What we expect and hope for isn't repetition, but something new. The past cannot and should not be repeated. But we have the haunting notion of a paradise lost – or the kingdom of God – we have lost something, lack something – which is our innocence.

Q To what extent can imagination be a tool helping us to move forward?

PR Indeed, it can. But we also need to introduce the word 'fantasy', deceiving imagination and its sophistry. There are *phantasmata* and there is the *eikōn*. Imagination is not more secure than memory: we can include everything unreal under the heading of imagination, as well as everything potential and possible. It's an undifferentiated concept: there is a true discourse [of imagination in the service of hope for the future – Ed.] and there is also its shadow.

PG Perhaps these thoughts explain Ricœur's approach to the Common Era at the end of his text: his insistence that we shouldn't be overimpressed by the importance of a past identity-in-culture or the correlation of cultural labels and realized identities or our ability to evaluate or even represent these variables accurately – but also his discreet assertion that the Judaeo-Christian matrix 'abides'. I asked him whether his own French word *demeure* should be translated in English 'remains' or 'abides', pointing out that there is a difference of connotation. The first is factual; the second implies a more long-lived indwelling and tends to refer the fact to its ground, while giving greater scope for interpretation – rather as the theological virtues of faith, hope and charity are said, in the AV text of Paul's Letter to the Corinthians, to 'abide'. He replied: 'of course, the latter'.

Other replies of his were also interesting in this regard.

PR Look at Exodus 3: 14: 'I AM WHO I AM' – God is unknowable as he is, ontologically; but he says to Israel, 'I will accompany you in time'. This doesn't admit a static notion of identity – as per e.g. Fichte – just the possibility of generating a history of faithfulness, of truthfulness. It allows us to search

CONCLUSION

– it raises a people of search and quest – and the possibility of making sense. The metaphysician's conception of God as intemporal essence is useless – and perhaps perilous.

Q But can't we say there is a convergence of ipse and idem in God?[26]

PR I'm not sure anthropomorphic concepts apply. There is danger of anthropocentrism. True: we speak of God's mercy, his memory, his will. But we must be cautious, especially concerning identity. We have no other access to the mystery than the promise that God will accompany us in time.

Q Isn't hope a matter of fulfilment, as well – of actual *jouissance*?[27] How does language accommodate a movement towards meaning, towards a fulfilment giving content to our hope?

PR We have a notion of fulfilment – in the negative. We know what the fulfilment of a threat is like – and of a promise too, when it doesn't happen and then does – given that the sense we make is made out of our experience.[28] That gives us a pre-understanding of something more fundamental. Fulfilment is a coincidence of meaning and event.[29]

PG The hope of the hermeneuticist ... really is hope, you know, in an age which has insistently explored to extremes – and beyond – how far we 'construct' and 'narrate' – and actually *make up entirely* – our own 'reality'! An age of the mirror: reflecting not so much on what the mind *encounters* in the real world, but on its own signs, images, representations, discourses; all hugely foregrounded in the intellectual culture of our time; and all fundamentally insecure, of uncertain reference. George Steiner asked pertinently: 'is there anything in what we say'?[30] All deconstructive theories of religion lean that way: they say in some form or other that we *merely* give ourselves the complement of our own demands; we mirror *merely* our own needs or our own desiring.

Against this background, these extracts from Paul Ricœur's seminar show pretty well what he means by the hermeneutic alternative, and how this 'this somehow ontological power of experienced subject-time at the root of cultural continuity, at the root of the cumulative character of historical experience' might relate to hope for the

CONCLUSION

task of 'renarrativizing' the Common Era, and of writing its future story differently.

Ricœur himself relates with relish the anecdote of an actual conversation of his with Jacques Derrida. Can the mind have access to truth? JD: 'Non, non, c'est *impossible!*' PR: 'Je dirais plutôt que c'est *difficile* . . .'[31] That strikes me as a brilliant recapitulation of the difference between these two French thinkers. Almost a parable for the way we ourselves go about telling the story – and writing the ongoing script – of the Common Era . . .

TH Two points strike me on the Common Era. Moltmann says: 'With increasing globalization, the Christian world became the Western world, and the Western world the modern world.' That's certainly how it feels to us from within our culture-zone and its era; but he wants to say as well: there are other worlds and other eras narrated by other peoples – and they are *different*, *Other*. It's easy to narrate it: pre-modern (up to the end of the Middle Ages), then modern (especially from the Enlightenment). The Enlightenment, while it certainly has a dialectic, love–hate relation with Christianity – but, notice, rather more with Christendom, than with Christianity – is nevertheless the child of the 'Christian' Middle Ages and of the Reformation, as much as it is an antithetical reaction to them. The pursuit of goodness, truth and beauty has its roots in Judaeo-Christian tradition – in the West anyway: I'm sure it has other roots in other traditions elsewhere. What happened was more an *immanentalizing* of the Christian story. And, quite rightly, also, the attempt to abolish Christendom as an institution. So the fact that the matrix of the Judaeo-Christian tradition 'abides' – even as culturally observable fact – ought not to be a surprise, because in a sense it never went away. In an immanentalized version, it's there through the Enlightenment and all the rest.

That's why Thiselton's chapter, unlike Gray's, seems to me as much a defence of Enlightenment ideals as it is a critical response to them. He clearly isn't in favour of the rhetorical and fragmented nature of value-pluralism. He wants to say, like Ricœur, that finally – or else we're in a mess – there has to be some basis for objectivity about truth and falsehood and evil and all the rest. For him too those things are rooted in a theological source. He certainly wants something like an Enlightenment basis for agreement and disagreement on all sorts of things – especially the lack of trust or *suspicion* that in his mind characterizes the postmodern period.

DA If you say the Enlightenment is the child of the Christian Middle

Ages, the response is going to be: 'this, however, is a child that's now grown up'. What is at the heart of the Enlightenment project is a belief in the possibility that progress lies solely within the province of humanity and its shared powers. As humans, we share a capacity in this – our – world to realize ideals; and for that we don't need anything transcendent.

TH Well, actually it's an act of miscegenation. The Enlightenment has two parents. One is Judaeo-Christian tradition. The other is rapid scientific and technical discovery, which gave a huge boost to the confidence of human beings in their ability to manipulate nature beneficently. That's proved by far the more problematic inheritance of the two, of course (as John Gray suggests). My point is: the genetic inheritance is mixed, complex.

DA Indeed. One reason some people think the Holocaust is so important – John Gray does, for instance – is that he thinks it declares the Enlightenment project to be extinguished or, at least, radically mistaken. This is a case in which the Enlightenment project rounds on itself: it characterizes a portion of humanity as less than human and uses the very tools of science and technology to exterminate it. Human reason serves the most extreme form of irrationality. That's not so far from Girard . . .

NR But that's a very different argument from that of people like Zygmunt Bauman who writes about the *modernity* of the Holocaust:[32] it's less to do with archaic eruptions *à la* Girard than the logic of modern bureaucracy which makes the personal impersonal and distanciates the Other . . .

PG What's so frightening about it, surely, is that it's *both* entirely modern *and* deeply archaic in all the ways Girard suggests – the very paradigm of emissary victimization; of the fascinated-horrified paroxysm of mimetic rivalry in 'divine' election; and of the violent, archaic sacralization of power. 'Ye shall be *as gods*' . . . when 'they' are *made vermin*. More than that: this scapegoating stands also in a deeply disturbing relation of mimetic rivalry *in the second degree*, i.e. *vis-à-vis* the more ancient anti-Jewish scapegoating not occasionally practised by Christendom. It *imitates* and *outdoes* it. That latter form too was a matter of vengeful sectarian hatred and blame-shifting – *we* are innocent, divinely elect, because *they* are uniquely guilty of the scapegoat sacrifice at the origin of *our* faith-tradition . . . Maybe there's room for everyone to see their particular part of Satan – the 'subject of the structure' – at work in the Holocaust . . .

NR When we say the Enlightenment was the rebel child of the Christian Middle Ages, one should distinguish. There's far more of the Judaeo-Christian substance in Marxism than in positivism. They're very different. The notion that things are going to get better by your own efforts is very different from the notion that we're all going to end up in one kind of heaven.

DA Yes, the Enlightenment project isn't a teleological project – it's a meliorist one – humanity has within its own capacities to progress and improve.

NR I've said I prefer Richard Rorty to John Gray on this front.[33] He does get to grips with the problem of marrying a notion of value-pluralism with the idea of a liberal state which has a regulatory system for declaring some values better than others, while not itself being substantively value-laden. I think that's a version of the Enlightenment project, because it says progress is possible, while not necessarily giving a direction to that progress. Improvement, but not defined in narrow terms. So there can be myriad kinds of improvement but still within the notion that it's within humankind's capacity to improve upon itself.

Irrespective of community traditions, quite independent of the contingencies of particular languages, individual human beings are 'equal in respect to their liability to suffering', to feel pain; and on this basis alone, 'there is something within human beings which deserves respect and protection'.[34] Truth may be lost as a criterion of value but humane behaviour remains.

TH There's a further distinction. Between 'progress' – the hope or expectation of things getting better – and 'Progress' as dogma – which says things will inevitably improve with the passage of time. Moltmann's option for rooting progress in a transcendent future rather than in an immanent process is in part that it justifies doing small-scale things, not obviously contributing to the envisaged utopia. If everything you do is done to contribute to some grand human project, then there will be little things along the way that are inherently worth doing but which you *don't* do because they're not contributing in a utilitarian sense. If we're *not* bound by this sense that we've got to *pull it off ourselves*, then the reason for doing the little things is that they're worth doing for their own sake: political acts, gestures of personal generosity, etc.

NR There's a lovely ending in George Eliot's *Middlemarch*, where Eliot describes how the goodness in Dorothea's life didn't translate into grand projects. Like millions of others she was a good person, she did honest deeds within a small canvas.

PG Yes, it is ... lovely. Now what about the Comaroffs?

NR Well, they're being purposively 'anthropological' in their paper. They're taking a non-value-laden stance. Neither hope nor lack of it: they're trying to describe a strange – or not so strange – contemporary coming together of religious forms and economic structures in their major ethnographic area, South Africa. In the same way as Weber and Marx tried to show the various kinds of relationships between economic and religious forms, and – more in Marx than Weber – to show the causal links between these and religious and cultural 'superstuctures', they are trying to explore a relation between a form of late capitalism, with its seeming magical arrival or advent through investments and non-productive means, to certain magical forms of Christian religiosity evidenced in the new churches of South Africa. What's interesting in the notion of 'millennial capitalism' is that capitalism itself becomes a religion: it's not that you have factory production, investment, etc. bearing the religious imprint of Calvinism, but that capitalism itself, in South Africa and throughout the capitalist world, becomes a religious orientation ...

PG I found that an enlightening and persuasive reading. Their final vision was haunting: the 'numinous magic of global enterprise' and the competing magics of a thousand cults born out of the despair of those who look on impotently from the outside, excluded from the enchanted circle of wealth and power ...

This is all about the interaction of the religious psyche and the economic determinants of the common culture, isn't it? Dominant cultural forms and forces, as I'm sure we would all agree, mould and inflect practices of religious belief. If we're Marxists, we say they reflect economic structures overwhelmingly, because these are what constitute the underlying model of causal reference. But even if we're not Marxists, we can still agree that the culture of an age – its ethos, ideology *and* economic structures – powerfully condition practices of belief and value, including religious ones. Reciprocally, in more Weberian vein, we can say that a given theology shapes and authorizes economic systems; in which case, it does *matter* very much what you believe theologically, and how.

The fruitful question here is what the Comaroffs' research tells us about the collective subject of our culture and society. The most basic narrative pattern it forms, in my view, is the story of how far 'we', in the neoliberal, third-phase capitalist West – the Comaroffs talk of a 'Judaeo-Protestant ideology' – of which America is now the irradiating centre – have come to adore and serve Mammon. That insight is particularly striking, perhaps, at the interface between third-world ex-colonial cultures and ourselves; there, our overt messages of belief and value (including Christian ones) are bound to be most strongly subverted, distorted and degraded by our overwhelmingly transmitted *second gospel* of Mammon. Remember, on a Girardian view, *any* form of sacralization, any 'invested' desire – the term is appropriate! – can be *religious in character* and highly contagious in a mimetic sense. How, then, would we *not* disseminate in the world our own confusion of belief and value?

How do you *distinguish*? I'm entirely prepared to believe that an economic organization, its ideology and ethos, breeds its inferior and spurious forms of religiosity. But I kept wanting to ask: is there a real McCoy? How do you *know* these forms are inferior, spurious ('conjuring with Christianity'), and a matter of religiosity merely? For the Comaroffs, I guess this natural religiosity isn't a parodic distortion of something else. It's all there is?

NR An anthroplogist might be loth to talk about natural religiosity . . . still less about 'something else'.

PG It seems to me that the brilliant maverick René Girard has dared to imagine just that. He finds the 'natural' or 'archaic' form everywhere – in mythology, in social practices, in political mystiques and intellectual fashions, in all times and places . . . pretty convincingly to my gaze. And then *something else*.

NR It's true that the anthropology conventionally practised in academe today has problems with a 'human nature' that goes beyond what's socially constructed. I wouldn't necessarily place myself in that category . . . The Comaroffs are not calling it spurious or false, though; they're just calling it 'religion'.

PG Yes. Their only real category distinction is between 'this-wordly' religions, and the inherited and official 'other-wordly' forms which these are seen to caricature; and both forms are, in any case, being read deconstructively, as signs of underlying economic and ideological determinants.

However, one could, it seems to me, discern an unsuspected compatibility between Girard and the Comaroffs. If there's one thing in the Comaroffs' chapter more fascinating than the 'numinous magic of global enterprise' – more central, more universal, more tangibly real! – it is in fact the propensity of human beings everywhere to generate mimetically myriad 'immanent' figures of religious desire. The dashing duo give us an absolute encyclopaedia of types: from the zombie cults and sorcery of the Third World, the voodoo economics and the unholy Pentecostalisms of the Second, and the cracked and cunning millenniarisms of the First. All stirred up and beckoned to, on their account, by the triumphal expansion post-1989 of the ethos and ideology of neoliberal capitalism. (But that's really *adverbial*, isn't it? It tells us at what moment, under which prevailing winds of society and culture; the real causative *explicandum* – the deeper subject of their very active verb – remains opaque.) And what is the common denominator of all these religious forms? It is that they 'involve the mimicking of [...] powerful new means of producing wealth'. In other words, we're back – but now on a globalized, intercultural scale – to the fundamental formula of archaic desire and mimetic rivalry...

And you see the pertinence for our debate of how we go about identifying 'religion'? If I perceive that a form of culturally inflected, economically determined natural religiosity *parodies* what Ricœur calls an *eikōn*, or 'true imaging', the difference is going to be considerable. I'm then no longer able simply to indict or dismiss it or even categorize it globally as 'religion', since it may well be uncomfortably close to, or involved with, something I myself naturally do or which our whole *secularized* culture naturally does. And if my *eikōn* is the crucifixion, I can't any more discharge my dissatisfaction with the caricature by simply blaming something or someone else. On the other hand, I do have a standard or model by which to recognize and evaluate the culturally distorted form *as such*, and an ethical imperative to *change it* into a true likeness, both within myself and in my society as far as I can. Beyond that, I may even have a basis on which to relate to what's going on in other culture-zones where there are also natural human beings, whose desires, cultural distortions of desire – and of sacrality – are visibly akin to mine and to ours...

NR You're wanting to say that the matrix of the Common Era actually gives you that? A model, an *eikōn* for renarrativizing our culture and for relating transculturally to its Others?

PG The faith matrix itself (as distinct from the increasingly immanentalized 'Judaeo-Protestant *ideology*' derived from it) – yes. Something like that. Think of Mammon and Islamic fundamentalists. Have we, on the Comaroffs' showing, any right to be surprised that the collective identity of our culture is widely seen as hypocritical and decadent in the Islamic world? Or even when fundamentalists *sacralize* that same judgment and, in *mimetic rivalry* with what *they* perceive to be our actual 'true' religion (i.e. a hegemony of wealth and power born out of our capitalist magic and their despair!), seek to do terrible injury to our seemingly complacent arrogance? The attack on the World Trade Centre was horrific and morally intolerable, yes; but, spiritually, it shouldn't astound us – it lies within a recognizable order of things human. As Gray has it: 'the Taliban warrior threatening to use new weapons of mass destruction in a holy war is an object of incredulous horror in liberal cultures; but he is not a historical anomaly'. Or as Girard might say, more profoundly: 'motes and beams'. The matrix of our own faith tradition tells us: 'You cannot serve both God and Mammon.'[35] *Cannot* refers us to a genuine material, moral and spiritual impossibility we hadn't actually noticed before. It says to us: if you didn't try so hard to do the impossible, wouldn't you be nearer to a common and communal era? (Ex-President Bill Clinton made a valiant attempt to spell out what that might actually mean in his recent Dimbleby Lecture for the BBC.)[36]

NR Well, we certainly need to get to grips with that commonality and with the notion of community. The problem of continuity or sameness through time, and in the globalized common space of our 'one world', is a hugely important aspect of these chapters. Thiselton is arguing that the difference between the Socratic and the pre-Socratic Greek philosophers is precisely the argument between modernism and postmodernism. Another interesting theme running through the chapters is the extent to which what we're seeing now is new, and must be new, given that everything is a reflection of socio-political, cultural-historical conditions that change. Or else isn't new. And one reason that it might *not* be new (in the sense of ever-changing) is the notion of human nature as a constant *à la* Girard.

PG Yes. Let's not say – I'm sure Girard doesn't – that human nature is a fixed or invariant *essence* pre-established and transcending time.

He's saying that there are constant variables of fundamental importance, and deeply recurring patterns, which are, empirically speaking, found in all cultures and times: look at the evidence of evolutionary biology, ethnology, cultural and social anthropology, literature, comparative mythology, the history of religions, etc. . . . But he thinks that these are open to modification, are 'plastic' . . . and that the key to changing them in the future is acting on the unseen, undeclared, unavowed and inavowable archaic 'religion' we *all actually do practise residually, with or without 'belief'*. Richard Schacht too thinks that human nature is plastic, only in a more metaphysically essentialist (and, for him, *de-essentialized*) sense, and a more robustly optimistic one. That's the point of the Humean legacy projected forwards in time courtesy of the metaphysical hypothesis dramatically worked out by Nietzsche. His narrative is articulated in terms of premodern essences, of their modern removal and postmodern deconstruction.

DA Schacht claims human nature in this sense goes together with 'God', disappears with 'God'.

PG In terms of the cultural history of the West, and of the story told about it by the period of anthropocentric humanism now largely closed, that's pretty much true. Already in 1926, Malraux has his Chinese observer of the West say: '*Man is dead* following God, and you seek anxiously to whom you may confide his strange inheritance.'[37] He means, can only mean legitimately, a certain 'absolutized', anthropocentric concept of each is dead, the second following on from the first; which leaves us, indubitably, in a fix for narrativizing the future . . . He's more sceptical, you see, than Nietzsche about our chances of standing on our own shoulders.

TH The challenge of Girard and Ricœur, I would say, and of Thiselton too, is to recognize at the same time that the Judaeo-Christian faith matrix transmitted by our culture emerges from this process genuinely intact. With Moltmann – and not *just* Moltmann – this faith-tradition is readier than it was to write the script out of God's coming future than out of our own historico-cultural past. It's useful to be reading from some sort of future-friendly script when you want to enact an actual historico-cultural future, a *newly* common and communal 'era' . . . Tentatively, often not very well yet, we're beginning to do this in our own, multicultural, pluri-faith societies. We're really only beginning to imagine it on a global scale . . .

CONCLUSION

PG Those who refer to the Judaeo-Christian matrix as determining for their own faith do have a present sense of what Ricœur calls the accompanying promise. But many secular minds, once they begin to unlearn the reflex that leads them to exorcize perpetually an inherited spectre of 'religion', and begin to discern the shape of the matrix informing their own cultural identity, can travel companionably with it a fair way, I would think, in secular space. It's a 'promising shape' in anyone's terms; though what's missing, clearly, in that case, when you think of theology as a form of anthropology and nothing more, is the carrying and justifying hope. I suppose such fellow-travellers would find their representation within the gospels in the 'ex-disciples' (as they must have thought of themselves at that time) walking the Emmaus road, following the death of Jesus...[38]

Ricœur's 'advanced' suggestion about the 'missing Body' belongs to just this narrative, this journey. There is still within faith – but it's 'always already there' before faith and outside it – an all-too-human need to clutch at, and cling to, the known quantity, the tangible form, the familiar corporeal presence; that's what confers the consoling evidence of religious rightness. Whereas what in fact encounters us, and that with which we have to do, is always a *truth* enlarged or at large of which others, out of their own traditions and resources, may be the mediators. This story is the ultimate paradigm of that case: here, the mediating stranger is ultimately recognized – but what a *delay* of non-recognition! – to be the divine Other: the Very One, known and unknown, who holds the key to narrativizing past and future, and who gives back to the travellers, vitally renewed, their own hope, and their own calling as inheritors of the promise. It's extraordinary and splendid – isn't it? – that the gospels anticipate *even* the redemption of our own post-'death-of-God' hangover! That's definitely... *promising*.

NR Promising to some of us, yes, but more so without its 'recognitions of faith', its divine transcendence. I mean, psychology and other sciences of human nature also allow for some kind of transcendence, not divinely linked. The death of God isn't necessarily the death of human nature...

PG Yes, true. That's promising, too... and companionable.

DA It's not that human nature dies with God's death. What dies is all certitude of an innately good nature – that's what all the scepticism and pessimism are about in the twenty-first century. We have no reassurance in the shared nature we have.

CONCLUSION

NR What about original sin. Wasn't that about human nature as intrinsically bad?

[General laughter] 'Highly problematic!', 'Guilty, M'lud!', 'Goodness!'.

PG I guess what you have in mind is an Augustinian notion, heavily inflected by its cultural background: Hellenic (neo-Platonic, ex-gnostic) estimates of the created world, Roman juridical models of inheriting property – that sort of thing. I'm not saying it didn't get a long innings in the mainstream of Catholic and Protestant belief – Jansenism, Luther, Calvin; but it was mostly turfed out ages ago. Not compatible with the matrix, really. Genesis says man is originally created in God's image, and that the whole of what's created is 'very good'.

What's problematic now is what the *cultural memory at large* retains under the name of 'original sin' – and its *own, autonomous and secular, development of that memory trace*. When secularized culture stops referring to the matrix as a 'live' or 'living' thing, secular man inherits exclusively the 'curse' of Genesis and picks up the whole of the tab... You can't *both* 'slay the Father' *and* have him bale you out! All you can do is keep exorcizing the baleful 'returns of the repressed' – and keep blaming 'religion' (or 'fundamentalism', or some other favoured liberal scapegoat) for them. Whereas, in the logic of the 'live' ongoing faith-matrix itself, you *can* correct the doctrine. There really is no revealed *theology*, you know – just 'accompanied' readings and rewritings of the theology of divine *self-revelation*...

NR The death of God is not necessarily the death of a 'good' notion of human nature, it may be the death of 'original sin' also.

TH That's importantly true, if we're referring to the cultural memory trace, and the concept it carries. We want to be free of a backward-looking cultural narrativization and the shadow it casts over us; and, largely, at the beginning of the twenty-first century, we've actually got to that point. Your suggestion is more problematic if you mean that because we jettison the Augustinian *formulation*, human nature itself becomes actually, magically, without a shadow side – innocent. You can imagine Girard limbering up again?

I think the doctrine of original sin, unhelpful as we may find some of its traditional formulations, was on to something; and, in fact, that it stands up rather well to contemporary reformulation. When I talk

CONCLUSION

about original sin to my classes, I talk – for example – *capitalism*. We're all in a context where certain patterns of behaviour are inevitable for us, because it's virtually impossible for us to struggle against them and prevail. We're free not to... but we're enmeshed in a 'logic of the system' and can't help ourselves. That can be interpreted nicely in terms of market forces and consumerism – just as the Comaroffs do! There's an inevitability in human beings doing bad things, or not doing good things, partly because they do (or don't) desire and will to do them, partly because we are in the thrall and sway of larger forces analogous to 'the market', bearing on every decision we make... Those determinations may be around us, and they may be in us, in our nature... the point is, they're before and beyond our power of choice – 'inherited', if you like. They are the accumulated, 'reified' weight of the world as *we* have made it – out of what is, in God's originating purpose, 'very good'.

DA With the 'death of God' perspective, there's no transcendent guarantee of the possibility of goodness. What goes is the *guarantee* of redemption or change or progress... It might turn out that human beings in a godless universe can do good; but it might turn out that they can't, or not enough of them, or not enough total good... It's entirely contingent. We foreswear the guarantee.

PG Yes. But allow me to put some distance between 'guarantees' and Ricœur's notion of 'accompanying promise'. Guarantees belong to insurance brokers and bankers (we British really are, as Napoleon said, a 'nation of shopkeepers'!). There isn't a genuinely comprehensive insurance policy 'all risks' to be had anywhere under the sun (not even from Sun-Alliance!). Not even for the Common Era *as future historico-cultural reality*. If there were, we wouldn't even be discussing the question of whether or not it makes sense to talk about a 'common era'. It would be a matter not of opinion, but of observation, rational certainty and common conviction. Historically, culturally, we have been used to thinking of it in just that way. 'Progress' was underwritten, guaranteed; and *we* were its bearers! We still have to adjust to the formidable dislocation of mind-set involved in *not* being guaranteed bearers in the banker's sense (and perhaps honour Nietzsche for making us so).

But that was always an anthropocentric misunderstanding in the first place, wasn't it? If we look to the crucifixion as *eikōn*, the very best, the most innocent imaginable human, is tortured to death by the conspiracy of reified forces and human wills, apparently failing utterly to bring about the kingdom of God . . . Why, after that, should we expect *any era of ours* to do better? Are *we* so much better? Or just, as Gray suggests, so much more powerful? On that view, God really is dead. We killed him – around 29 CE.

But then, improbably, amazingly, the narrative continues . . . and there is the paradigm 'resurrection', also delivered to us as foundational by the Common Era . . .

DA What's the actual difference between a banker's guarantee and a promise to come with somebody?

PG 'I promise to pay the bearer on demand . . .' And if not on demand, then as pie in the sky . . . The new relation isn't to the *thing promised* as such – which is what we all guzzlingly want and demand – remember Nietzsche's formula about 'nuzzling and pawing God'? – but now directly to the *subject of the promise*. We are being asked to *grow up* into a new form of relationality . . . The Johannine Christ says: 'I have called you *friends* . . .'[39]

TH I can see how the Emmaus road encounter might provide a paradigm for Christians in the post-'death of God' phase of our modern Western cultures and societies. One might even argue that it provides contemporary secularists with a model for imagining how and why the ending of Western Christendom might *not*, after all, signify the end for Christianity, so much as the renewal in history of its ongoingly recreated Common Era . . . Even in purely empirical terms, that's not such a wild projection, when you consider that there are more Christians *worldwide* than there have ever been . . . Really, this would be a good moment to look beyond the local headcounts of Western sociologists and cultural theorists; and, more importantly still, to lay to rest the – nineteenth-century, Eurocentric – ghost of Auguste Comte and his positivist model of history . . .

PG Yes. The Emmaus model reminds us – and we always forget! – that what Constantine founded (i.e. 'Christendom') is one thing; what founds *Christianity* quite another . . . The model even envisages a temporal interval, and a 'desacralized' social space, within which a novel religious (or relational) form, complete with a new type of communal bonding, emerges . . . To invoke another gospel analogy: you won't get good fruit, or good wine, if you don't cut back the vine . . . and what people think of in all naive philosophic literalness as the 'death of God' is really better described, in my view, as the radical pruning of

Christendom. It strikes me, though, that the Emmaus road disciples are totally *mindful* of the inherited promise, even when they think they've lost it. They do *remember*, albeit grievingly, out of which faith matrix they come; that's the condition of their being able to receive the gift of renewed insight and recreated hope ...

TH And the question then might be: how inclusive, potentially, is that matrix itself? How welcoming anthropologically?

NR How friendly, for instance, to feminist insights? (We asked a lot of women speakers, many of them feminists, who couldn't come and only *one* actually spoke in our series.)

PG At the risk of multiplying the continental cohort, the one I most missed is Julia Kristeva. From a psychoanalytical viewpoint, as well as from a feminist viewpoint, she was the ideal interlocutor. Her *Histoires d'amour* is a remarkable analysis of the notion and practice of love in the West – and a suggestive narrativization of the European culture-story. She stands somewhat outside the 'slaying of the Father' paradigm, the 'Oedipal moment' associated with Freud and Lacan, which Ricœur thinks was bound to happen in our culture, and has now largely run its course as a form of radical critique.

Remembering that she comes from a Freudo-Hegelian-Marxist background, complete with Nietzschean 'death-of-God' postulates, she thinks remarkably highly of love in the bible. The Song of Songs is the insurpassable model. Eucharistic *agape* is the exact antidote to the depressive and destructive tendencies of the Western, masculinist Narcissus and his complex of abandonment (cf. Ricœur). She describes the children of contemporary secular society, her patients in psychotherapy, by analogy with Spielberg's film *E.T.* They are – and we are – 'extra-terrestrials wanting for love'.[40] She looks to feminism to carry forward in a secular space the strange and splendid form of the sacred which she finds in Judaeo-Christianity. That's companionable. (One can always enquire on the way what is constituting reality, and what is cultural reflection ...)

She's one of our 'absent voices'. But let's also quote a real exchange between René Girard and Daphne Hampson, who's a 'post-Christian' theologian, as well as a feminist:

> **Daphne Hampson** Doesn't your theory leave out the whole context of gender? Sacrifice is a male scenario: a male solution to a male problem! Always the priests and 'sacrificers'

were men, weren't they, including still today, in most of Christianity? In response to your work, Luce Irigaray pertinently asks: why kill and cut up as a sign of the covenant? Isn't violence perpetrated to enable male bonding? Why did speech fail? Why was it not possible to talk out our differences?[41]

René Girard I don't see any opposition between us. You may be right about male sacrificers, I'm not sure. Women aren't specifically set apart among victims, anyway: victims are all forms of the marginalized – the stranger, prisoners, the handicapped, etc. Language does fail, as we know – despite the best efforts of the 'linguisticism' of the French school over past 30 to 40 years! [. . .] It fails because of human anger, jealousy, pride – only violent actions are left – giving the unexpected 'solution' – which is then seen as an intervention of God! My first philosophic interpretations of this phenomenon were and are naturalistic; but, it can be re-read from a Christian point of view – and then, this could be the very point at which the action of God in evolution (in society, in culture, in religion) really does work and happen.

DH I wouldn't think that. But I would agree Christianity is different in the archaic context. It makes sense in that light – but still, as a male solution to a male problem.

RG But then that's good, if it helps men (where they're 'in control', helping them helps everyone) – and isn't there some greater proximity between women and Jesus? It's women, mainly, who stand at the foot of the cross. I don't entirely accept your view of this violence as a form of 'male bonding' only. 'Bonding' moves us towards the biological. I see violence as creating a *spiritual* link between men who have no spiritual link. It's a very special bonding – the universal bond and bind of archaic religion, which, ideally, is *replaced* in Christianity by the very special Eucharistic 'bonding' in which both genders join, and which sets us free . . .

DH Luce Irigaray also suggests that male violence is part of the attempt to get away from nature. Isn't the real problem that all culture is a male creation, largely through religion; an attempt to get away from the cycles of nature, and impose culture?[42] So Irigaray asks: hidden from view in male culture, who actually is the sacrificial victim? It's woman/the Mother.

RG   Yes. But this 'culture' is largely gone in the West; it was a phase in human historico-cultural evolution...

DH   Christianity gone? I think women should reject Christianity as a profoundly masculinist religion.

RG   Christianity isn't intrinsically a masculinist religion. In so far as it centres on violence, it has to centre on the violent people in order to change them. The apparent marginality of women within it may be due to the fact they are central to nonviolence. The risen Jesus appears first to Mary Magdalene. But it's better, in my view, not to dwell on the institutional 'culture' of Judaeo-Christianity, which has changed and will change; better go back to its source texts. Institutional Christianity has been wrong, but wrong in the same way as everyone else was wrong: let's not scapegoat these institutional religions of Judaism and of Christianity, either!

DH   'Culture' was a male creation arising out of a patriarchal society – I take that to be an insight we owe to French thinkers. But, as we equalize society, our culture is now undergoing a major shift, and the shift will affect our symbolic systems...

RG   Yes... and the shift, you know, will have been part of the Christian revolution, the revolution of the Common Era! The immense work of deconstructing Christianity belongs to a necessary paradox of the modern age (often misnamed – it should never have been so named, since it contained so many 'archaic' elements – 'Christian culture'): anti-Christians are very often the first to discover its authentically Christian logic. It always takes two or three centuries to discover, for instance, the Christian elements in the Renaissance, or the Enlightenment. So Voltaire, defending the Protestant Calas, rediscovers Christian values opposable to the official Christian defenders of the French state. This is an inevitable paradox, too: 'normal' given the mimetic nature of the conflict playing beneath the concepts. The 'objection' becomes obvious and, is accepted as mainstream, even 'orthodox', once things quieten down and the scandal disappears. Maybe that rule is applicable to the women's movement as well? What happens in hostility and anger between factions that are quite temporary becomes acquired, and is replaced by a state of acceptance – which also, of course, brings new problems.

You could also quote the different, but not unrelated, example of the movement for animal rights – which has an immense resonance, despite its excesses, within a theory of mimetic violence and animal sacrifice. The deconstruction of Christianity as historically and culturally received 'AD' has to be pursued in all its aspects. All excluded minorities, all conceivable 'others' in culture have to pass through that breach or brokenness, and no doubt other breakings and breaches still to come, if Judaeo-Christianity is to resemble its own Future . . .

NR One last word . . . on Rorty's management of social and cultural inclusiveness. It isn't simply that a liberal polity is best because it recognizes and respects the diversity of cultures (and seeks to manage their just interaction), but because it recognizes and respects the individual diversity by which these cultures are constituted, and upon which their formal samenesses stand. A liberal polity allows and expects different individuals to flourish, to create themselves and attain self-autonomy: to make their own truths, to weave their own webs of belief and desire, to work their own private salvations. In short, the liberal polity which is to be globalized is one which publicly respects the right of individual citizens to their own civil freedoms against cultural prejudices, against social statuses, and against the language embodied in their self-expressions.

This is to be brought about, Rorty concludes, by 'maximizing the quality of education, freedom of the press, educational opportunity, opportunities to exert political influence, and the like', attempting to routinize social mobility, literacy, peace and leisure, so as to inculcate a 'free and open encounter' between the citizens of a polity engaging in undistorted, 'domination-free communication'.[43] Given such open communication and free discussion, Rorty is assured, individuals would not abide by (or expect others to abide by) concepts of the person or self, and of self-esteem, which ultimately violate the individual; females would not agree to genital mutilation, nor males to suicide-bombing, and no individual would condone the absolute certainty of a religious fundamentalism and the cruelties which inexorably follow. Through these liberal procedures, it may be hoped, individuals will seek to make the best selves for themselves that they can, not allow this potential to be curtailed by cultural, social or linguistic norms, and grant others the space to do likewise.

PG That's relatively companionable too . . . We could go on to examine the difference, and the relationship, between a tolerant social co-existence of diverse individualities, with their private salvations, and the Judaeo-Christian eschatalogical hope of genuinely reconciled human *community* . . .[44] But I fear this particular slice of Common Era time is running out and things need drawing together.

There isn't going to be a single or a simple answer to the question of whether we can speak of an *ongoing* Common Era, nor, if we can, in which continuity it stands with the particularized cultural identity we have had; which commonality it assumes, if any, beyond the current framing procedures of liberal democracy, nor which type of newness or renewal of potential for the future. Nor, fundamentally, in which relation this novelty stands to its generative and still informing faith matrix.

No simple answer is available, because 'we' in the West stand in a historical moment when the unifying metanarratives supplied by all official ideologies are running out; and because we ourselves mirror the emergence, within the shared culture-space of an increasingly globalized world, of multiple memories, plural narratives, diverse projects, different faiths. None of us, for differing reasons, wants to put the clock back. A certain progression of the 'modern world' – progress *perhaps* – leads that way . . . within the unfolding formal arithmetic of CE.

But we may hope to have clarified some of the issues, and glimpsed some types of possible answer. The Common Era has an unquestionable reality as a notion of cultural history and, even – though here with complex and important relativities – of collective memory and mindfulness. We are not free to suggest that the collective identity we have emerges predominantly out of an Islamic or a Hindu or a native American faith matrix. Even if Paul Ricœur reminds us that the Hellenic inheritance is entirely central, and not to be set aside from this same matrix; even if others still will point to other pieces of the mosaic of historico-cultural genesis (such as the Viking or Celtic legacies, the fertilizing presence of Islam in the European Renaissance, or of African Americans in North America). Cultural identities, as we

CONCLUSION

know so much better than we did in CE 900 or CE 1900, never were monolithic; and in the 'one world' we inhabit, they're becoming very much less so.

One of the good reasons for attending to the Judaeo-Christian matrix of the particular cultural identity we have historically assumed in the West must be to know ourselves better; without which we do not acknowledge Others better, but rather, much less and much worse . . . *Gnothi seauton*. Without memory, without a capacity of understanding our past, without knowing how to recognize ourselves collectively as a 'somebody', how would we begin to imagine or relate to 'somebody else'? Or to recognize the same in that Other, and the Other in this same or self? Still less to 'love our neighbour *as ourselves*'? Precisely in the logic of encounter, it is good to be mindful of the extent to which the Judaeo-Christian legacy is imprinted in the intimate and constituting tissue of our own cultural identity, not least in our secular negations and critiques of it . . .

We might perhaps all agree, at least, on the value of grasping adequately Judaeo-Christian distinctiveness. If the third millennium CE should, in the Western world, come to relegate these religious traditions to an erstwhile, distantly recalled developmental phase, then, given the formidable loss of hope entailed, it had better be on the basis of a sharper, more up-to-date, less culture-bound recognition of what is being rejected than is usually in evidence when images of 'religion', or 'monotheism' or 'the post-Christian era' are summoned up out of the fast-failing stock of common memory to become the currency of fashionable intellectual exchange. And if, inversely – evidence of a formidable eclipse of belief and practice within the Western world notwithstanding – the human future lies in God's own 'making new' of all things, then it will be even more crucially of the essence to avoid confusing a former identity-in-culture with a future identity-in-faith.

Reason enough, perhaps, to justify our invoking the framing device of the 'Common Era' which may at the outset have seemed to some questionable or partial, even if exactly appropriate, symbolically speaking, to the threshold year 2000 . . . As to the articulation of things past and things still to be, and for the hope of a communal human future transcending boundaries of cultural non-commonality (alterity, difference), there can only be plural – but perhaps also companionable? – answers.

NOTES

2 PROGRESS AND ABYSS: REMEMBERING THE FUTURE OF THE MODERN WORLD

1. R. Kaplan, *The Nothing That Is: A Natural History of Zero*, London: Allen Lane/The Penguin Press, 1999.
2. For a similar analysis cf. R. Bauckham and T. Hart, *Hope Against Hope. Christian Eschatology in Contemporary Context*, London: Darton Longman and Todd, 1991, Chap. 1: 'The Decline of Secular Hope', pp. 1–26.
3. G. W. F. Hegel, 'America is thus the country of the future in which in the times ahead of us . . . the whole significance of world history will be revealed', *Lectures on the Philosophy of World History. Introduction: Reason in History*, trans. H. N. Nisbet, Cambridge: Cambridge University Press, 1975 (the present quotation has been translated directly from the German). Just how unimportant the European powers were in 1492 in the context of the world as a whole is impressively described in P. Kennedy, *The Rise and Fall of the Great Powers*, New York: Random House, 1987.
4. B. Dietschy, 'Die Tücken des Entdeckens. Ernst Bloch, Kolombus und die Neue Welt' in *Jahrbuch der Ernst-Bloch-Gesellschaft*, Ludwigshafen: Verlag H. Duschmann, 1992/3, pp. 234–51.
5. E. Dussel, *The Invention of the Americas*, Eng. trans. (from Spanish), New York: Continuum, 1995. Among older studies see the important book by T. Todorov, *La Conquête de l'Amérique: la question de l'autre*, Paris: Seuil, 1982.
6. On the idea of a 'world soul' or the *anima mundi*, see H. R. Schlette, *Weltseele. Geschichte und Hermeneutik*, Frankfurt: Suhrkamp Verlag, 1993.
7. C. Merchant, *The Death of Nature. Women, Ecology and the Scientific Revolution*, San Francisco: Harper and Row, 1989; M. Suutala, *Zur Geschichte der Naturzerstörung. Frau und Tier in der wissenschaftlichen Revolution*, Frankfurt: Peter Lang Verlag, 1999.
8. E. Bloch, *The Principle of Hope*, trans. N. and S. Plaice and P. Knight, Oxford: Blackwell, 1986, on 'Eldorado and Eden' (German edn pp. 873ff.).
9. G. Guttiérrez, *Gott oder das Gold*, Freiburg: Herder Verlag, 1990 (German trans. of *Dios o el oro en las Indias*, 1989).
10. Cf. E. L. Tuveson, *Redeemer Nation. The Idea of America's Millennial Role*, Chicago: Chicago University Press, 1968.
11. For the development of this idea, see J. Moltmann, *The Coming of God*:

Christian Eschatology, trans. Margaret Kohl, London: SCM Press, and Minneapolis, Minn.: Fortress Press, 1996, Chap. 3: 'The Kingdom of God. Historical Eschatology'.

12 Karl Löwith, *Meaning in History*, Chicago: University of Chicago Press, 1949, p. 18. Löwith wanted to show that the modern faith in progress represents a secularization of Christian eschatology. But he did not perceive that it is the secularization only of Christian chiliasm, not of Christian eschatology as a whole. It is only if one hopes for a 'completion' of world history that one can talk about its 'progress'. Löwith took no account of Christian apocalyptic, which has to be seen as the reverse side of Christian chiliasm. That is why he called the later (1952) German version of his book 'World History and Saving Event' (*Weltgeschichte und Heilsgeschehen*), and not 'World History and the Events of Disaster', although this coupling would, after all, have been considerably more plausible after 1945.

13 See J. Taubes, *Abendländische Eschatologie* (1947), Munich: Matthes and Seitz Verlag, 1991. Since Taubes used only German sources, I may point to R. Bauckham, *Tudor Apocalypse. Sixteenth-century Apocalypticism, Millenarianism and the English Reformation: From John Bale to John Foxe and Thomas Brightman*, Abingdon: Sutton Courtney, 1978. Marjorie Reeves (*Joachim of Fiore and the Prophetic Future*, London: SPCK, 1976) shows how greatly English Protestantism and the English Enlightenment were coloured by Joachim's messianic spirit. Not least influential, finally, was the book *Spes Israelis* (1650), written by Manessah ben Israel, the Chief Rabbi of Amsterdam, which was dedicated to Oliver Cromwell, and brought about the readmission of Jews to the British Isles. See here Avilhu Zakai, *Exile and Kingdom: History and the Apocalypse in the Puritan Migration to America*, Cambridge: Cambridge University Press, 1992, and *idem.*, 'From Judgment to Salvation. The Image of the Jews in the English Renaissance', *Westminster Theological Journal*, 59 (1997), pp. 213–30.

14 See K. Aner, *Die Theologie der Lessingzeit*, Halle: Nachdruck G. Olms Verlag Hildesheim, 1964; W. Philipp, *Das Werden der Aufklärung in theologiegeschichtlicher Sicht*, Göttingen: Vandenhoeck und Ruprecht, 1957.

15 See Kant, *Das Ende der Dinge* (1794); *Ob das menschliche Geschlecht im beständigen Fortschreiten zum Besseren sei?* (1798). In his *Ideen zu einer allgemeinen Geschichte in weltbürgerlicher Absicht* (1784) he wrote: 'We see: philosophy too can have its chiliasm' (Eighth Proposition).

16 Joachim Ritter has already propounded this theory in connection with Hegel; see his *Hegel und die französische Revolution*, Cologne: Opladen, 1957.

17 W. Benjamin, *Illuminations*, trans. H. Zohn, New York: Harcourt Brace, 1973, reprint 1992, p. 249. The quotation in the present text has been translated directly from the German text in *Illuminationen. Ausgewählte Schriften*, Frankfurt, 1961, 268E (which, in spite of the title, is not identical in content with the selection in the English translation). See Gershom Scholem, *Walter Benjamin und sein Engel*, Frankfurt: Suhrkamp Verlag, 1983; S. Mosès, *Der Engel der Geschichte. Franz Rosenzweig, Walter Benjamin, Gershom Scholem*, Frankfurt: Suhrkamp Verlag, 1994.

18 Still of fundamental importance here is E. Galeano, *Open Veins of Latin America*, New York: Orbis Books, 1974. For the history of slavery, see D. P. Mannix and M. J. Cowley, *Black Cargoes: A History of the Atlantic Slave Trade*, New York: Viking, 1962.

19 See W. Leiss, *The Domination of Nature*, New York: Harper and Row, 1972; B. McKibben, *The End of Nature*, New York: Viking, 1989.
20 G. Werth (*Verdun. Die Schlacht und der Mythos*, Bergisch-Gladbach: Lübbe, 1982), writing on German strategy and military planning, says: 'Military thinking at the turn of the century was dominated by the idea of "annihilation".' At Verdun the German intention was not to win, as in Sedan in 1870, but to 'annihilate' (p. 53). See also M. Gilbert, *The First World War*, London: HarperCollins, 1995.
21 No enduring hope can be based on an 'ontology of not-yet-being' (E. Bloch, *Philosophische Grundfragen*, I, Frankfurt: Suhrkamp Verlag, 1961).
22 R. Wittram, *Das Interesse an der Geschichte*, Göttingen: Vandenhoeck and Ruprecht, 1958, p. 32.
23 'Consequently nothing in history can attempt of itself to relate to the messianic. Thus the kingdom of God is not the *telos* of historical dynamic ... Seen historically, it is not a goal but an end ... The secular is therefore not a category of the kingdom, but it is a category, and the most appropriate category, of its stealthiest approach' (Walter Benjamin, *Illuminationen*, p. 280; the passage is not included in the English selection: see note 17 above).
24 P. Tillich, *The Courage to Be* (1952), 2nd edn, New Haven, Conn., and London: Nisbet, 2000.
25 J. M. Lochman and J. Moltmann, *Das Recht und Menschenrechte*, Neukirchen: Neuhochener Verlag, 1977.
26 See H. Meier, *Die Lehre Carl Schmitts. Vier Kapitel zur Unterscheidung Politischer Theologie und Politischer Philosophie*, Stuttgart: Verlag J. B. Metzler, 1994, pp. 243–9.
27 G. Anders, *Die atomare Drohung*, 4th edn of *Endzeit und Zeitenwende* (1959), with an additional preface, Munich: C. H. Beck Verlag, 1983.
28 J. B. Metz, *Faith in History and Society: Toward a Practical Fundamental Theology*, trans. D. Smith, London and New York: Seaburg Press, 1980, Chap. 10: 'Hope as Imminent Expectation or the Struggle for Forgotten Time', pp. 169–79.
29 W. Stahel, *Die Beschleunigungsfalle oder der Triumph der Schildkröte*, Stuttgart: Kohlhammer Verlag, 1995.
30 See G. Müller-Fahrenholz, *Okumene – Glücksfall und ernstfall des Glaubens*, epol-Dokumentation 28/1998, 3–16, Frankfurt.
31 If this is correct, then a new ecological anthropology is now required. The modern anthropology of M. Scheler, A. Gehlen, H. Plessner, W. Pannenberg and others starts from the 'openness to the world' and the 'self-transcendence' of human beings, as a way of distinguishing them from animals. But this distinction goes back to J. G. Herder, *Essay on the Origin of Language* (1700), trans. A. Gode, Chicago: University of Chicago Press, 1966. Herder writes: 'Nature was his most severe stepmother, just as she was the most tender of mothers towards every insect.'
32 See R. Descartes, *Discourse on Method* (1637), trans. J. Veitch, London: Dent, 1948.
33 J. Moltmann, *God for a Secular Society. The Public Relevance of Theology*, trans. Margaret Kohl, London: SCM Press, and Minneapolis, Minn.: Fortress Press, 1999, 11.2: 'The Destruction and Liberation of the Earth: Ecological Theology', pp. 92–116.

NOTES

3 ENLIGHTENMENT HUMANISM AS A RELIC OF CHRISTIAN MONOTHEISM

1. I am not sure where the term 'Enlightenment project' originates. I use it here in the sense employed by Alasdair MacIntyre in his book, *After Virtue: A Study in Moral Theory*, London: Duckworth, 1981, chap. 5.
2. Salvific interpretations of history are not found only among Christians and Enlightenment humanists. They are found in Judaism, where they are confined to the history of the Jews, and in Islam, where they apply to all of humanity. In viewing human history as a whole as a salvific drama, Islam belongs with 'the West'.
3. The Soviet collapse was the defeat of a Western secular religion – Marxism – in Russia. It was briefly followed by another Westernizing Enlightenment project, neoliberalism, now also defunct. On the affinities between Marxism and neoliberalism in Russia, see my book, *False Dawn: The Delusions of Global Capitalism*, London and New York: Granta Books and The New Press, 1998, chap. 6.
4. I discuss Mill's debts to positivism in my book, *Mill on Liberty: A Defence*, second edition, London and New York: Routledge, 1966, pp. 116–19.
5. On Voltaire, see my book, *Voltaire and Enlightenment*, London: Phoenix/Orion, 1998.
6. Outside of Europe, Buddhism distinguished itself from traditional Indian beliefs by affirming that all humans could achieve nirvana, regardless of their caste (or gender).
7. For an interesting account of pagan ethics in which its deep differences from Christian morality are stressed, see John Casey, *Pagan Virtue: An Essay in Ethics*, Oxford: Clarendon Press, 1990.
8. *The Iliad*, trans. Robert Fitzgerald, New York: Anchor Press/Doubleday, 1974, p. 146.
9. For a fascinating account of mediaeval Christian millenarianism, see Norman Cohn, *The Pursuit of the Millennium: Revolutionary Millenarians and Mystical Anarchists of the Middle Ages*, revised and expanded edition, Oxford and New York: Oxford University Press, 1970.
10. I discuss the philosophy of history presupposed by standard sorts of liberal theory in my book, *Two Faces of Liberalism*, London and New York: Polity Press and The New Press, 2000, pp. 23–5.
11. Fukuyama's original article, 'The End of History', was published in *The National Interest*, summer 1989. See also his book, *The End of History and the Last Man*, New York: The Free Press, 1992.
12. I leave aside here, though not because they are uninteresting, the strands in Christian theology that are themselves variants of Platonism.
13. Hence the common Socratic and Christian preoccupation with weakness of will.
14. Following a particularistic religion may exclude belonging to other religions, as Judaism does; but not because its beliefs are inconsistent with those of other religions.
15. John Stuart Mill, *On Liberty and Other Essays*, Oxford: Oxford University Press, 1998, p. 15.
16. Stuart Hampshire, 'Justice Is Strife', *Proceedings and Addresses of the American Philosophical Association*, 65 (3), November 1991, pp. 24–5. Hampshire

develops this argument in his book, *Justice Is Conflict*, London: Duckworth, 1999.
17 Isaiah Berlin, 'Two Concepts of Liberty' in I. Berlin, *The Proper Study of Mankind*, Henry Hardy and Roger Hausheer (eds), London: Chatto and Windus, 1997, p. 197. Berlin's statement echoes one of his favourite quotes, Bishop Butler's 'Every thing is what it is, and not another thing.' See Henry Hardy, Editor's Preface in I. Berlin, *The Roots of Romanticism*, London: Chatto and Windus, 1999, p. ix.
18 "Tis not contrary to reason to prefer the destruction of the whole world to the scratching of my finger.' David Hume, *A Treatise of Human Nature*, in *Hume's Ethical Writings*, Alasdair MacIntyre (ed.), London, Collier-Macmillan, 1965, p. 180.
19 For an intriguing reconstruction of Hume's thought in which its relations with Christianity are explored, see Donald W. Livingstone, *Philosophical Delirium and Melancholy: Hume's Pathology of Philosophy*, Chicago and London: University of Chicago Press, 1998.
20 MacIntyre, *After Virtue*, p. 49.
21 For an illuminating exploration of Smith's thought, see Charles L. Griswold, Jr., *Adam Smith and the Virtues of Enlightenment*, Cambridge: Cambridge University Press, 1999.
22 For Voltaire's political relativism, see my *Voltaire and Enlightenment*, pp. 39–42.
23 See my *Two Faces of Liberalism*, chap. 2.
24 I have offered some speculations about the ethical outlook that might go with a consistent naturalism in my book, *Endgames: Questions in Late Modern Political Thought*, Cambridge: Polity Press, 1997, chap. 10, 'Beginnings'.

4 HISTORIOGRAPHY AND THE REPRESENTATION OF THE PAST

1 See the commentary by Richard Sorabaji, *Aristotle on Memory*, Providence, Rhode Island: Brown University Press, 1972.
2 *Ibid.*, 449b 15.
3 *Ibid.*, 449b 23.
4 Maurice Halbwachs, *La Mémoire collective*, Paris: Presses universitaires de France, 1950. English trans. *Collective Memory*, New York: Harper and Row, 1980. See also Patrick H. Hutton, 'Maurice Halbwachs as Historian of Collective Memory' in *History as an Art of Memory*, Burlington: University of Vermont Press, 1993 pp. 73ff.
5 See M. de Certeau, *L'Ecriture de l'histoire*, Paris: Gallimard, coll. 'Bibliothèques des histoires', 1975.
6 *Phaedrus*, 274c and 275b.
7 See Marc Bloch, *Apologie pour l'histoire ou métier d'historien*, Paris: Masson, Armand Colin, 1993–7 (1st edn Paris: Armand Colin, 1974). English trans. Peter Putnam, *The Historian's Craft*, Manchester: Manchester University Press, 1976.
8 See Carlo Ginzburg, 'Traces. Racines d'un paradigme indiciaire', Section 'Mythes, emblèmes, traces. Morphologie et histoire' in Marc Bloch, *Apologie pour l'histoire*, pp. 139–80.

9 See Fernand Braudel, *L'Identité de la France*, Paris: Flammarion, 1990, reprint 2000. English trans. S. Reynolds, *The Identity of France*, New York: Harper and Row, 1988.
10 See Lucien Lévy-Bruhl, *Carnets*, English trans. P. Rivière, *The Notebooks on Primitive Mentality*, Oxford: Blackwell, 1949. Geoffrey E. R. Lloyd has offered a devastating critique of this notion in *Demystifying Mentalities*, Cambridge: Cambridge University Press, 1990.
11 Louis Marin, *Le Portrait du roi*, Paris: Seuil, coll. 'Le Sens commun', 1981.
12 Louis Marin, *Des Pouvoirs de l'image*, Paris: Seuil, coll. 'L'Ordre philosophique', 1993.
13 *Temps et récit*, t. 1 'L'intrigue et le récit historique', 1983; t. 2 'La configuration dans le récit de fiction', 1984; t. 3 'Le Temps raconté', 1985, Paris: Seuil, coll. 'L'Ordre philosophique'. English trans. Kathleen McLoughlin and David Pellauer, vol. 1, 1984; vol. 2, 1985; vol. 3, 1988; Chicago: Chicago University Press.
14 See Hayden White, *Metahistory. The Historical Imagination in the XIXth Century*, Baltimore, Md., and London: The Johns Hopkins University Press, 1973; *Tropics of Discourse*, Baltimore, Md., and London: The Johns Hopkins University Press, 1978; *Content of the Form*, Baltimore, Md., and London: The Johns Hopkins University Press, 1987. See also, on these works, P. Ricœur, *Temps et récit*, t. 1, pp. 286–301, t. 3, pp. 273–82, and *La Mémoire, l'histoire, l'oubli*, Paris: Seuil, coll. 'L'Ordre philosophique', 2000, pp. 324–33.
15 Saul Friedlander (ed.), *Probing the Limits of Representation. Nazism and the 'Final Solution'*, Cambridge, Mass., and London: Harvard University Press, 1992, 2nd edn 1996.
16 Ibid., p. 2.
17 See White, *Tropics of Discourse* and *Content of the Form*.
18 George Steiner, *Language and Silence*, London: Penguin, 1967, p. 165.
19 Carlo Ginzburg, 'Just one witness!' in Friedlander (ed.), *Probing the Limits*, pp. 82–96.
20 Friedlander, *Probing the Limits*, p. 1.
21 *La Mémoire, l'histoire, l'oubli*, Paris: Seuil, coll. 'L'Ordre philosophique', 2000.
22 See H.-G. Gadamer, *Truth and Method*, trans. W. Glen-Doepel, London: Sheed and Ward, 1979.
23 See H. Arendt, *The Human Condition*, Chicago: The University of Chicago Press, 1958 and the preface by Paul Ricœur to the French translation, *Condition de l'homme moderne*, Paris: Calmann-Lévy, 1961, 1983.

5 THE FUTURE OF HUMAN NATURE

1 Portions of this essay are indebted to two of my previously published papers: 'Philosophical Anthropology: What, Why and How', *Philosophy and Phenomenological Research*, vol. L, Supplement, 1989, pp. 155–76; and 'Whither Determinism? On Humean Beings, Human Beings, and Originators,' *Inquiry*, 32 (3), 1989, pp. 55–77.
2 D. Hume, *A Treatise of Human Nature*, Oxford: Oxford University Press, 1978.
3 *Beyond Good and Evil*, tr. Walter Kaufman, New York: Vintage, 1966, s. 230.
4 *On the Genealogy of Morals*, tr. Walter Kaufman and R. J. Hollingdale, New York: Vintage, 1969, Second Essay, s. 1.

NOTES

5 *The Gay Science*, tr. Walter Kaufman, New York: Vintage, 1974, s. 108.
6 Ibid., s. 109.
7 *Beyond Good and Evil*, s. 230.
8 'Thus Spoke Zarathustra', in *The Portable Nietzsche*, tr. Walter Kaufman, New York: Vintage, 1954, First part, s. 4, 'On the Despisers of the Body'.
9 *On the Genealogy of Morals*, Second Essay, s. 16.
10 *Human, All Too Human*, tr. R. J. Hollingdale, Cambridge: Cambridge University Press, vol. 1, s. 2.

6 THE MIMETIC THEORY OF RELIGION: AN OUTLINE

1 E. O. Wilson, *Sociobiology, The Abridged Edition*. Cambridge, Mass.: Harvard, Belknap, 1980, p. 285.
2 'In turba ictus, Remus cecidit': Livy, VII, 2.
3 See *The Scapegoat*, trans. Yvonne Freccaro, London: Athlone, 1986, chap. 6.
4 Ibid., pp. 4–7.
5 J. C. Heestermann, *The Inner Conflict of Tradition*, Chicago: University of Chicago Press, 1985.

7 SECOND COMINGS: NEO-PROTESTANT ETHICS AND MILLENNIAL CAPITALISM IN AFRICA, AND ELSEWHERE

1 Some of the ideas developed here, along with the empirical examples required to illustrate them, were first aired in other essays, among them 'Occult Economies and the Violence of Abstraction: Notes from the South African Postcolony', *American Ethnologist*, 26 (3), 1999, pp. 279–301; '"Alien-nation": Zombies, Immigrants and Millennial Capitalism', *Codesria Bulletin*, 3/4, 1991, pp. 17–28; and 'Millennial Capitalism: First Thoughts on a Second Coming' in Jean and John Comaroff (eds), *Millennial Capitalism and the Culture of Neoliberalism*, special issue of *Public Culture*, 12 (2), 2000, pp. 291–343. A few passages included below are also taken from those essays, although they are deployed to rather different ends. The authors would like to express appreciation to Nigel Rapport, who invited them to present this lecture – and who extended warm hospitality to them during their visit to Scotland in November 2000.
2 See http://www.vissarion-unifaith.net. The phrases quoted in this paragraph are to be found in two places: the first, from the home page, by clicking on 'English', then on 'A Little Grain of Sand', then on 'Contents', and finally on 'Epilogue'; the second, directly from the home page on to 'Information Letter'. Vissarion has other linked sites as well, among them one in the USA (www.vissarion.com) and another in Russia (www.vissarion.ru).
3 Tom Whitehouse, 'Messiah on the Make in Sun City', *The Observer World*, 30 May 1999, p. 26. A documentary, made by Andrei Zhigalov, was screened by BBC2 as part of its series *Return from Wonderland* in 1999.
4 See Vernon Blankenship, 'Buildings for the Post-Christendom Church: From Meeting House to Megachurch', *Cutting Edge*, 29 (2), 2000, p. 1.

NOTES

5 *Ibid.*, p. 2, following L. Schaller, *The New Reformation – Tomorrow Arrived Yesterday*, Nashville, Tn.: Abingdon Press, 1999.
6 *Specters of Marx: The State of Debt, the Work of Mourning, and the New International*, trans. Peggy Kamuf, New York: Routledge, 1994.
7 For instance, Benjamin J. Barber, 'Jihad vs. McWorld', *The Atlantic Monthly*, 269 (3), March 1992, pp. 53–65.
8 See Marina S. Brownlee *et al.* (eds), *The New Medievalism*, Baltimore, Md.: Johns Hopkins University Press, 1991; Matthew Connelly and Paul Kennedy, 'Must It Be the Rest against the West?', *The Atlantic Monthly*, 274 (6), December 1994, pp. 61–84.
9 See Paul Hirst and Grahame Thompson, *Globalization in Question: The International Economy and the Possibilities of Governance*, Cambridge: Polity Press, 1996.
10 See Saskia Sassen, *Losing Control? Sovereignty in an Age of Globalization*, New York: Columbia University Press, 1996.
11 See Antonio Negri, 'The Specter's Smile' in M. Sprinker (ed.), *Ghostly Demarcations: A Symposium on Jacques Derrida's Specters of Marx*, London and New York: Verso, 1999, p. 9; and John L. Comaroff and Jean Comaroff, 'Postcolonial Politics and Discourses of Democracy in Southern Africa: An Anthropological Reflection on African Political Modernities', *Journal of Anthropological Research*, 53 (2), 1997, pp. 123–46.
12 See Derrida, *Specters of Marx*, p. 83; D. Blaney and M. K. Pashsa, 'Civil Society and Democracy in the Third World: Ambiguities and Historical Possibilities', *Studies in Comparative International Development*, 28 (1), 1993, pp. 3–24.
13 See Susan Gal, 'Feminism and Civil Society' in J. Scott, C. Kaplan and D. Keats (eds), *Transitions, Environments, Translations*, New York: Routledge, 1997; George Yudice, 'Civil Society, Consumption and Governmentality in an Age of Global Reconstruction', *Social Text*, 45, 14 (4), 1995, pp. 1–25.
14 See Negri, 'The Specter's Smile,' p. 9.
15 See Comaroff and Comaroff (eds), *Millennial Capitalism*.
16 Arif Dirlik, 'Looking Backwards in an Age of Global Capital: Thoughts on History in Third World Cultural Criticism' in X. Tang and S. Snyder (eds), *Pursuit of Contemporary East Asian Culture*, Boulder, Col.: Westview Press, 1996, p. 194.
17 See Wim van Binsbergen (ed.), *The Social Life of Things Revisited*, Raleigh, N.C.: Duke University Press, forthcoming.
18 See Richard Sennett, *The Corrosion of Character: The Personal Consequences of Work in the New Capitalism*, New York: W. W. Norton, 1998.
19 The mural, *Paid Programming*, by Jeffrey Zimmerman, was to be found, at the time of writing, on Honore Street at North Avenue. It has been reproduced in *Public Culture*, 12 (2), 2000, pp. 348–9.
20 George F. Will, 'Hooked on Gambling: Other Comment', *Herald Tribune*, 26–27 June 1999, p. 8.
21 Jane Bryant Quinn, 'Capital Gains: The Lottery on Lives', *Newsweek*, 15 March 1999, p. 55.
22 'Viaticals' are policies bought from the terminally ill, especially in the late stages of AIDS.
23 'Lottery Mania Grips Madya Pradesh, Many Commit Suicide' in *India Tribune* (Chicago), 23 (1), 2 January 1999, p. 8.

24 See Robert Weller, 'Living at the Edge: Religion, Capitalism and the End of the Nation-State in Taiwan' in Comaroff and Comaroff (eds), *Millennial Capitalism*, p. 482; Heather Hartel, 'Roadside Religion and the Decorated Shade', paper presented at the joint conference of the Popular Culture and American Culture Associations, Nashville, Tennessee, 5 October 2000.
25 Brett Pulley, 'Compulsion to Gamble Seen Growing', *New York Times*, 7 December 1997, p. 22.
26 Will, 'Hooked on Gambling'.
27 Michael Tackett and Ted Gregory, 'Gambling's Lure Is Still a Divisive Issue', *Chicago Tribune*, 20 May 1998, p. 3; the words quoted are those of James Dobson, president of Focus on the Family, a Christian media ministry. They echo observations made by a range of witnesses to the US National Gambling Impact Study Commission, set up in 1996 to study the effects of gambling.
28 Derrida, *Specters of Marx*, following J. Rifkin, *The End of Work: The Decline of the Global Labor Force and the Dawn of the Post-Market Era*, New York: G. P. Putnam's Sons, 1995.
29 Comaroff and Comaroff, 'Occult Economies'.
30 Lesley Fordred, 'Narrative, Conflict and Change: Journalism in the New South Africa', PhD diss., University of Cape Town, 1999.
31 Peter Geschiere, *The Modernity of Witchcraft: Politics and the Occult in Postcolonial Africa*, Charlottesville, Va.: University of Virginia Press, 1997.
32 Misty L. Bastian, 'Bloodhounds Who Have No Friends: Witchcraft and Locality in the Nigerian Popular Press' in J. and J. L. Comaroff (eds), *Modernity and Its Malcontents*, Chicago: University of Chicago Press, 1993, pp. 133ff.
33 See Asonzeh Ukah, 'Media and Material Culture of Nigerian Pentecostalism'. Proposal Submitted to the Social Science Research Council Program on African Youth in a Global Age, July 2001.
34 See Rosalind Morris 'Modernity's Media and the End of Mediumship? On the Aesthetic Economy of Transparency in Thailand' in Comaroff and Comaroff (eds), *Millennial Capitalism*, pp. 457–76.
35 See Uli Schmetzer, 'Letter from Bangkok: Thai Seers Dealt Reversal of Fortune', *Chicago Tribune*, 18 November 1997, p. 4.
36 S. Žižek, *The Plague of Fantasies*, London: Verso, 1997, p. 10.
37 See Nancy Scheper-Hughes, *Death without Weeping: The Violence of Everyday Life in Brazil*, Berkeley: University of California Press, 1992.
38 See Jean Comaroff, 'Consuming Passions: Nightmares of the Global Village' in E. Badone (ed.), *Body and Self in a Post-Colonial World*, special issue of *Culture*, 17 (1–2), 1997, pp. 7–19.
39 See J. S. La Fontaine, *Speak of the Devil: Allegations of Satanic Child Abuse in Contemporary England*, Cambridge: Cambridge University Press, 1997. There have been many stories in British tabloids about such matters. For an especially vivid one, see Brian Radford, 'Satanic Ghouls in Baby Sacrifice Horror', *News of the World*, 24 August 1997, pp. 30–1. Its two subtitles – 'Cult is cover for pedophile sex monsters' and 'They breed tots to use at occult rituals' – reflect well the moral panic to which they speak.
40 According to this myth, whose telling is always accompanied by authenticating detail, the victim is offered a drink and, sometime later, awakes in a hotel bath, body submerged in ice. A note, taped to the wall, warns him

NOTES

not to move, but to call the emergency services number. He is asked by the operator to feel for a tube protruding from his back. If he finds one, he is instructed to remain still until paramedics arrive: his kidneys have been harvested.

41 See e.g. Celestine Bohlen, 'Albanian Parties Trade Charges in the Pyramid Scandal', and Edmund L. Andrews, 'Behind the Scams: Desperate People, Easily Duped', *New York Times*, 29 January 1997, p. 3.

42 Leslie Eaton, 'Investment Fraud Is Soaring Along with Stock Market', *New York Times*, 30 November 1997, pp. 1, 24.

43 'Charity Pyramid Schemer Sentenced to 12 Years', *Chicago Tribune*, 23 September 1997, p. 6.

44 African Press Association; published on the Web by IOL on 13 July 2000 (http://www.iol.co.za/general/newsprint.php3?art_id=t20000731204009474M624397).

45 Selby Bokaba and Vivian Warby, 'Fury as Cash "Miracle" Turns to Dust', *The Star* (Johannesburg); published on the Web by IOL on 13 July 2000 (http://www.iol.co.za/general/newsprint.php3?art_id=t2000071321401 7362L300819).

46 Selby Bokaba, 'Hero's Welcome for Miracle 2000 Mastermind', *The Star* (Johannesburg); published on the Web by IOL on 31 July 2000 (http:/www.iol.co.za/general/newsprint.php3?art_id=ct2000007312040 09474M624397).

47 Report on e-news at 6 p.m., e-TV (South Africa), 17 October 2001.

48 Jane Schneider, 'Rumpelstiltskin's Bargain: Folklore and the Merchant Capitalist Intensification of Linen Manufacture in Early Modern Europe' in A. Wiener and J. Schneider (eds), *Cloth and Human Experience*, Washington: Smithsonian Institution Press, 1989.

49 Eric Kramer, 'Possessing Faith: Commodification, Religious Subjectivity, and Community in Brazilian neo-Pentecostal Church', PhD diss., University of Chicago, 1999.

50 The phrases in quotes were uttered by a Universal Church pastor in Mafeking, South Africa, where the denomination is growing fast: by January 2000 it had two storefront chapels, several rural centres, and a much watched programme on the local TV channel.

51 Kramer, 'Possessing Faith', p. 35.

52 P. M. Worsley, *The Trumpet Shall Sound: A Study of 'Cargo' Cults in Melanesia*, London: Macgibbon and Kee, 1957.

53 Honoré de Balzac, *Cousin Bette*, Part I 'Of Poor Relations', trans. Marion Ayton Crawford, Harmondsworth: Penguin, 1965 (1st edn 1847).

54 Joseph Conrad, *Under Western Eyes*, Harmondsworth: Penguin, 1957 (1st edn 1911).

55 M. Gluckman, 'The Magic of Despair', *The Listener*, 29 April 1959 (republished in *Order and Rebellion in Tribal Africa*, London: Cohen and West, 1963).

56 See Comaroff and Comaroff, '"Alien-nation"'.

57 See Comaroff and Comaroff, *Modernity and Its Malcontents*, pp. xvff.

58 We were struck by a recent instance, since it resonates so obviously with our concerns here: Michael Metelits, speaking of labour legislation in the 'new' South Africa, referred to it as a 'tricky, not to say occult business'. See Michael Metelits, 'Toiling Masses and Honest Capitalists', *Work to Rule: A*

NOTES

Focus on Labour Legislation, supplement to *Mail and Guardian*, 15–21 October 1999, p. 11.
59 See Derrida, *Specters of Marx* and Žižek, *Plague of Fantasies*.
60 *The Protestant Ethic and the Spirit of Capitalism*, trans. T. Parsons, New York: C. Scribner's, 1958, p. 175.

8 CAN A PREMODERN BIBLE ADDRESS A POSTMODERN WORLD?

1 J. Moltmann, *God for a Secular Society: The Public Relevance of Theology*, London: SCM, 1999, pp. 11–17.
2 R. J. Bernstein (ed.), *Habermas and Modernity*, Cambridge: Polity Press, 1985.
3 Paul Ricœur, 'The Hermeneutics of Revelation' in L. S. Mudge (ed.), *Essays on Biblical Interpretation*, London: SPCK, 1981, esp. pp. 85–93.
4 I have argued this case, in effect, over a sustained exegesis and theological exposition of some 1,450 pages in Anthony C. Thiselton, *The First Epistle to the Corinthians: A Commentary on the Greek Text* (The New International Greek Testament Commentary, Grand Rapids, Mich.: Eerdmans, and Carlisle: Paternoster, 2000) esp. pp. 12–17, 120–75, 204–39, 669–76, 900–1214.
5 Wolfhart Pannenberg, *Systematic Theology* (3 vols, Edinburgh: T. and T. Clark and Grand Rapids, Mich.: Eerdmans, 1991, 1994 and 1998), vol. 1, pp. 65 and 71.
6 Cf. Karl Rahner, *Foundations of Christian Faith*, New York: Seabury, 1968, p. 48; and W. Pannenberg, *Basic Questions in Theology* (3 vols), London: SCM, 1970, 1971 and 1973, esp. vol. 1, pp. 39–50 and 164–74 and vol. 2, p. 25.
7 See Pannenberg, *Basic Questions*, vol. 1, pp. 46–8, and vol. 3, pp. 14–68.
8 David Harvey, *The Condition of Postmodernity*, Oxford: Blackwell, 1989, p. 9.
9 Ibid.
10 The phrase and argument is amplified by Kevin Vanhoozer, *Is There a Meaning in This Text? The Bible, The Reader, and the Morality of Literary Knowledge*, Grand Rapids, Mich.: Zondervan, 1998, pp. 65–97; cf. J. Derrida, *Writing and Difference*, London: Routledge, 1978, and *Of Grammatology*, Baltimore, Md., and London: Johns Hopkins University Press, 1976.
11 Richard Rorty, *Philosophy and the Mirror of Nature*, Princeton, N.J.: Princeton University Press, 1979.
12 Harvey, *Condition*, p. 9.
13 J.-F. Lyotard, *The Postmodern Condition: A Report on Knowledge*, Minneapolis: University of Minnesota Press, and Manchester: Manchester University Press, 1984, p. xxiv.
14 Bill Readings, *Introducing Lyotard: Art and Politics*, London and New York: Routledge, 1991, p. xxxiii.
15 Roland Barthes, 'Death of the Author' in *The Rustle of Language*, New York: Hill and Wang, 1986, p. 54; Vanhoozer, *Is There a Meaning?*, p. 30.
16 Vanhoozer, *Is There a Meaning?*, p. 48.
17 Harvey, *Condition*, pp. 5 and 6.
18 See Wayne A. Meeks, *The First Urban Christians. The Social World of the*

NOTES

Apostle Paul, New Haven, Conn.: Yale University Press, 1983, p. 34; and Thiselton, *First Epistle*, pp. 12–17 and throughout (See Index, Postmodernity).

19 F. Nietzsche, *Complete Works* (18 vols), London: Allen and Unwin, 1909–13, vol. 15, *The Will to Power*, ii, II, Aphorism 481.
20 *Ibid.*, 12, Aphorism 481.
21 *Ibid.*, 11, Aphorism 480.
22 *Ibid.*, 16, *The Antichrist* 186, Aphorism 43.
23 Anthony C. Thiselton, *Interpreting God and the Postmodern Self: On Meaning, Manipulation and Promise*, Edinburgh: T. and T. Clark and Grand Rapids, Mich.: Eerdmans, 1995, throughout.
24 M. M. Mitchell, *Paul and the Language of Reconciliation: An Exegetical Investigation into the Language and Composition of 1 Corinthians*, Louisville, Ky.: Knox/Westminster 1992, esp. pp. 1–99 and 198–201; L. L. Welborn, *Politics and Rhetoric in the Corinthian Epistles*, Macon, Ga.: Mercer University Press, 1997, pp. 1–42; cf. Thiselton, *First Epistle*, pp. 107–33, which includes a detailed bibliography of sources.
25 Richard Rorty, *Truth and Progress: Philosophical Papers*, vol. 3, Cambridge: Cambridge University Press, 1998, p. 7.
26 *Ibid.*, p. 8.
27 A. J. Ayer, *Language, Truth and Logic*, London: Gollancz, 2nd edn 1946 (also Penguin edn 1971) and Rorty, *Truth*, pp. 8–12 and 19–42.
28 Rorty, *Truth*, p. 21.
29 *Ibid.*, p. 4.
30 *Ibid.*, p. 25.
31 A. C. Thiselton, 'Signs of the Times: Towards a Theology for the Year 2000 . . .' in David Fergusson and Marcel Sarot (eds), *The Future as God's Gift: Explorations in Christian Eschatology*, Edinburgh: T. and T. Clark, 2000, pp. 9–40.
32 R. Ambler, 'The Self and Postmodernity' in K. Flanagan and P. C. Jupp (eds), *Postmodernity, Sociology and Religion*, New York and London: Macmillan, 1996, p. 134; cf. pp. 134–51.
33 F. Jameson, *Postmodernism: Or, the Cultural Logic of Late Capitalism*, London: Verso, 1991, p. 55.
34 S. Benhabib, *Situating the Self: Gender, Community and Postmodernism in Contemporary Ethics*, Cambridge: Polity, 1992, p. 2.
35 E. D. Ermarth, *Sequel to History: Postmodernism and the Crisis of Representational Time*, Princeton, N.J.: Princeton University Press, 1992.
36 T. Doherty, 'Postmodernist Theory: Lyotard, Baudrillard and Others' in Richard Kearney (ed.), *Twentieth-Century Continental Philosophy*, Routledge History of Philosophy, vol. 8, London: Routledge, 1994, p. 475; cf. pp. 474–505.
37 R. H. Roberts, 'A Postmodern Church? Some Preliminary Reflections on Ecclesiology and Social Theory' in D. F. Ford and D. L. Stamps (eds), *Essentials of Christian Community*, Edinburgh: T. and T. Clark, 1996, pp. 179–95, esp. 182–3.
38 D. W. Hardy, 'The Future of Theology' in D. W. Hardy (ed.), *God's Ways with the World*, Edinburgh: T. and T. Clark, 1996, p. 31; cf. pp. 31–50; and esp. 'Magnificent Complexity' in Ford and Stamps, *Essentials*, pp. 336–7.

39 Thiselton, *First Epistle*, pp. 12–17, 40–3, 50–1, 75, 548, 1002, 1054–9, 1255 and throughout.
40 Meeks, *First Urban Christians*, p. 54.
41 *Ibid.*
42 *Ibid.*; cf. also pp. 72–3, and Thiselton, *First Epistle*, pp. 12–17.
43 Donald Engels, *Roman Corinth: An Alternative Model for the Classical City*, Chicago and London: University of Chicago Press, 1990, throughout.
44 Strabo, *Geography* 8: 6: 20; Pausanias, *Description of Greece* 2: 1: 5–7; in modern literature James Wiseman, 'Corinth and Rome, I, 228 BC – AD 267' in *Aufstieg und Niedergang der römischen Welt* 2: 7: 1, Berlin: deGruyter, 1979, esp. pp. 439–47; and Engels, *Roman Corinth*, pp. 8–21.
45 Listed in Thiselton, *First Epistle*, pp. 6–12, esp. *Hesperia* 6 (1937), pp. 261–56; 10 (1941), pp. 143–62; 41 (1972), pp. 143–84; 44 (1975), pp. 1–59; 51 (1982), pp. 115–63; 58 (1989), pp. 1–50; 59 (1990), pp. 325–56.
46 J. Murphy-O'Connor, *St Paul's Corinth: Texts and Archaeology*, Wilmington, Del.: Glazier, 1983, p. 171.
47 See e.g. W. Schrage, *Der erste Brief an die Korinther*, Zürich: Benziger, and Neukirchen-Vluyn: Neukirchener, 3 vols to date, 1991, 1995, 1999 [Ev.-Kath. Kom. z. N.T. VII, 1–3], vol. 1, pp. 25–9.
48 B. Witherington, *Conflict and Community in Corinth*, Carlisle: Paternoster, and Grand Rapids, Mich.: Eerdmans, 1995, p. 20.
49 B. W. Winter, *Philo and Paul among the Sophists*, Cambridge: Cambridge University Press [SNTS Monograph Series 96], 1997, pp. 238.
50 Rorty, *Truth*, p. 25.
51 *Ibid.*, p. 4.
52 Schrage, *Der erste Brief*, vol. 1, p. 165.
53 Seneca, *Controversiae*, 9: 1; Quintilian, *Institutio Oratoria*, 2: 2: 9, 12; further references in S. Pogoloff, *Logos and Sophia. The Rhetorical Situation of 1 Corinthians*, Atlanta, Ga.: Scholars Press [SBL Diss. Ser. 134], 1992, pp. 175–8.
54 Pogoloff, 'Rhetoric and Antifoundationalism' in *Logos and Sophia*, pp. 26–35; see further pp. 171–2.
55 *Ibid.*, pp. 173–235.
56 A. D. Clarke, *Secular and Christian Leadership in Corinth. A Socio-Historical and Exegetical Study of 1 Corinthians 1–6*, Leiden and New York: Brill [Arb. z. Gesch. des Ant. Jud. und des Urchr. 18] 1993, p. 25.
57 *Ibid.*, p. 32.
58 *Ibid.*, p. 39.
59 J. D. Moores, *Wrestling with Rationality in Paul*, Cambridge: Cambridge University Press [SNTS Monograph Series 82], 1995, pp. 133–4.
60 S. Fish, *Doing What Comes Naturally. Change, Rhetoric and the Practice of Theory in Literary and Legal Studies*, Oxford: Clarendon Press, 1989, pp. 482 and 483.
61 *Ibid.*
62 J. B. Skemp, *The Greeks and the Gospel*, London: Carey Kingsgate, 1964, esp. pp. 1–45 and 90–120.
63 A. Deissmann, *Light from the Ancient East*, London: Hodder and Stoughton, 1927. Deissmann made no secret of his own 'egalitarian' political agenda.
64 E. A. Judge, *The Social Pattern of Early Christian Groups in the First Century*,

NOTES

London: Tyndale Press, 1960; Meeks, *First Urban Christians*; G. Theissen, *The Social Setting of Pauline Christianity*, Philadelphia, Pa.: Fortress, 1982; B. W. Winter, *Philo and Paul; Seek the Welfare of the City*, Grand Rapids, Mich.: Eerdmans, 1994; B. W. Winter, *After Paul Left Corinth*, Grand Rapids, Mich.: Eerdmans, 2001. Cf. however also J. J. Meggitt, *Paul, Poverty and Survival*, Edinburgh: T. and T. Clark, 1998.

65 A. Eriksson, *Traditions as Rhetorical Proof. Pauline Argumentation in 1 Corinthians*, Stockholm: Almqvist and Wiksell [Con. Bib. N.T. Ser. 29], 1998, pp. 251–78. See also Thiselton, *First Epistle*, pp. 1169–1314.

66 N. Schneider, *Die rhetorische Eigenart der paulinischen Antithese*, Tübingen: Mohr [HUT, 11], 1970.

67 M. Bünker, *Briefformular und rhetorische Disposition im 1 Korintherbrief*, Göttingen: Vandenhoeck and Ruprecht, 1983.

68 Moores, *Wrestling*, pp. 6–10, 25–8, 132–8.

69 Thiselton, *First Epistle*, pp. 43, 154, 173–5, 240, 325–6, 469, 499–500, 560–1, 602, 627, 930, 996 and 1024.

70 See W. L. Lane, *Hebrews*, 2 vols, Dallas, Tx.: Word, 1991, pp. lxix–lxxxviii; A. Vanhoye, *Homilie für halfbedürftige Christen*, Regensburg: Pustet, 1981; W. G. Überlacker, *Der Hebräebrief als Appell*, Stockholm: Almqvist and Wiksell [Con. Bib. N.T. Ser. 21], 1989.

71 See Wesley A. Kort, *Story, Text and Scripture. Literary Interests in Biblical Narratives*, University Park, Pa.: Pennsylvania State University Press, 1988, p. 44.

72 F. Kermode, *The Genesis of Secrecy. On the Interpretation of Narrative*, Cambridge, Mass.: Harvard University Press, 1979.

73 R. W. Hepburn, 'Demythologizing and the Problem of Validity' in A. Flew and A. MacIntyre (eds), *New Essays in Philosophical Theology*, London: SCM, 1955, pp. 227–42; A. C. Thiselton, *The Two Horizons*, Grand Rapids, Mich.: Eerdmans, and Exeter: Paternoster, 1980, pp. 252–63; and the varied discussions in H.-W. Bartsch (ed.) *Kerygma und Mythos: ein theologisches Gespräch*, 6 vols, Hamburg: Reich and Heidrich, from 1948.

74 R. Bultmann, *Jesus Christ and Mythology*, London: SCM, 1960, pp. 322–34.

75 Ibid., p. 32.

76 R. Bultmann, 'The Case for Demythologizing: A Reply' in H.-W. Bartsch (ed.), *Kerygma and Myth*, vol. 2, London: SCM, 1964, pp. 182–3.

77 G. Theissen, *Psychological Aspects of Pauline Theology*, Edinburgh: T. and T. Clark, 1987, p. 63.

78 A. C. Thiselton, 'The Logical Role of the Liar Paradox in Titus 1: 12, 13: A Dissent from the Commentaries in the Light of Philosophical and Logical Analysis' *Biblical Interpretation*, 1994, 2, pp. 207–23; cf. Thiselton, 'Truth' in C. Brown (ed.), *The New International Dictionary of NT Theology*, Exeter: Paternoster, and Grand Rapids, Mich.: Zondervan, vol. 3, 1978, pp. 1123–46.

79 A somewhat simplified but nevertheless useful exploration of these logical issues in the framework of the later Wittgenstein is offered by D. M. High, *Language, Persons and Belief*, New York: Oxford University Press, 1967.

80 Thomas Aquinas, *Summa Theologiae*, 60 vols, Latin and English, Oxford: Blackfriars, 1963, Part Ia: qu. 47: art. 1 and art. 2.

81 See D. B. Martin, *The Corinthian Body*, New Haven, Conn., and London:

NOTES

Yale University Press, 1995, pp. 3–61 and 94–103; and Thiselton, *First Epistle*, pp. 990–1011.
82 Vanhoozer, *Is There a Meaning?* pp. 37–280; N. Wolterstorff, *Divine Discourse*, Cambridge: Cambridge University Press, 1995, pp. 37–170 and throughout.
83 A. C. Thiselton, *The Two Horizons*, Exeter: Paternoster, and Grand Rapids, Mich.: Eerdmans, 1980, p. 389; cf. pp. 386–407.

CONCLUSION: DIALOGUE ON THE 'COMMON ERA'

1 The initials PG, NR, TH and DA refer to the Editors. Other contributors to the original seminars which followed the lectures given at St Andrews are designated by their own initials where they have been identified (otherwise, by the letter Q). Material quoted from the 'live' seminars given by volume contributors is indented for ease of recognition; the printed text of these interventions has been revised and approved by the speakers and represents new material in relation to the chapters.
2 See Paul Ricœur, *Temps et récit*, t. 3, 'Le Temps raconté', Paris: Seuil, 1985 (trans. Kathleen McLoughlin and David Pellauer, *Time and Narrative*, vol. 3, Chicago and London: Chicago University Press, 1988) and *Soi-même comme un autre*, Paris: Seuil, 1990 (trans. Kathleen Blaney, *Oneself as Another*, Chicago and London: Chicago University Press, 1992).
3 Paul Ricœur, 'Narrative Hospitality' in R. Kearney (ed.), *The Hermeneutics of Action*, London: Sage, 1996.
4 Matthew 24: 30.
5 The Book of Revelation 21: 5.
6 See 'Ebauche d'un serpent' in the collection *Charmes* (1922).
7 Cf. John 5: 17: 'My Father is working still, and I am working.'
8 F. Nietzsche, *Beyond Good and Evil*, London: Penguin, 1979, no. 251.
9 F. Nietzsche, *Human, All Too Human*, London: Penguin, 1986, no. 475.
10 Calas was a French Protestant from Toulouse who in 1762 was accused of having conspired with the rest of his family to kill his eldest son in order to prevent him from converting to Catholicism. The father was sentenced to death and broken on the wheel. Voltaire campaigned in defence of the accused against what he saw as unjust religious persecution and protected the rest of the family; he succeeded, after three years, in getting further proceedings against them quashed.
11 See René Girard, 'Mimetische Theorie und Theologie' in *Vom Fluch und Segen der Sündenböcke: Raymond Schwager zum 60. Geburtstag*, Thauer: Kulturverlage, 1995, pp. 17–29. Reprinted in French in *Celui par qui le scandale arrive*, Paris: Desclée de Brouwer, 2001, pp. 63–8.
12 John 10: 15.
13 John 1: 11, 5.
14 1 Corinthians 2: 8.
15 Isaiah Berlin, *Four Essays on Liberty*, Oxford: Oxford University Press, 1969, p. 172.
16 Jules Michelet, *Histoire de la Révolution française*, Paris: Gallimard, Pléiade, 1952 (1st edn 1847–53), p. 21.
17 Hebrews 11: 1.
18 Richard Rorty, 'On Ethnocentrism: A Reply to Clifford Geertz', *Michigan Quarterly Review* (Winter 1986), 25, pp. 525–34.

19 *Ibid.*, p. 532.
20 Personal communication to Nigel Rapport, 4 June 1994.
21 Comte's progressive theory of history distinguishes a mythological age, followed by a religious and metaphysical age, in turn superseded by the age of science or positivism.
22 See R. Girard, 'Le Meurtre fondateur dans la pensée de Nietzsche' in P. Dumouchel (ed.), *Colloque de Cerisy 'Violence et Verité. Autour de René Girard'*, Paris: Grasset, 1985, p. 603: 'Admire the efficacy of the manoeuvre, all the cleverer since it is unaware of its own cunning. Nietzsche is quoted fully and accurately in appearance, but actually in truncated form because of the aphoristic foregrounding. The slogan "God is dead" which circulates around our world doesn't summarise the thought of the Madman at all, it falsifies it grossly. For Enlightenment philosophy, God can only die a natural death. Once the naive period of humanity is over, all things religious cease to be "credible", as we say these days. [...] The "death of God" operation evacuates Nietzsche's idea in order to tiptoe back to this facile, banal, *vulgar* idea. [...] The true difference between the atheism of the crowd and the thought of the Madman is none other than the difference between death and murder.'
23 See N. Frye, *The Great Code: The Bible and Literature*, London: Routledge and Kegan Paul, 1982.
24 See Paul Ricœur, *De l'interprétation. Essai sur Freud*, Paris: Seuil, 'L'Ordre philosophique', 1965 (trans. D. Savage, *Freud and Philosophy: An Essay on Interpretation*, New Haven, Conn., and London: Yale University Press, 1970); and *Le Conflit des interprétations. Essais d'herméneutique 1*, Paris: Seuil, 'L'Ordre philosophique', 1969 (trans. Don Ihde, *The Conflict of Interpretations: Essays in Hermeneutics*, Evanston, Ill.: Northwestern University Press, 1974).
25 John 20: 13.
26 See *Soi-même comme un autre*. The distinction turns on the notions of 'sameness' and of 'ipseity' which are both operative in judgments of 'identity': the overwhelmingly used identity-criterion of 'one and the same' is commonly made to do duty for 'the very one'.
27 The French word has multiple senses: 'pleasure, delight, enjoyment, well-being; satisfaction, fulfilled possession; orgasmic climax'. The 'libidinal' connotation, much enlarged in its range of reference, has tended to dominate in post-structuralist theory in France since 1968 [Ed.].
28 The pre-understanding of promise from the experience of threat has particularly interesting application to the Book of Genesis. See Paul Ricœur, 'The Hermeneutics of Revelation' in Lewis S. Mundy (ed.), *Essays on Biblical Interpretation*, London: SPCK, 1981.
29 This formula might be interestingly applied to expressions used in the gospels: 'the Kingdom of God is at hand'; 'It is finished' [Ed.].
30 See George Steiner, *Real Presences; Is There Anything in What We Say?*, London: Faber and Faber, 1989.
31 'No, no, it's *impossible!*' 'I'd prefer to say, it's *difficult* ...'.
32 Zygmunt Bauman, *Modernity and the Holocaust*, Ithaca, N.Y.: Cornell University Press, 1989.
33 Richard Rorty, *Contingency, Irony and Solidarity*, Cambridge: Cambridge University Press, 1992.

34 *Ibid.*, p. 88.
35 See Matthew 6: 24; Luke 16: 18.
36 BBC Richard Dimbleby Lecture, 'The Struggle for the Soul of the Twenty-first Century', December 2001. See http://www.bbc.co.uk/arts/news_comment/dimbleby/print-clinton.shtml
37 André Malraux, *La Tentation de l'occident*, Paris: Grasset, 1926; 'Le Livre de poche' (1972), p. 128.
38 See Luke 34: 13–35.
39 John 15: 15.
40 See Julia Kristeva, 'Des extra-terrestres en mal d'amour', *Histoires d'amour*, Paris: Denoel, 1983, pp. 462–74 (trans. Leon S. Roudiez, *Tales of Love*, New York, Guildford: Columbia University Press, 1987).
41 On these questions of 'women in relation to our sacrificial societies', see Luce Irigaray, 'Women, the Sacred and Money', *Paragraph* 8 (1986), special number on 'Feminism' edited by Diana Knight. Reprinted in Gillian C. Gill (trans.), *Sexes and Genealogies*, New York: Columbia University Press, 1993.
42 *Ibid.*
43 Rorty, *Contingency, Irony and Solidarity*, pp. 67–8.
44 The notion of 'community' defined on this model refers to a common belonging and calling, transcending cultural and social forms. In the Judaeo-Christian scriptures, it is linked to a *reconciliation* between humankind and nature, and between human beings; both are predicated on the primary reconciliation between mankind and God (see e.g. Isaiah 11: 1–9; Romans 15: 4–13). For Christian reflections on this notion in its modern, cultural and societal application, see e.g. Emmanuel Mounier, *Refaire la renaissance*, Pt. 1, 'Révolution personnaliste et communautaire', Paris: Seuil, coll. 'Points', 1961, 2000.

BIBLIOGRAPHY AND FURTHER READING

Ambler, R., 'The Self and Postmodernity' in K. Flanagan and P. C. Jupp (eds), *Postmodernity, Sociology and Religion*, New York and London: Macmillan, 1996.
Anders, G., *Die atomare Drohung*, 4th edn of *Endzeit und Zeitenwende* (1959), with an additional preface, Munich: C. H. Beck Verlag, 1983.
Aquinas, Thomas, *Summa Theologiae*, 60 vols, Latin and English, Oxford: Blackfriars, 1963.
Archard, David (ed.), *Consciousness and Unconsciousness*, London: Hutchinson, 1984.
—— (ed.), *Philosphy and Pluralism*, Cambridge: Cambridge University Press, 1996.
Arendt, H., *The Human Condition*, Chicago: The University of Chicago Press, 1958.
Ayer, A. J., *Language, Truth and Logic*, London: Gollancz, 2nd edn 1946; Penguin edn 1971.
Balzac, Honoré de, *Cousin Bette*, Part I 'Of Poor Relations', trans. Marion Ayton Crawford, Harmondsworth: Penguin, 1965 (1st edn 1847).
Barber, Benjamin R., 'Jihad vs. McWorld', *The Atlantic Monthly*, 269 (3), March 1992, pp. 53–65.
Barthes, Roland, 'Death of the Author' in *The Rustle of Language*, New York: Hill and Wang, 1986.
Bartsch, H.-W. (ed.), *Kerygma und Mythos: ein theologisches Gespräch*, 6 vols, Hamburg: Reich and Heidrich, from 1948.
Bastian, Misty L., '"Bloodhounds Who Have No Friends": Witchcraft and Locality in the Nigerian Popular Press' in J. and J. L. Comaroff (eds), *Modernity and Its Malcontents: Ritual and Power in Postcolonial Africa*, Chicago: University of Chicago Press, 1993
Bauckham, R., *Tudor Apocalypse. Sixteenth-century Apocalypticism, Millenarianism and the English Reformation: From John Bale to John Foxe and Thomas Brightman*, Abingdon: Sutton Courtney, 1978.
—— *The Bible in Politics: How to Read the Bible Politically*, London: SPCK, 1981.

BIBLIOGRAPHY AND FURTHER READING

―― *The Fate of the Dead: Studies in Jewish and Christian Apocalypse*, Leiden, Boston: Brill, 1998.
―― *'God will be all in all': The Eschatology of Jürgen Moltmann*, Edinburgh: T. and T. Clark, 1999.
―― and David Bebbington, *History and Christianity: A Bibliography Prepared for the Historians' Study Group of the UCCF Associates*, Leeds: Dept of Theology, 1977.
―― and T. Hart, *Hope Against Hope. Christian Eschatology in Contemporary Context*, London: Darton Longman and Todd, 1999.
Bauman, Zygmunt, *Modernity and the Holocaust*, Ithaca, N.Y.: Cornell University Press, 1989.
Benhabib, S., *Situating the Self: Gender, Community and Postmodernism in Contemporary Ethics*, Cambridge: Polity Press, 1992.
Benjamin, W., *Illuminations*, trans. H. Zohn, New York: Harcourt Brace, 1973, reprint 1992.
Berlin, Isaiah, *Four Essays on Liberty*, Oxford: Oxford University Press, 1969.
―― 'Two Concepts of Liberty' in I. Berlin, *The Proper Study of Mankind*, Henry Hardy and Roger Hausheer (eds), London: Chatto and Windus, 1997.
―― *The Roots of Romanticism*, London, Chatto and Windus, 1999.
Bernstein, R. J. (ed.), *Habermas and Modernity*, Cambridge: Polity Press, 1985.
Binsbergen, Wim van (ed.), *The Social Life of Things Revisited*, Raleigh, N.C.: Duke University Press, forthcoming
Blaney, David L. and Pasha, Mustapha Kamal, 'Civil Society and Democracy in the Third World: Ambiguities and Historical Possibilities', *Studies in Comparative International Development*, 28 (1), 1993, pp. 3–24.
Blankenship, Vernon, 'Buildings for the Post-Christendom Church: From Meeting House to Megachurch', *Cutting Edge*, 29 (2), 2000, pp. 1–4.
Bloch, E., *The Principle of Hope*, trans. N. and S. Plaice and P. Knight, Oxford: Blackwell, 1986.
Bloch, Marc, *Apologie pour l'histoire, ou métier d'historien*, Paris: Masson, 1993–7 (1st edn Paris: Armand Colin, 1974). English trans. Peter Putnam, *The Historian's Craft*, Manchester: Manchester University Press, 1976.
Braudel, F., *L'Identité de la France*, 3 vols, Paris: Arthaud-Flammarion, 1986, reprinted 1990, 2000. English trans. S. Reynolds, *The Identity of France*, New York: Harper and Row, 1988.
Brownlee, Marina S., Brownlee, Kevin and Nichols, Stephen G. (eds), *The New Medievalism*, Baltimore, Md.: Johns Hopkins University Press, 1991.
Bultmann, R., *Jesus Christ and Mythology*, London: SCM, 1960.
―― 'The Case for Demythologizing: A Reply' in H.-W. Bartsch (ed.), *Kerygma and Myth*, vol. 2, London: SCM, 1964, pp. 182–3.
Bünker, M., *Briefformular und rhetorische Disposition im 1 Korintherbrief*, Göttingen: Vandenhoeck and Ruprecht, 1983.
Camus, Albert, *La Peste*, Paris: Gallimard, 1947.
Casey, John, *Pagan Virtue: An Essay in Ethics*, Oxford: Clarendon Press, 1990.
Certeau, M. de, *L'Ecriture de l'histoire*, Paris: Gallimard, coll. 'Bibliothèques des histoires', 1975.

BIBLIOGRAPHY AND FURTHER READING

Clark, Elisabeth and H. Richardson, *Women and Religion: A Feminist Sourcebook of Christian Thought*, New York: Harper and Row, 1977.

Clarke, A. D., *Secular and Christian Leadership in Corinth. A Socio-Historical and Exegetical Study of 1 Corinthians 1–6*, Leiden and New York: Brill, 1993.

Cohn, Norman, *The Pursuit of the Millennium: Revolutionary Millenarians and Mystical Anarchists of the Middle Ages*, London: Secker and Warburg, 1957, revised and expanded edition, Oxford and New York: Oxford University Press, 1970.

Comaroff, Jean, 'Consuming Passions: Nightmares of the Global Village' in E. Badone (ed.), *Body and Self in a Post-colonial World*, special issue of *Culture* 17 (1–2), 1997, pp. 7–19.

Comaroff, Jean and Comaroff, John L., *Body of Power, Spirit of Resistance: The Culture and History of a South African People*, Chicago: University of Chicago Press, 1995.

—— *Ethnography and the Historical Imagination*, Boulder, Col.: Westview Press, 1992.

—— (eds), *Modernity and Its Malcontents: Ritual and Power in Postcolonial Africa*, Chicago: University of Chicago Press, 1993.

—— 'Postcolonial Politics and Discourses of Democracy in Southern Africa: An Anthropological Reflection on African Political Modernities', *Journal of Anthropological Research*, 53 (2), 1997, pp. 123–46.

—— 'Occult Economies and the Violence of Abstraction: Notes from the South African Postcolony', *American Ethnologist*, 26 (3), 1999, pp. 279–301.

—— '"Alien-nation": Zombies, Immigrants, and Millennial Capitalism' in G. Schwab (ed.), *Forces of Globalization*, New York: Columbia University Press, 1999.

—— 'Millennial Capitalism: First Thoughts on a Second Coming' in J. L. Comaroff and J. Comaroff (eds), *Millennial Capitalism and the Culture of Neoliberalism*, special edition of *Public Culture*, 12 (2), 2000, pp. 291–343.

Connelly, Matthew and Kennedy, Paul, 'Must It Be the Rest against the West?' *The Atlantic Monthly*, 274 (6), December 1994, pp. 61–84.

Conrad, Joseph, *Under Western Eyes*, Harmondsworth: Penguin, 1957 (1st edn 1911).

Deissmann, A., *Light from the Ancient East*, London: Hodder and Stoughton, 1927.

Derrida, J., *Of Grammatology*, Baltimore, Md., and London: Johns Hopkins University Press, 1976.

—— *Writing and Difference*, trans. Alan Bass, London: Routledge, 1990 (original edn 1978).

—— *Specters of Marx: The State of Debt, the Work of Mourning, and the New International*, trans. Peggy Kamuf, New York: Routledge, 1994.

Descartes, R., *Discourse on Method; and the Meditations*, trans. F. E. Sutcliffe, Harmondsworth: Penguin, 1968.

Dietschy, B., 'Die Tücken des Entdeckens. Ernst Bloch, Kolumbus und die Neue Welt', *Jahrbuch der Ernst-Bloch-Gesellschaft*, 1992/3, pp. 234–51.

Dirlik, Arif, 'Looking Backwards in an Age of Global Capital: Thoughts on

History in Third World Cultural Criticism' in X. Tang and S. Snyder (eds), *Pursuit of Contemporary East Asian Culture*, Boulder, Col.: Westview Press, 1996.

Doherty, T., 'Postmodernist Theory: Lyotard, Baudrillard and Others' in Richard Kearney (ed.), *Twentieth-Century Continental Philosophy*, Routledge History of Philosophy, vol. 8, London: Routledge, 1994.

Dussel, E., *The Invention of the Americas*, trans. M. Barber, New York: Continuum, 1995.

Engels, Donald, *Roman Corinth: An Alternative Model for the Classical City*, Chicago and London: University of Chicago Press, 1990.

Eriksson, A., *Traditions as Rhetorical Proof. Pauline Argumentation in 1 Corinthians*, Stockholm: Almqvist and Wiksell, 1998.

Ermarth, E. D., *Sequel to History: Postmodernism and the Crisis of Representational Time*, Princeton, N.J.: Princeton University Press, 1992.

Fish, S., *Doing What Comes Naturally. Change, Rhetoric and the Practice of Theory in Literary and Legal Studies*, Oxford: Clarendon, 1989.

Friedlander, S. (ed.), *Probing the Limits of Representation. Nazism and the 'Final Solution'*, Cambridge, Mass. and London: Harvard University Press, 1992, 1996.

Frye, Northrop, *The Great Code: The Bible and Literature*, London: Routledge and Kegan Paul, 1982.

Fukuyama, Francis, *The End of History and the Last Man*, New York, The Free Press, 1992.

Gadamer, H.-G., *Truth and Method*, trans. W. Glen-Doepel, London: Sheed and Ward, 1979.

Gal, Susan, 'Feminism and Civil Society' in J. Scott, C. Kaplan and D. Keats (eds), *Transitions, Environments, Translations*, New York: Routledge, 1997.

Galeano, E., *Open Veins of Latin America*, New York: Orbis Books, 1974.

Geschiere, Peter, *The Modernity of Witchcraft: Politics and the Occult in Postcolonial Africa*, Charlottesville: University of Virginia Press, 1997.

Gifford, P., *Paul Valéry, le dialogue des choses divines*, Paris: J. Corti, 1989.

—— 'Au Miroir de l'Orient. Valéry, Malraux et la tentation de l'Occident' in Kunio Tsunekawa (ed.), *Paul Valéry, orient et occident. Actes du colloque international de Tokyo 24–27 septembre, 1996*, Paris: Minard, 'Les Lettres Modernes', pp. 97–115.

—— and Gratton, J. (eds), *Subject Matters: Subject and Self in French Literature from Descartes to the Present*, Amsterdam: Rodopi, 1999.

Gilbert, Martin, *The First World War*, London: HarperCollins, 1995.

Ginzburg, Carlo, 'Traces. Racines d'un paradigme indiciaire', Section 'Mythes, emblèmes, traces. Morphologie et histoire' in Marc Bloch, *Apologie pour l'histoire, ou métier d'historien*, Paris: Masson, 1993–7 (1st edn Paris: Armand Colin, 1974). English trans. Peter Putnam, *The Historian's Craft*, Manchester: Manchester University Press, 1976, pp. 139–80.

—— 'Just one witness!' in S. Friedlander (ed.), *Probing the Limits of Representation. Nazism and the 'Final Solution'*, Cambridge, Mass. and London: Harvard University Press, 1992, 1996, pp. 82–96.

BIBLIOGRAPHY AND FURTHER READING

Girard, René, 'Le Meurtre fondateur dans la pensée de Nietzsche' in P. Dumouchel (ed.), *Colloque de Cerisy 'Violence et Verité. Autour de René Girard'*, Paris: Grasset, 1985.

—— *The Scapegoat*, trans. Yvonne Freccaro, London: Athlone, 1986.

—— *To Double Business Bound: Essays on Literature, Mimesis and Anthropology*, London: Athlone, 1988.

—— *Des Choses cachées depuis la fondation du monde, recherches avec Jean-Michel Oughourlian et Guy Lefort*, Paris: Grasset, 1987. Trans. Stephen Barnes, Michael Matteer, *Things Hidden from the Foundation of the World*, London: Athlone, 1989.

—— *A Theater of Envy: William Shakespeare*, New York: Oxford University Press, 1991.

—— *La Violence et le sacré*, Paris: Grasset, 1972. Trans. Patrick Gregory, *Violence and the Sacred*, London: Athlone, 1995.

—— *Vom Fluch und Segen der Sündenböcke: Raymond Schwager zum 60. Geburtstag*, Thauer: Kulturverlage, 1995.

—— *Celui par qui le scandale arrive*, Paris: Desclée de Brouwer, 2001.

Gluckman, Max, 'The Magic of Despair', *The Listener*, 29 April 1959 (republished in *Order and Rebellion in Tribal Africa*, London: Cohen and West, 1963).

Gray, John, *Mill on Liberty: A Defence*, London: Routledge and Kegan Paul, 1983.

—— *Enlightenment's Wake: Politics and Culture at the Close of the Modern Age*, London and New York: Routledge, 1995.

—— *Endgames: Questions in Late Modern Political Thought*, Cambridge: Polity Press, 1997.

—— *Voltaire and Enlightenment*, London: Phoenix/Orion, 1998.

—— *False Dawn: The Delusions of Global Capitalism*, London and New York: Granta Books and The New Press, 1998.

—— *Two Faces of Liberalism*, London and New York: Polity Press and The New Press, 2000.

Griswold, Charles L., Jr., *Adam Smith and the Virtues of Enlightenment*, Cambridge: Cambridge University Press, 1999.

Guttiérrez, G., *Gott oder das Gold*, Freiburg: Herder Verlag, 1990 (German trans. of *Dios o el oro en las Indias*, 1989).

Halbwachs, Maurice, *La Mémoire collective*, Paris: Presses universitaires de France, 1950. English trans. *Collective Memory*, New York: Harper and Row, 1980.

Hampson, Daphne, *The Challenge of Feminism to Christianity*, London: SPCK, 1985.

—— *After Christianity*, London: SCM, 1996.

Hampshire, Stuart, 'Justice Is Strife', *Proceedings and Addresses of the American Philosophical Association*, 65 (3), November 1991, pp. 24–5.

—— *Justice Is Conflict*, London, Duckworth, 1999.

Hardy, D. W., 'The Future of Theology' in D. W. Hardy (ed.), *God's Ways with the World*, Edinburgh: T. and T. Clark, 1996.

Hart, Trevor, *Faith Thinking: The Dynamics of Christian Theology*, London: SPCK, 1995.

—— *Regarding Karl Barth: Essays Toward a Reading of His Theology*, Carlisle: Paternoster Press, 1999.
Harvey, David, *The Condition of Postmodernity*, Oxford: Blackwell, 1989.
Hegel, G. W. F., *Lectures on the Philosophy of World History. Introduction: Reason in History*, trans. H. N. Nisbet, Cambridge: Cambridge University Press, 1975.
Hepburn, R. W., 'Demythologizing and the Problem of Validity' in A. Flew and A. MacIntyre (eds), *New Essays in Philosophical Theology*, London: SCM, 1955, pp. 227–42;.
Herder, J. G., *Essay on the Origin of Language* (1700), trans. A. Gode, Chicago: University of Chicago Press, 1966.
High, D. M., *Language, Persons and Belief*, New York: Oxford University Press, 1967.
Hirst, Paul and Thompson, Grahame, *Globalization in Question: The International Economy and the Possibilities of Governance*, Cambridge: Polity Press, 1996.
Hume, David, 'A Treatise of Human Nature' in Alasdair MacIntyre (ed.), *Hume's Ethical Writings*, London: Collier-Macmillan, 1965.
Hutton, Patrick H., 'Maurice Halbwachs as Historian of Collective Memory' in *History as an Art of Memory*, Burlington: University of Vermont, 1993.
Irigaray, L., *Speculum de l'autre femme*, Paris: Minuit, 1974. Trans. Gillian C. Gill, *Speculum of the Other Woman*, Ithaca, NY: Cornell University Press, 1985.
—— *Ce sexe qui n'en est pas un*, Paris: Minuit, 1977. Trans. Catherine Parker with Caroline Brooke, *This Sex Which Is Not One*, Ithaca, NY: Cornell University Press, 1985.
—— 'Women, the Sacred and Money', *Paragraph* 8 (Oct. 1986), pp. 7–23.
Jameson, F., *Postmodernism: Or, the Cultural Logic of Late Capitalism*, London: Verso, 1991.
Judge, E. A., *The Social Pattern of Early Christian Groups in the First Century*, London: Tyndale Press, 1960.
Kant, I., 'Schriften zur Anthropologie, Geschichtsphilosophie, Politik und Pädagogik', vol. 6 of *Werke*, 6 vols, ed. Wilhelm Weischedel, Darmstadt: Wissenschaftliche Buchgesellschaft, 1964.
Kaplan, R., *The Nothing That Is: A Natural History of Zero*, London: Allen Lane/The Penguin Press, 1999.
Kennedy, P., *The Rise and Fall of the Great Powers*, New York: Random House, 1987.
Kermode, F., *The Genesis of Secrecy. On the Interpretation of Narrative*, Cambridge, Mass.: Harvard University Press, 1979.
Kort, Wesley A., *Story, Text and Scripture. Literary Interests in Biblical Narratives*, University Park, Pa.: Pennsylvania State University Press, 1988.
Kramer, Eric, 'Possessing Faith: Commodification, Religious Subjectivity, and Community in a Brazilian Neo-Pentecostal Church', PhD diss., University of Chicago, 1999.
Krige, Eileen Jensen and Comaroff, John L. (eds), *Essays on Marriage in Southern Africa*, Cape Town: Juta, 1981.
Kristeva, Julia, *Histoires d'amour*, Paris: Denoel, 1983. Trans. Leon S. Roudiez, *Tales of Love*, New York, Guildford: Columbia University Press, 1987.

—— *Etrangers à nous-mêmes*, Paris: Fayard, 1988. Trans. Leon S. Roudiez, *Strangers to Ourselves*, New York, London: Harvester Wheatsheaf, 1992.
La Fontaine, Jean S., *Speak of the Devil: Allegations of Satanic Child Abuse in Contemporary England*, Cambridge: Cambridge University Press, 1997.
Lane, W. L., *Hebrews*, 2 vols, Dallas, Tx.: Word, 1991.
Le Doeuff, Michèle, *Hipparchia's Choice: An Essay Concerning Woman, Philosophy, etc.*, Oxford and Cambridge, Mass.: Blackwell, 1991.
Leiss, W., *The Domination of Nature*, New York: Harper and Row, 1972.
Lévy-Bruhl, Lucien, *Carnets*, English trans. P. Rivière, *The Notebooks on Primitive Mentality*, Oxford: Blackwell, 1949.
Livingstone, Donald W., *Philosophical Delirium and Melancholy: Hume's Pathology of Philosophy*, Chicago and London: University of Chicago Press, 1998.
Lloyd, Geoffrey E. R., *Demystifying Mentalities*, Cambridge: Cambridge University Press, 1990.
Lochman, J. M. and Moltmann, J., *Das Recht und Menschenrechte*, Neukirchen: Neuhochener Verlag, 1977.
Löwith, Karl, *Meaning in History*, Chicago: University of Chicago Press, 1949.
Lyotard, J.-F., *The Postmodern Condition: A Report on Knowledge*, Minneapolis: University of Minnesota Press, and Manchester: Manchester University Press, 1984.
MacIntyre, Alasdair, *After Virtue: A Study in Moral Theory*, London: Duckworth, 1981.
McKibben, B., *The End of Nature*, New York and London: Viking, 1989.
Malraux, A., *La Tentation de l'occident*, Paris: Grasset, 1926; 'Le Livre de Poche', 1972.
Mannix, D. P. and Cowley, M. J., *Black Cargoes: A History of the Atlantic Slave Trade*, New York: Viking, 1962.
Marin, Louis, *Le Portrait du roi*, Paris: Minuit, coll. 'Le Sens commun', 1981.
—— *Des Pouvoirs de l'image*, Paris: Seuil, coll. 'L'Ordre philosophique', 1993.
Martin, D. B., *The Corinthian Body*, New Haven, Conn., and London: Yale University Press, 1995.
Meeks, Wayne A., *The First Urban Christians. The Social World of the Apostle Paul*, New Haven, Conn.: Yale University Press, 1983.
Meggitt, J. J., *Paul, Poverty and Survival*, Edinburgh: T. and T. Clark, 1998.
Meier, H., *Die Lehre Carl Schmitts. Vier Kapitel zur Unterscheidung Politischer Theologie und Politischer Philosophie*, Stuttgart: Verlag J. B. Metzler, 1994, pp. 243–9.
Merchant, C., *The Death of Nature. Women, Ecology and the Scientific Revolution*, San Francisco: Harper and Row, 1989.
Metz, J. B., *Faith in History and Society: Toward a Practical Fundamental Theology*, trans. D. Smith, London and New York: Seaburg Press, 1980.
Mill, John Stuart, *On Liberty and Other Essays*, Oxford: Oxford University Press, 1998.
Mitchell, M. M., *Paul and the Language of Reconciliation: An Exegetical Investigation into the Language and Composition of 1 Corinthians*, Louisville, Ky.: Knox/Westminster, 1992.

BIBLIOGRAPHY AND FURTHER READING

Moltmann, J., *Theology of Hope: On the Ground and the Implications of a Christian Eschatology*, second edition, London: SCM, 1967.
—— *The Coming of God: Christian Eschatology*, trans. Margaret Kohl, London: SCM, and Minneapolis, Minn.: Fortress Press, 1996.
—— *God for a Secular Society: The Public Relevance of Theology*, London: SCM, 1999.
—— *The Crucified God: The Cross of Christ as the Foundation and Criticism of Christian Theology*, trans. R. A. Wilson and John Bowden, London: SCM, 2001.
Moores, J. D., *Wrestling with Rationality in Paul*, Cambridge: Cambridge University Press, 1995.
Morris, Rosalind, 'Modernity's Media and the End of Mediumship? On the Aesthetic Economy of Transparency in Thailand' in J. Comaroff and J. L. Comaroff (eds), *Millennial Capitalism and the Culture of Neoliberalism*, special edition of *Public Culture*, 12 (2), 2000, pp. 457–76.
Mosès, S., *Der Engel der Geschichte. Franz Rosenzweig, Walter Benjamin, Gershom Scholem*, Frankfurt: Jüdischer Verlag, 1994.
Mounier, Emmanuel, *Refaire la renaissance*, Paris: Seuil, 1961, Coll. 'Points', 2000.
Murphy-O'Connor, J., *St Paul's Corinth: Texts and Archaeology*, Wilmington, Del.: Glazier, 1983.
Negri, Antonio, 'The Specter's Smile' in M. Sprinker (ed.), *Ghostly Demarcations: A Symposium on Jacques Derrida's Specters of Marx*, London and New York: Verso, 1999.
Niebuhr, Reinhold, *Moral Man and Immoral Society*, London: SCM, 1963 (1st edn 1932).
Nietzsche, F., *Complete Works* (18 vols), London: Allen and Unwin, 1909–13.
Pannenberg, Wolfhart, *Basic Questions in Theology* (3 vols), London: SCM, 1970, 1971 and 1973.
—— *Systematic Theology* (3 vols), Edinburgh: T. and T. Clark and Grand Rapids, Mich.: Eerdmans, 1991, 1994 and 1998.
Philipp, W., *Das Werden der Aufklärung in theologiegeschichtlicher Sicht*, Göttingen, 1957.
Pogoloff, S., *Logos and Sophia. The Rhetorical Situation of 1 Corinthians*, Atlanta, Ga.: Scholars Press, 1992.
'Questions of a Common Era', special edition of *Signs: Journal of Women in Culture and Society* (Chicago: Chicago University Press), 25 (4), Summer 2000.
Rahner, Karl, *Foundations of Christian Faith*, New York: Seabury, 1968.
Rapport, N., *Transcendent Individual: Towards a Literary and Liberal Anthropology*, London and New York: Routledge, 1997.
—— and Overing, J., *Social and Cultural Anthropology. The Key Concepts*, London and New York: Routledge, 2000.
Readings, Bill, *Introducing Lyotard: Art and Politics*, London and New York: Routledge, 1991.
Reeves, Marjorie, *Joachim of Fiore and the Prophetic Future*, London: SPCK, 1976.

BIBLIOGRAPHY AND FURTHER READING

Ricœur, Paul, *De l'interprétation. Essai sur Freud*, Paris: Seuil, 'L'Ordre philosophique', 1965. Trans. D. Savage, *Freud and Philosophy: An Essay on Interpretation*, New Haven, London: Yale University Press, 1970.

—— *Le Conflit des interprétations. Essais d'herméneutique 1*, Paris: Seuil, 'L'Ordre philosophique', 1969. Trans. Don Ihde, *The Conflict of Interpretations: Essays in Hermeneutics*, Evanston, Ill.: Northwestern University Press, 1974.

—— *La Metaphore vive*, Paris: Seuil, 'L'Ordre philosophique', 1975, trans. Robert Czeray, *The Rule of Metaphor: Multidisciplinary Studies of the Creation of Meaning in Language*, Toronto, Buffalo: University of Toronto Press, 1977.

—— 'The Hermeneutics of Revelation' in L. S. Mudge (ed.), *Essays on Biblical Interpretation*, London: SPCK, 1981.

—— *Temps et récit*, t. 1 'L'Intrigue et le récit historique', 1983; t. 2 'La Configuration dans le récit de fiction', 1984; t. 3 'Le Temps raconté', 1985; Paris: Seuil, coll. 'L'Ordre philosophique'. Trans. Kathleen McLoughlin and David Pellauer, vol. 1, 1984; vol. 2, 1985; vol. 3, 1988; Chicago: Chicago University Press.

—— *Soi-même comme un autre*, Paris: Seuil, 'L'Ordre philosophique', 1990, trans. Kathleen Blaney, *Oneself as Another*, Chicago and London: University of Chicago Press, 1992.

—— 'Narrative Hospitality' in R. Kearney (ed.), *The Hermeneutics of Action*, Sage, 1996.

—— and Alistair MacIntyre, *The Religious Significance of Atheism*, Bampton Lectures in America, no. 18, New York, Columbia, London: Columbia University Press, 1969.

Rifkin, Jeremy, *The End of Work: The Decline of the Global Labor Force and the Dawn of the Post-Market Era*, New York: G. P. Putnam's Sons, 1995.

Ritter, Joachim, *Hegel und die französische Revolution*, Cologne: Opladen, 1957.

Roberts, R. H., 'A Postmodern Church? Some Preliminary Reflections on Ecclesiology and Social Theory' in D. F. Ford and D. L. Stamps (eds), *Essentials of Christian Community*, Edinburgh: T. and T. Clark, 1996.

Rorty, R., 'On Ethnocentrism: A Reply to Clifford Geertz', *Michigan Quarterly Review*, 25 (Winter, 1986), pp. 525-34.

—— *Contingency, Irony and Solidarity*, Cambridge: Cambridge University Press, 1992.

—— *Truth and Progress: Philosophical Papers*, vol. 3, Cambridge: Cambridge University Press, 1998.

Saint-Exupéry, A., *Terre des hommes*, Paris: Gallimard, 1937.

Sassen, Saskia, *Losing Control? Sovereignty in an Age of Globalization*, New York: Columbia University Press, 1996.

Schacht, Richard, *Hegel and After: Studies in Continental Philosophy Between Kant and Sartre*, Pittsburgh: University of Pittsburgh Press, 1975.

—— *Nietzsche*, London: Routledge and Kegan Paul, 1983.

—— *The Future of Alienation*, Urbana: University of Illinois Press, 1994.

—— (ed.), *Nietzsche, Genealogy, Morality*, Los Angeles: University of California Press, 1994.

—— *Making Sense of Nietzsche*, Urbana: University of Illinois Press, 1995.

—— (ed.), *Nietzsche's Postmoralism: Rethinking Nietzsche's Prelude to Philosophy's Future*, New York: Cambridge University Press, 1996.
—— (ed.), *On Human Nature, Readings in Philosophical Anthropology*, New York: Prentice Hall, 2001.
Schaller, Lyle, *The New Reformation – Tomorrow Arrived Yesterday*, Nashville, Tn.: Abingdon Press, 1999.
Scheper-Hughes, Nancy, *Death without Weeping: The Violence of Everyday Life in Brazil*, Berkeley: University of California Press, 1992.
Schlette, H. R., *Weltseele. Geschichte und Hermeneutik*, Frankfurt: Suhrkamp Verlag, 1993.
Schneider, Jane, 'Rumpelstiltskin's Bargain: Folklore and the Merchant Capitalist Intensification of Linen Manufacture in Early Modern Europe' in A. Weiner and J. Schneider (eds), *Cloth and Human Experience*, Washington: Smithsonian Institution Press, 1989.
Schneider, N., *Die rhetorische Eigenart der paulinischen Antithese*, Tübingen: Mohr [HUT, 11], 1970.
Scholem, Gershom, *Walter Benjamin und sein Engel*, Frankfurt: Suhrkamp Verlag, 1983.
Schrage, W., *Der erste Brief an die Korinther*, Zürich: Benziger, and Neukirchen-Vluyn: Neukirchener, 3 vols to date, 1991, 1995, 1999 [Ev.-Kath. Kom. z. N.T. VII, 1–3).
Sennett, Richard, *The Corrosion of Character: The Personal Consequences of Work in the New Capitalism*, New York: W. W. Norton, 1998.
Skemp, J. B., *The Greeks and the Gospel*, London: Carey Kingsgate, 1964.
Sorabaji, Richard, *Aristotle on Memory*, Providence, Rhode Island: Brown University Press, 1972.
Sprinker, Michael (ed.), *Ghostly Demarcations: A Symposium of Jacques Derrida's Specters of Marx*, London: Verso, 1999.
Stahel, W., *Die Beschleunigungsfalle oder der Triumph der Schildkröte*, Stuttgart: Kohlhammer Verlag, 1995.
Steiner, George, *Language and Silence*, London: Penguin, 1967.
—— *Real Presences: Is There Anything in What We Say?*, London: Faber and Faber, 1989.
Suutala, M., *Zur Geschichte der Naturzerstörung. Frau und Tier in der wissenschaftlichen Revolution*, Frankfurt: Peter Lang Verlag, 1999.
Taubes, J., *Abendländische Eschatologie* (1947), Munich: Matthes and Seitz Verlag, 1991.
Theissen, G., *The Social Setting of Pauline Christianity*, ed. and trans. John H. Schütz, Philadelphia, Pa.: Fortress, 1982.
—— *Psychological Aspects of Pauline Theology*, Edinburgh: T. and T. Clark, 1987.
Thiselton, Anthony C., 'Truth' in C. Brown (ed.), *The New International Dictionary of NT Theology*, Exeter: Paternoster, and Grand Rapids, Mich.: Zondervan, vol. 3, 1978.
—— *The Two Horizons*, Grand Rapids, Mich.: Eerdmans, and Exeter: Paternoster, 1980.

—— *New Horizons in Hermeneutics: The Theory and Practice of Transforming Biblical Reading*, London: HarperCollins, 1992.

—— 'The Logical Role of the Liar Paradox in Titus 1: 12, 13: A Dissent from the Commentaries in the Light of Philosophical and Logical Analysis', *Biblical Interpretation*, 2, 1994, pp. 207–23

—— *Interpreting God and the Postmodern Self: On Meaning, Manipulation and Promise*, Edinburgh: T. and T. Clark and Grand Rapids, Mich.: Eerdmans, 1995.

—— 'Signs of the Times: Towards a Theology for the Year 2000 . . .' in David Fergusson and Marcel Sarot (eds), *The Future as God's Gift: Explorations in Christian Eschatology*, Edinburgh: T. and T. Clark, 2000.

—— *The First Epistle to the Corinthians: A Commentary on the Greek Text*, The New International Greek Testament Commentary, Grand Rapids, Mich.: Eerdmans, and Carlisle: Paternoster, 2000.

Tillich, P., *The Courage to Be* (1952), 2nd edn, New Haven and London: Nisbet, 2000.

Todorov, T., *La Conquête de l'Amérique: la question de l'autre*, Paris: Seuil, 1982.

Torrance, Alan, *Persons in Communion: An Essay on Trinitarian Descriptions and Human Participation, with Special Reference to Volume 1 of Karl Barth's 'Church Dogmatics'*, Edinburgh: T. and T. Clark, 1996.

—— and Regan, Hilary (eds), *Christ and Context: The Confrontation between Gospel and Culture*, Edinburgh: T. and T. Clark, 1992.

Tuveson, E. L., *Redeemer Nation: The Idea of America's Millennial Role*, Chicago: Chicago University Press, 1968.

Überlacker, W. G., *Der Hebräerbrief als Appell*, Stockholm: Almqvist and Wiksell [Con. Bib. N.T. Ser. 21], 1989.

Valéry, Paul, 'Genesis' in *Charmes*, Paris: Gallimard, 1922.

Vanhoozer, Kevin, *Is There a Meaning in This Text? The Bible, The Reader, and the Morality of Literary Knowledge*, Grand Rapids, Mich.: Zondervan, 1998.

Vanhoye, A., *Homilie für halfbedürftige Christen*, Regensburg: Pustet, 1981.

Weber, Max, *The Protestant Ethic and the Spirit of Capitalism*, trans. T. Parsons, New York: C. Scribner's, 1958.

Welborn, L. L., *Politics and Rhetoric in the Corinthian Epistles*, Macon, Ga.: Mercer University Press, 1997.

Weller, Robert P., 'Living at the Edge: Religion, Capitalism, and the End of the Nation-State in Taiwan' in J. L. Comaroff and J. Comaroff (eds), *Millennial Capitalism and the Culture of Neoliberalism*, special edition of *Public Culture*, 12 (2), 2000, pp. 477–98.

Werth, G., *Verdun. Die Schlacht und der Mythos*, Bergisch-Gladbach: Lübbe, 1982.

White, Hayden, *Metahistory. The Historical Imagination in the XIXth Century*, Baltimore, Md., and London: Johns Hopkins University Press, 1973

—— *Tropics of Discourse*, Baltimore, Md., and London: Johns Hopkins University Press, 1978.

—— *Content of the Form*, Baltimore, Md., and London: Johns Hopkins University Press, 1987.

Whitehouse, Tom, 'Messiah on the Make in Sun City', *The Observer World*, 30 May 1999, p. 26
Wilson, E. O., *Sociobiology, The Abridged Edition*, Cambridge, Mass.: Harvard, Belknap, 1980.
Winter, B. W., *Philo and Paul; Seek the Welfare of the City*, Grand Rapids, Mich.: Eerdmans, 1994.
—— *Philo and Paul among the Sophists*, Cambridge: Cambridge University Press, 1997.
—— *After Paul Left Corinth*, Grand Rapids, Mich.: Eerdmans, 2001.
Wiseman, James, 'Corinth and Rome, I, 228 BC – AD 267' in *Aufstieg und Niedergang der römischen Welt* 2: 7: 1, Berlin: deGruyter, 1979.
Witherington, B., *Conflict and Community in Corinth*, Carlisle: Paternoster, and Grand Rapids, Mich.: Eerdmans, 1995.
Wolterstorff, N., *Divine Discourse*, Cambridge: Cambridge University Press, 1995.
Worsley, Peter M., *The Trumpet Shall Sound: A Study of 'Cargo' Cults in Melanesia*, London: Macgibbon and Kee, 1957.
Yudice, George, 'Civil Society, Consumption, and Governmentality in an Age of Global Reconstruction', *Social Text*, 45, 14 (4), 1995, pp. 1–25.
Zakai, Avilhu, *Exile and Kingdom: History of the Apocalypse in the Puritan Migration to America*, Cambridge: Cambridge University Press, 1992.
—— 'From Judgment to Salvation. The Image of the Jews in the English Renaissance', *Westminster Theological Journal*, 59 (1997), pp. 213–30.
Žižek, Slavoj, *The Plague of Fantasies*, London: Verso, 1997.

INDEX

absolutism 159
Africa 13: post-colonial Southern Africa 111; West Africa 116
age (era): 'age of anxiety' 28, 118; age of catastrophes 23–6; golden age 21; new age of enchantment (neoliberal capitalism) 124; premodern, modern, postmodern 14, 168–9; 'Third Age of the Spirit' 21; age of utopias 22; *see also* bi-millennium; 'Common Era'; millennium; postmodernism; time (temporality)
alienation 11
Ambler, Rex 136
America: South America 131; United States 9, 18, 20, 28, 118, 131, 178
Anders, Gunter 30
'Angel of history' (*Angelus Novus*) 8, 23, 26
anthropology 71; philosophical 76–7
apartheid, death of 114
Apocalypse Now 25
Aquinas, Thomas 145
Arendt, Hannah 67
Aristophanes 141
Aristotle 39, 41, 50, 52, 67, 97
Asian societies 9
Auden, W. H. 25
Augustine (saint) 40, 51, 53, 182
Auschwitz 17, 25, 27, 64; *see also* Holocaust
Ayer, A. J. 135
Aztecs 18

Bacon, Francis 18, 43

Balzac, H. de 123
Barth, Karl 128, 144
Barthes, Roland 14, 61
Bauman, Zygmunt 7, 174
Benjamin, Walter 8, 23, 26, 28
Bentham, Jeremy 38, 44, 47
Benveniste, E. 56, 58
Bergson, Henri 3, 52, 54, 67, 170
Berlin, Isaiah 9, 45, 159
Bernstein, Richard 127, 129
bible 11, 15, 146: biblical idea of new creation 148–9; as 'common code' 169; Hebrew bible 101, 142; and postmodernism 127–46; selfhood and otherness in 168; uniqueness of biblical tradition 104
bible, New Testament 15, 143, 144: gospels 105 (Matthew 126, 128, 144, Luke 128, 144, Mark 128, 142, John 126, 128, 143, 157); epistles (Romans 126, 143, 146, 1 Corinthians 129, 130, 133, 139, 141–5, 2 Corinthians 127–46, Ephesians 126, 2 Thessalonians 30, Hebrews 28, 128, 142); Revelation 30, 34
bible, Old Testament 12: Genesis 128, 145, 182; Exodus 133; Job 101, 131; Psalms 120; Ecclesiastes 131, 143; Isaiah 101; Jeremiah 143; Ezekiel 8; 27–8, 34; Daniel 20
bi-millennium 1; *see also* millennium
Blair, Tony 9
Bloch, E. 161
Bloch, Marc 57, 66
Body Zone 1

INDEX

Boxer rising 22
Bragg, Melvyn 3
Braudel, F. 60
British Empire 2
Buddhist 43
Bultmann, Rudolf 14, 128, 142

Calvin, Jean 40, 182
Camus, Albert 150
capitalism 13: model for understanding 'original sin' 183; neoliberal capitalism (end of the world of work, primacy of consumption, stimulation of desire, preternatural production of wealth, 'casino capitalism') 112–14, 119; 'numinous magic of global enterprise' 111, 120; 'second coming' (as salvation gospel) 13, 106–26; and Western ideology (Judaeo-Protestant) 115
catholic(ism) 47, 72, 182; *see also* Aquinas; Augustine; Christianity; Jansenism; etc.
Celsius 102
Certeau, Michel de 56, 66
Chartier, Roger 66
Chernobyl 17
chiliasm 21, 113
Christendom 2, 163, 173–5, 184: 'post-Christendom' and 'post-Christian' 166
Christianity 1, 10, 43, 149, 184: Christ 138, 139; Christian particularity ('exceptionalism') 154, 186; and civilization 48, 98; and Corinthian 'spirituality' 130; the Cross 138, 148; and deconstruction 127–46, 135, 187–8; divine sovereign initiative 129, 146; and the Enlightenment 35–50; and European colonization 18; and feminism 186–7; grace as givenness 15, 128, 138; and holism of creation 32, 157; Kingdom (of God) 2, 21, 31; and 'original sin' 40, 182–3; *parousia* 13, 107–9, 121; 'post-Christian' 166; the resurrection 8, 148, 184; the Spirit (Paraclete) 138, 156; universally

relevant foundation 15, 40, 49, 127; *see also* Christendom; church; Jesus of Nazareth
church: Christian 2, 21, at Corinth 134–46; Last Testament Church 106; New Life Church in South Africa 107, 119, 125; Orthodox Church 107; post-Christendom Church in America 108; Universal Church of the Kingdom of God (Pentecostal) in Brazil, Nigeria 120–1
Cicero 138
Clarke, Andrew 138, 139, 141
Clinton, Bill 179
Cold War 66, 114
colonization 18; colonial empires 22
Columbus, Christopher 19
'Common Era' 2, 4, 6, 10, 15, 66, 144–89; *see also* age; time (temporality)
Comaroff, Jean and John 12, 106–26, 166, 177–9, 183
community 2, 3, 96–7, 123, 125, 159, 163, 179, 189
Comte, Auguste 22, 38, 88, 184
Condorcet, M.-J.-A.-N. 39
conflict: East–West 32; civil strife 109; mimetic nature of 89–93
Confucianism 43
conquista 18
Conrad, Joseph 123
Constantine 2, 184
consumerism 109, 113–14
Copernicus 18
Corinth 137–46
creation: the Creator 157; 'new creation' 148, 161, 162
crimes against humanity 17, 30
critical theory 70
Cromwell, Oliver 21
cross (Christian): as critique of secular society 14; crucifixion-resurrection as determining event 148; as *eikōn* 179
culture: 'casino culture' in America 112; cultural difference 90; variety of 47, 164; *see also* ethnocentrism; identity(ies)

221

INDEX

Dante 94
dead, raising of the 27–8
death, overcoming of 28, 156; death of Jesus 181
deconstruction(ism) 15, 70, 131, 133, 172
de Gaulle, Charles 150
Deissmann, Adolf 141
democracy 29: democratic decision making and nuclear power 32; and genetically modified foodstuffs 33, 109; democratization movements in South Africa 114; liberal democracy 158–9
demythologizing 14, 142; demystification 14
Deng Xiaoping 111
Derrida, Jacques 6, 14, 109, 113, 125, 132–3, 144, 168, 173
Descartes, René 18, 33, 140; Cartesian duality 80–1
desire 89; global economy of 114, 122
Dewey, John 70
Diderot, Denis 47
Docherty, Thomas 14, 136
Drabble, Margaret 7
Durkheim, E. 88

Eco, Umberto 139
ecology 6, 32
economy: economic change 60; global economy of desire 122; occult economies (pyramid schemes, sale of body parts) 115–19, 121–5; and religion 13
ecumenism 32
Eliot, George 176
emancipation 9, 50
embodiment 12, 79
Emmaus road 184
end-time *see* eschatology
Engels, Donald 137
English-speaking world 8
Enlightenment 160, 164, 173–5: deconstructionist rage against 127, 130, 136; post-Enlightenment 163; as project 9, 35; as secular version of Christianity 35–50; supposing monotheistic belief 49
environment 9

Epicurus 39
Eriksson, Anders 14, 141
eschatology 15, 30, 34, 189
essence 172, 179
ethics 9: consensus on 46; conservation ethics 32; ethical goals 21; ethical imperative 162; ethical subjectivism 46; objective pluralism in 49
ethnocentrism 134, 164; ethnic cleansing 25
Europe, rise of 20; abuse of children and theft of human tissue in 117
evil: power of radical evil unbroken 25; *see also* Satan
existentialism 11, 70, 73

fascism 25
feminism 6, 11, 70, 73, 170, 185–8
Feuerbach, Ludwig 70
'Final Solution' 17, 25, 44, 63, 66, 71
First World War 24–5, 160
Fish, Stanley 138, 139, 140
Foucault, Michel 11, 14, 69, 72, 74, 128, 131–4, 141, 143–4
foundational myths 91–2
foundationalism 133; anti-foundationalism 139
Free World 2
freedom 9, 167; 'liberticide' 38
French Revolution 2, 22, 28, 65, 66
Freud, Sigmund 6, 10, 50, 54, 92–3, 130, 185
Friedlander, Saul 63–4, 92, 93
Frye, Northrop 169
Fukuyama, Francis 39, 41
fundamentalism 109, 167, 189
Furet, Stanislas 66
future: bound up with contradictions of past 17; bridges to future 26; foregrounded as dimension of human time (paradigm of transcendence) 20, 22; God's future 161, 180; and 'narrative identity' 147

Gadamer, H.-G. 67, 140
gambling 112; *see also* capitalism, 'casino capitalism'
Gandhi, M. 154

INDEX

genome 19
Germany 8; basic law of Federal Republic 29
Ginsburg, Carlo 57, 64, 66
Girard, René 12, 88–105, 148, 151–3, 166, 169, 174, 177–85
globalization 32: of capitalist economy 110; global economy of desire 122; global electronic integration 115; globalized world 189; of power and responsibility 33
God: 'God is dead' 5, 11, 166, 180–1, 183, 184, 185; human 'God-complex' 33; image of 18; righteousness and justice of God 30
grace 15, 128, 138–9, 146
Gray, John 9, 147, 148, 164, 166, 174–5, 179, 184
Greek tragedy 91
Grey, Sir Edward 24
Gulag Archipelago 17

Habermas, Jürgen 39
Halbwachs, Maurice 53, 57
Hampshire, Stuart 44
Hampson, Daphne 169–70, 185–7
Harvey, David 131–3
Hayek, F. von 9, 39
Heesterman, J. C. 100
Hegel, G. F. 11, 18, 22, 67, 70, 71, 72, 81, 128, 140
Heidegger, M. 54, 67, 60, 128, 140, 157, 170
Heracleitus 140
hermeneutics 10, 14
Herodotus 55
Hinduism 43
Hiroshima 17, 27
historiography 10, 56: critical realism in history-writing 58; literary phase of 61; and postmodernism 62, 168; as representation (problems in representing the past) 51–68
history: and genealogy 77; history of truth (faithfulness) 171; of mankind 41; meaning in the face of 26; and memory 10, 65; of mentalities 60; philosophy of 22; pressure exerted by history in the making 10–11; rewriting of 11; as a series of catastrophes 36; truth of 65; *see also* 'Angel of history'
Hitler 25, 30, 63, 70
Hobbes, T. 40, 48, 81, 83
Holocaust ('Shoah') 10, 63, 67, 168, 174
Holy Roman Empire 2
Homer 41
hope 7, 20, 147–8, 162–3, 190: apocalypse without hope 25; Christian theology of 8, 26; end-time (eschatological) hope 22; Enlightenment hopes 49; hope against hope 28; the hope of truth 10; and human rights 29; and identity 163; messianic 17; and millennial capitalism 122; as motivating European discovery of world 19; for political world 30; of resurrection 27; transcendent 8–9, 27
Horkenheimer, Max 19
human nature 11, 12, 73–4, 85, 179: 'ban on man' 72; confidence in 181–3; dying with 'death of God'? 181; future of 69–87; models of (Platonic, Aristotelian, Cartesian, Hobbesian, Humean, Kantian, Hegelian, Heideggerian, Sartrean, Christian) 80; the 'no longer merely animal animal' 76, 77
human rights 29, 109; fetishization of 115
humanism: and deconstructionism 127; of the Enlightenment 35–8, 44, 76; 'man is dead' 11, 49–50, 160, 180
Hume, David 11, 46, 47, 69, 70, 74–5, 80, 166
Husserl, E. 54

identity(ies): 'our' collective identity-in-culture 1, 5, 54, 165, 177, 189–90; construction of identity in neoliberal capitalism 111, 114; criteria of personal identity 54, 64; human subject-identity 147, 154, 166, 171, 172, 190; narrative identity (Ricœur) 147; as

INDEX

personhood 131; as response to *kerygma* 139
imagination 171; deceiving imagination (fantasy) 52–3, 172
Incas 18
industrial revolution 31
intersubjectivity 12, 79
Irigaray, Luce 186, 187
ironism 158–60
Islam 121, 172, 179

James, William 135
Jansenism 182
Jesus of Nazareth 15, 42, 104, 111–12, 121, 142, 144, 155, 158: as emissary victim 100 (death of 181, 'Lamb of God' 105, Passion of 156); parables of 145, 158; risen Jesus 170; and social constructions 128; and women 186
Jews 2, 20, 27, 150, 158, 169; Judaeo-Protestant ideology 177
Joachim of Fiore 19–20, 21
Judaeo-Christianity 12: eschatology of 159–60, 189; inheritance of 7, 67; matrix of religious or cultural identity 1, 4, 5, 68, 163, 168, 169, 171, 173–5, 180, 181, 187, 189, 190; particularity of 6, 66, 147–9, 159–60, 168, 169, 173–5, 180–1, 187, 189, 190
Judaism 1, 43, 187
Judge, E. A. 141
justice 9; and spirit of Jesus 31

Kant, I. 19, 21, 38, 47, 67, 71, 127, 132
Kermode, Frank 7, 142
Kierkegaard, Søren 47, 70, 135
Kingdom of God (of Heaven) 3, 20, 31, 184
Klee, Paul 23
knowledge, scientific 9, 123, 126; as power 19; *see also* Enlightenment; historiography: representation; postmodern; truth
Kristeva, Julia 7, 185
Kuhn, T. 132

Lacan, J. 6, 155, 170, 185, 170
language 129: and rhetorical argument 141; code-switching 142; indeterminacy 145
Lessing, Ephraim von 21
Lévy-Bruhl, L. 60
liberalism 9: and progress 39; society of liberal democracy 164–5, 175, 188; values of 38, 44
linguistics: Saussurian model 58, 168; Benveniste 58
Livy 92, 145
Locke, John 54, 69
'lost body' (of risen Jesus) 170
'lost object of desire' (Lacan) 170
Luce, Henry 20
Luther, Martin 182
Lyotard, J.-F. 132–3

Machiavelli 40
MacIntyre, Alistair 36, 47
magic: capitalist 11, 116–17, 120, 122, 124; sorcery, witchcraft and occult activity in South Africa 116
Malraux, André 180
Mammon 177, 179
Mao Zedong 25
Marcus Aurelius 43
marginality (boundaries) 144
Marx(ism) 6, 11, 13, 22, 38, 39, 41, 46, 66, 70, 72, 73, 110, 122, 125, 176, 185
Mayas 18
Meeks, Wayne 136, 141
memory 7: collective 10, 53, 189; duty of remembrance (*devoir de mémoire*) 55, 66; faithfulness of memory 50, 55; and hope 170; impeded, manipulated, constrained 54–5; pragmatics of 54; subject of 54; and the truth of history 65; *see also* historiography; history
messianism: and birth of modernity 18–22; Jewish messianism 20; messianic banquet 144, 148; messianic spirit and capitalism 126; new messiahs 106, 119
Michelet, Jules 160
Mill, J. S. 9, 38, 39, 44, 46
millenarianism 2: millennial capitalism 115; 'Thousand years empire of Christ' 19; *see also* chiliasm; messianism

INDEX

millennium: millennium and bi-millennium 1–2; Millennium Dome 1; as mystic moment 1, 17
mimetic theory of religion 88–107: mimetic crisis 90, 95, 97, 98, 101; mimetic desire 12, 89; mimetic rivalry 12, 78; mimetic violence 100
mind, mentality 79–80; *see also* history: of mentalities
Mitchell, Margaret 134, 142
Mithraism 39
modernity 7, 127: modernity as new time 20, 21; shadow side of 23
Moltmann, Jürgen 1, 8, 16–34, 127, 147–51, 162, 180
Montesquieu, C.-L. de S. 48
Moores, John 138, 139, 141–2
morality 48, 50
Morin, Louis 61
Morris, Rosalind 117
Moses 133
Mott, John 22
Mother Earth 18; symbolic Mother 187
myth(s): and censorship 93; of death and resurrection 103; mythology and religion radically critiqued by Judaeo-Christianity 156; Oedipus 93, 94, 96, 155, 170; *see also* demythologizing

narrative hospitality 147
nature 18, 26, 23, 33; nature and nurture 72, 78–9
Nazis 150, 165, 167
negativities 7
New Labour 9
Newton, Isaac 18
Niebuhr, Reinhold 144
Nietzsche, Friedrich 5, 11, 12, 67, 69, 70, 75–8, 80–1, 83, 127, 128, 130, 133–4, 143–4, 148–50, 160, 166–8, 183–5
nuclear threat 30
Nussbaum, Martha 7

objectification 12, 79
Oedipus complex 96, 155, 170; 'Oedipal moment' of twentieth-century thought 181, 185

O'Goran, Edmundo 18
ontology 15, 133
Origen 102
Other (culture zones) 178; acknowledging Others 190; divine Other 181
Overman 148, 150, 160, 167

paganism 40–3
Paine, Thomas 39
Pannenberg, Wolfgang 130
Parmenides 140
past 8, 77, 147, 168, 169, 170–1, 185
Paul (apostle) 14, 128, 130, 133, 134, 141–3, 158
Perelman, C. 139
philosophy: analytical 70; Catholic 72; historical 77; linguistic 70; phenomenology 11, 73; pre-Socratic 140, 179; Socratic 179; *see also* Derrida; Irigaray; Nietzsche; Plato; etc.
Plantinga, A. 7
Plato 42–3, 52, 57, 65, 67, 93, 169
pluralism 6–7, 10, 137; *see also* values: value pluralism
Pogaloff, Stephen 138, 141
Pol Pot 25
positivism 2, 44, 46, 70; *see also* Comte
post-Christian 5, 102
post-colonialism 6, 107, 153, 177
postmodern(ism) 7, 10, 62, 67, 127–46, 173; does not constitute an era (Docherty, Ricœur) 7, 136, 160, 169, 175; as 'palace of mirrors' 168; postmodern person, made with objects 111; postmodern pessimism 124; postmodern world 14, 173; as suspicion of ideology and power interests 128, 131, 144, 173
post-structuralism 70
progress: devouring its own children 24, 27–8; as dogma 175, 182–3; Enlightenment ideas of progress 21–2, 37; linked to linear chronology 16; only a means to an end 32; not to be expected from human animal on a naturalistic

view 152; possibility of 9, 30, 31, 36, 39, 42, 160, 161, 166; profits and losses of 16
Protagoras 140
Protestant 182: Judaeo-Protestant ideology 177; neo-Protestantism 111, 123
psycho-somaticity 12, 79

Quintilian 138
Quintomonarchists 19

Rahner, Karl 130
Ranke, Leopold von 28
Reagan, Ronald 9
reason 35, 46–9, 63, 131
relativism 7, 10, 48, 63, 134
religion 12: African, ritual and symbolism 13; archaic religion 88–105 (binding/bonding role 89, 180; cultural origins of 90, 98; myths 90; ritual sacrifice and deception 100); capitalism as a religion 176; deconstructing idolatrous religion 135, 156, 172; identifying 'religion' 178; liberal 'spectre' of religion 181–2; 'natural religiosity' 177; new religious movements linked to neoliberal capitalism 28, 115–25; non-exclusivity of religions outside Judaeo-Christianity 43; polytheistic cults 36; private salvations 188; redemption (of past) 28; truth claims of Judaeo-Christian religion 14
Renaissance 4
Renan, Ernest 3
revolution 2, 11, 107: American 28; Christian 187; Nazi 167; Soviet 167; Velvet 167; *see also* French revolution
Ricœur, Paul 10, 51–68, 129, 147, 168–73, 180–1, 185–6, 189–90
Roberts, Richard 136
Robinson, Mary 7
Rorty, Richard 39, 127, 134–5, 137–8, 158, 164–5, 175, 188
Rousseau, Jean-Jacques 40, 153
Russell, Bertrand 39

Ryle, Gilbert 140

sacrifice 12, 99, 104; archaic and Christian 150–1, 152, 156–8
Saint-Exupéry, A. 149
Sartre, Jean-Paul 81
Satan 123, 155–6, 158
Saussure, F. de 58
scapegoat(ing) 12, 93, 103–5, 151–2, 174, 187; new world with the end of 105; occulted in myth 104; and political correctness 152; scapegoat figures (Joseph, Job, Suffering servant 101; Jesus 174)
Schacht, Richard 11, 69–97, 148, 166, 180
Schmitt, Carl 30
science and technology 18, 34, 38, 45, 117, 174
Second World War 25, 93
secular(ism) 1, 10, 42, 166: as Christian category 4, 42; morality promoted by Enlightenment 50
Seneca the Elder 138
Shakespeare, William 12, 155
Shekinah (cosmic incarnation of God) 34
Shintoism 43
skandalon (stumbling-block, affront) 141, 154–6
Skemp, J. B. 141
slavery 23; 'slave morality' (Nietzsche) 168
Smith, Adam 47, 125
society: communist 46; social bonding 89; social constructivism 141
socio-biology 71
Socrates 42, 49, 65
sophists 65
Sophocles 91
soteriology 45
soul 40, 76, 80, 79, 162
Soviet Union 25
Spengler, O. 25
Spinoza, B. 40
spirit(uality) 67, 72, 80, 113, 161
Stalin 25
Stalingrad, Battle of 17, 27
Steiner, George 7, 64, 172

INDEX

stoicism 43
structuralist (ism) 6, 73
supernaturalism ('true') 78
symbol systems 82; symbolic order 85

taboos 18; *see also* Freud; religion
Taliban 44, 179
Taoists 43
Thatcher, Margaret 9
theism 129
Theissen, Gerd 141, 143, 144
Third Way 9
Third World 8; and First World 23
Thiselton, Anthony C. 13, 148, 161, 173, 180
Thousand Year Reich, thousand years' empire, *see* millenarianism
Tillich, Paul 28
time (temporality): experienced subject time (*la durée*) 67, 170, 172; 'God will accompany us in time' 172; as intemporal essence 172; scales of duration 60
transcendence 3, 147–8; appropriated transcendence ('horizontal', 'from below') 160, 165; the future as paradigm of transcendence 22
Troetschke 67
truth (access to, truth claims) 86, 127–8, 135, 144, 173

Ukah, Asonzeh 117
United Nations 29
United States *see* America
universal(ity) 15, 37, 45–50, 127–35

Valéry, Paul 149
valley of dry bones (Ezekiel) 8, 28

values: conflicts of value 49; 'defensible only in terms of Christian monotheism' 35–50; rational consensus on 9, 36, 46; revaluation of (Nietzsche) 11, 75, 148, 167; shared 167; universal values of the Enlightenment 48; value pluralism 9, 49, 147, 161, 164–5, 175; value relativism 48
Venter, Craig 19
Verdun, Battle of 17, 24, 27
victim(ization) 23–6, 85, 95; *see also* scapegoat
violence 12, 91: and catharsis 97; in Christianized Europe 152; of Crucifixion 102; propensity to mimetic violence 100; stoning of Stephen 102
Virgil 21
Vissarion (Sergei Torop) 106–7, 125
Voltaire 39, 48, 187

Weber, Max 13, 18, 39, 109, 122, 126, 176
Weil, Simone 67
Weizhäcker, Richard von 29
Welborn, L. L. 134
White, Hayden 62, 63
Wilson, E. O. 88
Winter, Bruce 141
witchcraft 116, 154
Wittgenstein, Ludwig 81

xenophobia 115

Yad Vashem (Jerusalem) 28

Zeno of Elea 140
Zwi, S. 20

For Product Safety Concerns and Information please contact our EU representative GPSR@taylorandfrancis.com
Taylor & Francis Verlag GmbH, Kaufingerstraße 24, 80331 München, Germany

www.ingramcontent.com/pod-product-compliance
Lightning Source LLC
Chambersburg PA
CBHW060601230426
43670CB00011B/1924